Harry's Favo

Harry's Favourite Thing

By Al Gale

HARRY'S FAVOURITE THING
Copyright © Al Gale 2017

All Rights reserved

No part of this book may be reproduced in any form by photocopying or by any electronic or mechanical means, including information storage or retrieval systems, without permission in writing from both the copyright owner and the publisher of this book.

Front cover image courtesy of Mother Hen Films Ltd.

Harry's Favourite Thing

In loving memory of our son,
Harry Oliver Thomas Gale

My thanks once more go to the magnificent staff at Acorns Children's Hospice, for being there, and for helping us through our ordeal.

Thanks too to my family, for putting up with my continued madness, from physical challenges to book writing.

Harry's Favourite Thing

Part One:

Harry

Harry

Harry deserves the first word. Without him there would have been no impetus or requirement for much of what followed. His short life changed our own ones to an unimaginable degree, and I feel that it's important to clarify why I went about taking on the challenge of the English Channel - an event ridiculously outside of my personal comfort zone.

Harry was a planned child. Esta and I already had Lewis, who was five years old when his brother arrived on the scene, and we thought that two children would complete our little family. I had two older children already, Sean and Connagh, but they lived with their mum on the Isle of Wight at the time, so until Harry turned up it was just the three of us at home in Worcester.

There was nothing particularly remarkable about Harry's birth, once the miracle of childbirth itself is set aside. Like Lewis before him he was overdue, though with Harry, Esta had to bear with the indignity and discomfort of an induced birth to hurry him along. It was either that or face a caesarian. And Esta was adamant that she wanted a natural birth.

Our son arrived on a wet, miserable day in October. Whilst waiting for the drugs to do their work on the contraction process, Esta and I walked around the soulless hospital car park in the drizzle. When the rain increased and drove us inside, we resorted to laps of the anaesthetic-smelling hospital corridors, all in an attempt to let gravity help out. A fire test put paid to our internal wanderings, as each of the magnetic retainers on the doors was released, automatically swinging the heavy fire doors into action. Instead we retreated to the coffee shop, sipping a beverage there as Esta proof-read one of my assignments for my Open University degree in literature whilst I read Pride and Prejudice for the third time. It was just a regular day.

An induced birth, so Esta tells me, does not give the body time to come to terms with what is happening. From having only minor contractions, Esta was very quickly in intense pain, desperately wanting to push but being told she was not dilated enough to do so. The hours of waiting for anything to begin quickly turned into a relatively manic hour or so as our second son abruptly entered the world. The standard procedures were duly followed: ten fingers, ten toes, eyes open and a good set of lungs judging by the wailing he was making. Slightly grey, but nothing unusual - certainly nothing that could not be fixed by wafting some oxygen under his nose. All in all, a seemingly normal and healthy baby. I left Esta and our baby together so that I could go and take care of Lewis.

Harry would not settle at all that night, howling each time he was put down. In the end, Esta had to rest him on her chest so that she could get any peace, snatching just a few hours precious sleep herself.

I was back at the hospital the next morning, having dropped Lewis off at school. On the way to the ward I happened to notice that the small on-site registry office was open, so I popped in to enquire about getting a birth certificate. The registrar was only too happy to take all of the details, made all that much easier by Harry being born only a hundred or so meters away. Within just 16 hours of his birth our boy was fully and legally registered in the system. I proudly showed Esta his birth certificate when I went to collect them both immediately afterwards.

We brought Harry home to our small three bedroom house that day. The nursing staff were happy that both mother and child were fine, and Esta simply wanted to rest in the comfort of her own bed and in the surrounding of our own house. Lewis wanted to meet his new brother too, though naturally he had expectations of being able to play games with him immediately, so was quickly disappointed. For him, as with many other older siblings I'm sure, the novelty of a small baby in the house wore off very quickly.

Lewis had always been a very good baby. He was lively, and didn't need much sleep, but he was generally healthy, happy and content. Harry quickly revealed himself to be anything but content. In fact, he cried almost continually, and slept very seldom. His feeds were short, and Esta was convinced he was not taking enough milk. Surely, I thought, all babies take as much as they need, if they can get it? Harry was simply his own boy. We had to accept that he would not be a facsimile of Lewis. And as for the crying, that too would pass. We simply had to bear with it.

The latter part was easier for me to say than it was for Esta to deal with. At the time I was a contractor, working away down in

London five days a week, meaning that I was only home for three nights at a time. Though in time he would have his own room, as with Lewis when he was a baby Harry slept in our room in a small basket next to Esta's side of the bed. He was never in it very long. It seemed that Harry's sleeping patterns governed our own lives. When he finally stopped crying and fell asleep in the evening, we immediately retired to bed too. But the expectation was that this would all be very temporary. It was a sacrifice we had made before with Lewis, putting our adult-time together on hold whilst our lives adjusted. And when Harry woke up in the night, seemingly minutes after we had dropped off, Esta would quietly slip out of bed, pick him up, and take him downstairs to feed him. She confessed that she often dozed off slightly whilst he was at her breast, and I can hardly blame her.

In the meantime, Lewis also adjusted to having a more demanding individual in the house than himself. He was remarkably good at chatting to Harry and trying to get him to laugh, though at best we only ever seemed to achieve a temporary respite from the wailing.

After just three weeks I could see that Esta was losing weight, was dead on her feet, and had seriously lost her normal, lively spark. Harry's crying was sucking the living energy from my wife, and exhaustion was all she seemed to know or remember. Esta's mother, Pat, and my own, Vicky, were doing as much to help as they could. I just hoped that Harry would settle down soon, and I tried to ensure our lives returned to some semblance of normality. As keen rugby fans we were season ticket holders to our local Premiership side, Worcester Warriors. We took Harry with us to a match in a sling around my front, and miraculously he fell asleep at one point, only to be awoken moments later to the celebratory shouts of thousands of fans when Worcester scored a try.

On reflection, it's amazing how unaware and dismissive I was of exactly how unsettled Harry was. I cannot be the only parent to be guilty of such a crime. Hindsight is wonderful of course, but every time Esta expressed her concerns I assured her that everything was fine: Harry was just a grizzly baby, I'd tell her.

To be fair, this opinion was very much backed up by the health visitor assigned to Esta. Harry was weighed and measured as usual, and because he continued to grow and put on weight as expected, he was simply viewed as a somewhat unhappy child who fed less than might be expected. But clearly he must have been eating enough, or he would not have been within the safe sentinel line which human growth is measured against.

Days turned into weeks. I'm not sure where Esta found the strength or energy to continue, as she barely slept. And Harry simply cried and cried. Esta's constant worrying about him was a further drain to her already depleted reserves of energy. She felt alone in her concern, either because I was away with work, or because the health visitor gently but firmly assured her Harry was growing and developing exactly as could be expected.

At six weeks, fearing she would go insane if someone did not confirm her own worries, Esta took Harry to the doctor. Unable to find any reason for his crying or his general upset, the doctor could only advise us that Harry was suffering from colic. We'd been through this hell with Lewis, and knew it was unpleasant for the child. But our experience was that each episode of colic with our older son would generally end in a huge belch, an almost satisfied smile, and then a very contented sleep. Nothing of this sort was happening with Harry, and Esta left the surgery feeling as powerless and frustrated as when she'd entered.

It's important to emphasise that we are not trying to establish any blame. We are convinced that every healthcare worker we had contact with did the best they could under the conditions, and within the work and time constraints by which they were bound. And at the very first indication that something was genuinely amiss, Harry was immediately referred to a doctor. In our son's case, this occurred when he was just under seven weeks old, and he abruptly stopped growing as expected.

Because on the 22nd November, Esta was told our tiny baby boy was suddenly losing weight.

The events of the next few days quickly became an incohesive blur. One day quickly merged and blended into another, and yet contradicting this fantasy was the mirage of days appearing to last forever. A year or more later I discovered the notes I had made at the time. We were astounded to discover just how much had occurred in such a short space of time. I carried those notes around with me for seven years before I finally managed to put them to full use.

On being told the news of Harry's weight loss, Esta was flooded with mixed emotions. On the one hand her assumed paranoia was suddenly replaced with confirmation that something was really wrong with our boy, and on the other hand, that latter realisation in turn led to the natural panic of a concerned mother. All Esta wanted to know was why Harry had been crying for almost seven weeks, and why he was now beginning to lose weight.

Harry had never been a chubby baby at any point. He appeared to eat just enough to sustain his crying, and though he had been growing as predicted, he somehow always managed to look undernourished. Now though, as the doctor began to check him over, he looked positively scrawny.

The GP who had been appointed to us was a man by the name of Dr. Felix Blaine. He was a young-ish man who spoke quietly and acted, as you would want your doctor to, very calmly. He spoke to Esta as he examined Harry, explaining what he was doing and asking clarifying questions of her. The baby notes he had in front of him confirmed that Harry was now below the important sentinel line, so was underweight according to his age. This may have been less alarming had he always tracked below this line, but the sudden dip was what really concerned everyone right now. What Dr. Blaine found made him stop, pause, and check again.

During the escalation of Esta's visit to the GP, my mother had been texting me, pleading with me to come home. I was aware of Harry's loss of weight, but I was in no better position than Esta to do anything about it. Obviously I could be there for moral support, but I wanted to be sure there was something that could actually be done first. As the only bread winner, and one who was a contractor to boot, I could not afford to drop everything and come home with an open ended calendar. I had a contractual obligation to have my bum on a seat in London, and I only got paid for any days I actually worked. I needed the doctor to confirm whether we were blowing this out of proportion.

The next communication I got was from Esta herself. She and Harry had been rushed to Worcester Royal Infirmary, the same one in which Harry had been born. Things were not clear at that stage, but Esta thought that Dr. Blaine may have detected an irregularity in our son's heartbeat. Quite whether he was correct, or how serious it was, no-one was yet sure. Naturally my wife was worried, but she was also exhausted too. The hospital staff had offered to take Harry away in order to try and feed him so that Esta could sleep. With motherly instincts, Esta had resisted at first. She felt as though she had failed in being able to breastfeed her son. She was also used to having him by her immediate side 24 hours a day. But with gentle determination the staff persuaded her that extra tests were needed to be carried out, and that the best possible thing all round was for Esta to get some much-needed rest. When we discussed the prospect of me coming home, we agreed to wait another day. We would hopefully know more the next day, and Esta could go back and get some sleep.

    For both of us, the start of the next morning gave us no indication as to what the day would bring. News on Harry was sparse, with doctors unwilling to speculate on information they were unsure of. All we knew was that our boy was in the best possible place if something was seriously amiss, and that at least our concerns over Harry's continual crying were now being addressed. I returned to work as normal, and waited for an update.

    From my point of view, the 23rd November was a day of mixed and often contradictory messages as information began to trickle out about Harry's condition. Dr. Blaine had originally detected a possible heart murmur, and the hospital was now eager to ascertain the exact cause and extent of this problem. But with Esta being unable to keep me constantly updated due to a weak phone signal within the hospital, my mum would text me with the latest news. Typically, a message from Esta would then belatedly arrive, confusing the issue from my perspective. All I did know was that it appeared that Harry did had a heart problem to some degree. What I could not clarify was the seriousness, which could range between anything from a hole in his heart to a blocked or under-developed aortic valve. Nevertheless, any heart condition was of course devastating news to us, and I envisaged Harry relying on immediate surgery and probable medication for the remainder of his life. I instantly left London and headed home to Worcester.

    Our nightmare had begun.

BCH

Like in a well-directed suspense movie, I clearly remember the tension and anxiety building within me during the train journey home. We'd fallen into a communications black hole for a while, partly because there were no updates to be passed along, and secondly because when things did begin to move once more, they did so at such an escalated pace that Esta was unable to even text me.

The various heart scans and readings taken from Harry had been sent to Birmingham Children's Hospital, known throughout the region as BCH. Some of the world's best medical consultants are employed here, and if anyone were able to confirm the original suspicions of Dr. Blaine, it was the senior cardiologist at BCH.

But by the time I arrived back in Worcester, I learnt that Harry and Esta were no longer in the Royal Infirmary there. What had been seen at BCH had caused sufficient consternation to order the immediate transfer of mother and son directly to the specialist care of the Children's Hospital. They were both ushered rapidly into an ambulance and blue-lighted 40 or so miles across to Birmingham.

With Esta already having spent one unexpected night in hospital, I firstly needed to go home and collect a few essentials for my wife to change into. I also wanted to check on my mother-in-law, Pat, who was looking after Lewis, and to reassure our older son that everything was going to be fine: Harry was in hospital, and that was the best thing for everyone. They'd soon make him better there, because that's what hospitals did, after all.

Another train took to me to Birmingham, and I made my way quickly via the well-signposted entrance for BCH and onto the relevant ward. Though the exhaustion had not entirely vanished from Esta's face, it had now been eclipsed by a mask of terror and worry.

We knew little more about Harry's condition at this stage. Our son had been put on a drip with no fewer than four IV feeds into his body, one in each hand and foot. Esta had been asked to leave the room when this was done, with staff only too aware of the anxiety this procedure caused to parents. A nurse came out to clarify some questions about Harry, and we prepared ourselves for what we assumed would be another round of explaining his lack of sleep and irregular feeding habits.

Instead, she asked about his 'body tone'.

'Does he often go very rigid, as though stretching every muscle in his body at once? We've witnessed him do it once or twice already.'

Harry hated being fussed or disturbed. Whenever we had to change his nappy, he went into such a frantic state that his muscles would contract, his back would tense, and his entire body became as solid as a piece of wood. But as he had been doing this since his very first days, we now took it as standard. Esta had simply got into the habit of performing a formula-one style nappy change. She had it down to a matter of seconds. Without knowing any better, we were actually somewhat proud of our son's almost extraordinary strength. We confirmed what the nurse had asked.

'And does he ever hold his breath, as though he cannot exhale?'

Yes, Harry did that whilst he was in his tantrum. We could get away without this occurring if the nappy change were quick enough, but otherwise a short puff of breath into his mouth would get him breathing again.

'And what about his eyes? Do they ever sort of flicker, as though he's dreaming with his eyelids open?'

Again, yes, this was part of Harry's character.

'When was the first time you noticed any, or all of these?'

Harry had been doing all of those things since he'd first been born.

The nurse thanked us and left, but we were left unsure as to whether our answers pleased her or not.

Sometime later in the evening we were told that there would be no further update to the situation that day. Harry was comfortable, sedated and sleeping, and being fed by IV tubes. Our son was being kept under close observation. If we wanted, we could go home and return the next day. Esta refused to leave. She wanted me to go back and relieve her mum of babysitting duties for one night, but then she wanted me to return again in the morning. She hoped she'd know more by then. We both hoped so. The strain of not knowing was becoming unendurable.

Waiting in hospitals is torture. I really don't know how Esta could stand any more of it. I'd only been there a matter of hours, and I'd had enough already. Esta thinks it's a lack of control, which could be right. The feeling of helplessness is pure hell to me, yet Esta chose to stay the night at BCH. By some miracle there was a spare bed in one of the children's rooms, and the nurses took pity on my wife and let her sleep in the comfort of a bed.

    The 24th of November dawned and regular everyday chores had to be done. I washed, fed and helped Lewis to dress, then took him to school as normal. When dropping the car back home in readiness to catch the train back to BCH, I bumped into our next door neighbour who ran the little shop around the corner. I remember explaining to him that Harry had a heart murmur and was at the Children's hospital, with both of us agreeing in a neighbourly way that this was the best thing, and that everything would be fine now that Harry was at BCH.

    And indeed, arriving at the hospital it certainly looked as though things were in hand. A cardiologist was due to speak to us and tell us the full detailed schedule for the day, but we understood that it was currently planned for Harry to have surgery at the next available opportunity. We were unclear at this point as to the nature or scale of that surgery, and all we could do was be as optimistic as possible.

    It was a good while later before we met the cardiologist, a man by the name of Dr. Rakesh. He informed us that Harry needed immediate heart surgery, and stressed in no uncertain terms that this was undoubtedly a major operation. However, he had personally conducted such procedures many times, and the hospital had an excellent record of successes. Everything medically possible was being done for our son.

    We enquired as to when the operation would begin, and here we detected the first indications of a system under tremendous strain. Harry was currently in the Intensive Care Unit (ICU). He had suffered a bad night and had effectively 'died' twice. Resuscitation had been successfully performed, but his need for immediate treatment made him a top priority patient now. Today, the initial wait had been for a bed on a ward for Harry. Once a bed had come free, it then transpired that an anaesthetist required for the operation was not available - so the bed had been re-allocated to a child not awaiting any surgery. The scarce availability of resources was suddenly all too apparent, and we realised just how incredible it had been for Esta to be given a bed to sleep in the night before.

The waiting continued, and the day dragged on. Whenever we enquired as to progress we were told that it was just a matter of time. As soon as everything and everyone was available, we would be told. We waited, we paced, and we waited some more.

At 17:00 we were apologetically told that no further surgery was scheduled for that day. We, and Harry, would have to wait until tomorrow. It was a crushing blow after an anxious day of optimism. Our slim hopes of some progress, some forward momentum, were dashed, only to be replaced by the likelihood of more anxious waiting.

Frustrated as we were, we knew better than to take it out on overworked staff. We didn't have the money to move to a private hospital, so we had to accept that there were other children who also needed care. We were reassured again that Harry was comfortable, that he was sleeping peacefully down in ICU, and we were advised to get as much rest as possible in preparation for another potentially stressful and traumatic day.

As with previously, Esta wanted to stay at BCH so that she was as close as possible to Harry. We knew there were no beds available this time, but my wife said something would turn up. How she could remain at all optimistic, I had no idea. The lack of any ability to influence the course of events was driving me crazy. I was completely sympathetic to the use of limited resources, and the staff at the hospital had all been magnificent. There was nothing to complain about apart from the lack of positive news, and everyone was doing everything they could about that.

It's incredible to look back on such a day, one that we had originally considered to be unbearably horrendous, and to subsequently realise how ordinary and mundane it was when compared to later events.

Saturday 25th November was to unequivocally reveal itself as the most horrific and shocking day of our lives.

I received a call from Esta early in the day to tell me that Harry was going in for a pre-op scan. Surgery would follow immediately. Naturally, there was no way I could leave Esta alone at the hospital whilst our son was being operated on, so I knew I had to get there by the fastest possible means. I called Esta's mum, Pat, and informed her that I would be getting a taxi. If she wanted to come with me, she needed to come to our house immediately. I don't think she has ever made the journey between our homes in a faster time.

The rapidity of progress was not to last, though. The northbound traffic on the M5 motorway was horrendous, and we gradually receded from a crawl into a complete stop just shy of our exit. The sense of growing anxiety I'd experienced previously on the train was now eclipsed by the frustration I was feeling at this hold up, and I felt the urgent need to do something to get us moving. The hard shoulder of the motorway ended just a short way ahead due to the strut of an overhead bridge occupying that part of the road. If we could get past the bridge we could then utilise the hard shoulder and make a fast exit to the junction. Except that the traffic was at a standstill as far ahead as I could see, and it was giving no indication that it was about to move any time soon.

I jumped out of the car and began to run up the motorway. I started to knock on car windows like a madman, asking everyone to nudge up close to the car in front so that we could pull ahead of the bridge. Some of the drivers turned away from me and ignored my initial pleas, but I continued knocking and hammering on their windows until they complied. As I looked back towards my taxi, I could see it gradually approaching the bridge strut, slowly closing the gap between me and the car. It was an agonising spectacle, witnessing such a slow progression, me pleading with more drivers to please inch up another tiny bit. But finally the taxi was through the gap, pulling onto the hard shoulder and quickly driving up to collect me.

We were on the move once again.

But if I thought that would be an end to our problems, I was utterly mistaken. Our next issue was that the taxi driver had no idea how to get to BCH. We told him to drive to Snow Hill train station, and that the hospital would be signposted from there. He then confessed he never been to Birmingham, and that he had no Sat-Nav in the car. It was unbelievable. I had only ever been to BCH via train, so fortunately Pat began to give the driver directions, relying upon the one time she herself had driven to the hospital at the beginning of this whole episode.

Upon arrival I flew out of the taxi and into the hospital,

ungallantly leaving Pat to follow me and to bring Lewis. I arrived at the ward on the run, mechanically grabbing some sanitising gel and rubbing my hands clean even as I rushed towards a stricken-looking Esta.

'He's had his scans, but they won't take him in for surgery,' she explained.

'What? Why not?'

'I've no idea yet. There seems to be some confusion. I'm waiting for them to get back to me.'

Again that word, waiting. It was like a mantra now, and it was all we seemed to know. Within a few short days our lives had been reduced to stress, anxiety, uncertainty, but above all, waiting: Waiting for a bed; waiting for news; waiting for a doctor. I take my hat off to all doctors and nursing staff. Constantly working in such an environment, they all deserve medals.

Esta had been reduced to spending the previous night on some plastic chairs in the waiting room. Nothing better had presented itself, and she already felt grimy with lack of sleep. Over the past two days she had gradually made friends with a nurse called Gill, who'd taken pity on my wife's plight. As we waited now, we saw Gill approaching the waiting room with a solemn face, accompanied by a smartly dressed Indian man whose countenance and bearing undoubtedly identified him as a very experienced and senior doctor. It was 11:30.

We were asked, in that hypothetical 'would you like to..' fashion that broaches no argument, whether we would accompany them both to somewhere more private. It was an unnerving and truly ominous short walk to the small, secluded meeting room. Esta and I took a seat on a small settee, unconsciously sitting closely together in a naturally protective fashion.

Dr. Chickermane introduced himself, explaining that he was the senior cardiologist who had been put in charge of our son. As Gill sat by silently, he began to firstly describe the normal constructs and operation of a healthy heart. We asked a few questions to confirm our limited understanding of cardiology, allowing him to elaborate on his initial description. After a gentle pause, Dr. Chickermane subsequently began to tell us of Harry's problem.

'You son has a serious blockage in his aorta. This has placed his heart under an incredible amount of strain. He has been in severe pain for a long time, I'm afraid.'

So that was why our boy had been crying. No wonder he never wanted to eat much. Agony contributes little towards a regular and healthy appetite.

'But you can operate? You can remove the blockage?'

There was another slight pause. Gill glanced towards the doctor, perhaps wondering if he wanted her to take it from here, but he ignored her and continued gently.

'I'm afraid there are some extenuating circumstances.' Another pause, a slight intake of breath, perhaps whilst he considered the best possible way of explaining the situation, or perhaps to give us time to mentally prepare ourselves for whatever was to follow. 'There is evidence of brain damage, I'm sorry to say. I cannot say too much at this stage, as we have a neurologist on his way here now. He is best qualified to confirm our findings. All I do know is that the results are consistent with a stroke. This looks to have happened at least a few weeks ago.'

The room, our whole world, shrank in upon us with those words. No amount of pausing or self-preparation could have equipped us for this shock. We were utterly speechless. We looked at him as though he'd lost his mind, and then we glanced at Gill in that incredulous way that pleads, 'This is a joke, right?' It was painfully obvious now why she was present: to provide the calming influence of a rational and educated woman. Without the requirement for any words, her face silently told us, 'I'm so terribly sorry. He's absolutely correct.'

There wasn't much to say, even had we been capable of speech. We simply sat motionless, tightly squeezed up against one another on the hospital settee, numb and uncomprehending. We'd been asked no questions, and no answers were required at this stage. Dr. Chickermane informed us that naturally we could stay in the private room and take as much time as we needed to absorb this news. The neurologist would be here in around an hour. As soon as he arrived, everyone would come and find us. We would know more then.

In the meantime, we had more waiting to contend with.

Except that this subsequent period of waiting had suddenly taken on a whole new realm of dread. From desperately wanting news, we had abruptly been transposed into parents who now dreaded hearing any more. What if the next glut of information was worse? How bad could things be? Or would the subsequent news actually come as a relief to our worst-case-scenario assumptions?

After all: brain damage! Our boy had cerebral palsy! How much worse can news get?

I stood up and walked to the small window that looked down into a rectangular courtyard one floor below. Whilst working as a contractor in London I had plenty of spare time on my hands in the evenings and of course whilst commuting to and from work on public transport. To make the most of this time I was presently studying towards an honours degree with the Open University. Though the main degree was in literature, a subject I could satisfactorily study whilst on the move commuting, my current module was on the subject of childhood development. Whilst 300 points of the degree involved selecting modules from a pre-defined list, the extra 60 units necessary for the honours part were optional. I'd selected childhood development so that I would understand the phases of Harry's mental progression. That seemed cruelly ironic at this moment, and I stood gazing blankly into the courtyard, the horrific words 'brain damage' dominating my thoughts.

The shock of this news caused an incredible internal noise within my head, making it impossible to think. But as this began to subside, I gradually began to think rationally again. Quite suddenly I began to appreciate that the module was not wasted or ironic at all - it was abruptly completely appropriate. I kept my thoughts to myself for a moment. I needed the neurologist to clarify a few points first.

Esta came up and put her arms around me. I turned round to face her, and it was only then that I became aware that I was crying. The mental shock of hearing about our son had hit me harder than anything I'd ever known. I'd been totally unprepared for this. I'd been expecting heart surgery, an operation, maybe an extended stay in hospital as he recovered. But everything had revolved around the likelihood, the parental expectation, of complete recovery.

Personal thoughts and attitudes on pro-life issues may not normally be a subject that many couples have to discuss. We had certainly never had a conversation on the issue. But it was sounding now as if our child was going to be mentally handicapped. The degree of severity was yet to be determined, as was our ability to live with a disabled child. Our thoughts and hopes at this stage were that

Harry would be able to function at some level. Somehow, we would all have to adapt and cope.

We found ourselves unable to go and tell Esta's mum, Pat. We couldn't find the words, and until we knew exactly what we were facing, we thought that limited news was worse than no news. Suddenly it was us keeping others waiting. As soon as we knew more, we'd let the family know.

I phoned my mum to try and find out where she was. Her and my step-father, Graham, were on the way to the hospital. They too thought that Harry was going in for heart surgery. Knowing what we did about the brain damage our son was suspected to have suffered, we were worried that Pat would simply crumble when we told her. We wanted my mum to get to the hospital to take Pat and Lewis home. We had enough to face without also worrying about Pat. It all sounds very selfish now, of course. The family all wanted to be at the hospital in the same way that Esta had wanted to stay overnight. They wanted to support us. Unfortunately, we weren't in the condition to think at our most rational and considerate levels.

Gill returned and asked if we'd like to go and see Harry whilst we waited for the neurologist to arrive. We were taken downstairs to ICU and introduced to a nurse called Ruth who was responsible for Harry. She was a lovely lady, but we found that the image of our son in that room, wired up to monitors and various machines, with tubes and various lines running into his tiny, fragile frame was just too much. I don't know what we'd been expecting, but seeing him like this was a massive shock to us. Our son looked so helpless, so ill, so vulnerable. We had to get out of the building and get some air. I called my mum again, trying to gently convey the seriousness of the situation without actually giving any details. It turned out that they still had not left home.

We returned to the private room where the news had been broken to us. The facility seemed to have been set aside for us for the time being, so we had Gill fetch Lewis for us to give Pat a short break, and we did our best to pretend nothing was amiss with the world as we played with our eldest son.

When a text arrived from my mum, I was flooded with relief. Such emotion was short-lived, however, when we realised that they were only just about to board the train. It would be over another hour before they arrived. Having kept the secret from Pat for this long had been torture to us, and was cruel to her, so we decided we simply had to break the bad news. Esta wanted to be alone with her mum, knowing that the latter would want to grieve without her son-in-law present, so she found Pat and took her down to ICU. Another benefit of breaking the news privately was that they'd also have the professionals on hand to comfort and support both of them.

It was 16:00 when Dr. Chickermane returned with a different nurse, Theresa. The two medical staff were accompanied by a third man, smartly but casually dressed in simple shirt and trousers. The man was introduced as the senior neurologist for the region, Mr. Smith.

'Call me Martin,' he said in a soft Northern accent.

I thanked him for coming in to the hospital on a Saturday, and he gave me a sad smile. 'Vocations like ours are never nine to five, I'm afraid.' He paused. 'I have something I need to show you. Could you follow me, please?'

We were led to a very small room indeed. There was a computer monitor in one corner, a big and cumbersome device of the old cathode ray tube style. Martin took control of the mouse, as Esta, myself and the two other staff members squeezed ourselves into the room.

'What you are about to see,' began Martin, quietly and calmly, 'is a series of images showing Harry's brain. Imagine it's a photo of the top slice of his brain, and with each new image we are moving horizontally downwards towards his toes. Understand?'

We waggled our heads, Indian-style, thinking, but not sure, that we understood.

An image was displayed on the screen, looking a bit like a photograph of a dinosaur egg. The distinctive cauliflower pattern of a brain was easy to make out inside the 'shell' of Harry's skull. There were a few very small patches of light-grey in amongst the mostly dark-grey matter.

Martin began to click the mouse button. We were visually moving down through Harry's brain. Every few slides we'd see more of the light-grey blotches.

When we'd reached the last image, Martin asked, 'Tell me what you saw.'

'A few light-grey patches. But not many. There were only a few!' I said this as though my positivity could somehow change things, or convince Martin to alter the opinion he'd clearly already reached.

What Martin had done had not been a trick or an attempt to deliberately deceive us, I realised a little later. It had been a way to ensure we could not deny the evidence or pretend things were any different.

Because next, Martin gently told us, 'The light-grey parts are live tissue. The dark-grey parts are dead tissue.'

We had been partially prepared for such news from the outset, but it was still in a sense of disbelief and dumb shock that we followed Martin back to the larger private room.

'I hope you can forgive me for having to show you that? I looked at the images earlier myself, of course, and I knew you needed to see the reality, the seriousness of the situation. If I'd have simply told you the degree of damage, that would not have been enough.'

We didn't know what to say. Asking just how bad it really was seemed irrelevant. I kept thinking about those tiny light-grey patches, and how few of them there had been.

'I'd wanted to ask about the possibility of plasticity...' I began.

Martin raised his eyebrows in appreciation of my terminology. During my degree module on childhood development, research into brain damage had actually been covered in a dedicated section of the course. However, this had primarily been done in the case of adults who'd suffered a head injury, as this allowed 'before and after' scenarios for contrast and comparison. In some cases, the human brain had shown the capability to 're-program' other healthy areas of tissue to compensate for the damaged areas. Victims of such head trauma may have to relearn to walk or use their limbs under full control as a different part of the brain took on this responsibility, but it was something that had proven to be possible. This ability was known as 'plasticity', and the theory went that if this were possible in adults subsequent to an injury, then surely it must be possible during the normal development stage within an infant.

'I'm afraid there is just not enough live tissue,' Martin said. 'If I'm completely honest, I'm not even medically sure how Harry is still alive. You probably don't want to hear this right now, but it looks as if your son suffered two, possibly three massive strokes before he was even born. I'm afraid that the serious heart deformity ultimately lead to his brain being starved of oxygen.'

The discussion continued for some time, but I cannot recall any more of it. Essentially, there was nothing good whatsoever to report. Harry was alive, just, but even the top expert in the surrounding counties did not know how this was actually possible. As far as could be determined, Harry would undoubtedly be quadriplegic. He probably could not see, he had only the most basic and instinctive sense of touch (which was primarily restricted to his sense of pain), and on top of this he also still had a life-threatening blockage in his heart.

'Where is Harry now?' I asked.

'He's still downstairs in ICU. He's completely sedated, and he's asleep.' We were further told, in a calm and gentle way, that Harry was being kept alive by a ventilator that was breathing for him.

I glanced at Esta. We'd had no time to discuss things this far, so when I asked the following question, it was as much to see if we were on the same wavelength as it was to find out the answer.
'I think it's best if we cancel the heart operation.' I began.

Dr. Chickermane instantly agreed. He added that the complications of proceeding due to the cerebral palsy may even be such that we had no choice anyway.

'What would happen if we turned the ventilator off?' I said, almost in a whisper.

Again there was a pause. I was looking at Esta, and she nodded slightly, consenting to my line of thought. I didn't catch if the doctors and Theresa all glanced at each other, but I could well imagine it.

Though both Dr. Chickermane and Martin were the experts in their own relevant fields, the latter seemed to have naturally taken command within the room.

'Are you asking what may theoretically happen, or if we are authorised to do this?'

'Both.'

'OK. Well the extreme likelihood is that your son will be unable to begin breathing on his own. And yes, in an instance such as this, we are allowed to authorise the withdrawal of artificial assistance.' He paused, moving from a professional to a personal stance. 'Would you like my opinion?'

Esta and I both nodded.

'If it were me, as both a parent and as a medical professional... I would personally request the removal of the ventilator.'

To our astonishment, both Theresa and Dr. Chickermane verbally agreed they would do the same.

I genuinely don't think that either I or Esta were expecting this. Suddenly, after days of frustration and the complete lack of ability to influence any outcome, we had unexpectedly been presented with the ultimate of all decisions: Life, or death? It is cruelly ironic that we now had to ask the medical staff if they would wait a while. Naturally, they told us to take all the time we needed. In reality of course, I think everyone in that room knew what the final decision was going to be. The 'thinking time' was more out of respect than with any real intention of reversing the decision.

Naturally, we did discuss it. This is not a decision to be taken lightly, after all. Days and weeks later we were often told of tragedies whereby couples disagreed on such crucial issues. Almost without exception, such relationships are doomed, and the couples invariably split up. It was with a massive degree of relief that we were both 100% of the opinion that we would let nature take its course, whatever the outcome. The ventilator was to be turned off.

'Please bear with us a little while,' Martin requested. 'We'll need to make them aware down in ICU. We'll be as quick as we possibly can.' His acknowledgement of the need for haste was particularly sensitive: We didn't want this drawn out for any longer than was absolutely necessary.

Telling our parents of our decision was heart-breaking. Though there was no disagreement or argument about our proposed course of action, my step-father nevertheless burst into tears. My mum and mother-in-law both began to pray quietly. Lewis, off playing somewhere quietly, was blissfully unaware that the grown-ups were all crying.

Memory is a selective thing. When I came to constructing these chapters many years later, my recollection of the sequence of events turned out to be very different from the notes I'd taken the trouble to record at the time. I found it impossible back then to capture our emotions, and I probably assumed it was not necessary anyway. My notes appear sanitised, as though recorded by an independent and unrelated observer. I probably also reasoned that I'd not actually need to refer to the words ever again, assuming that they would be indelibly etched into my brain. If that was the case, I'm happy that I was wrong. It goes without saying that this was a deeply disturbing and emotional time.

Other, equally unpleasant things went on during this final wait too, such as the necessity to discuss the post mortem that would have to be carried out on Harry's body. There was a further requirement for a biopsy and the taking of blood samples too, and we were even asked, albeit gently, if we would allow our son to help with future medical research. We gathered exactly what was meant by that, and we both declined. Harry had already suffered enough indignation.

I think that those discussions were so traumatic that our brains refused to retain any substantial recollection of them. Were it not for my notes, I would completely have forgotten that such conversations had ever taken place.

Similarly, we must have told Lewis something of what was about to take place. I cannot recall where we spoke to him, or even how we may have framed what we said. We agreed that he had the right to be there at the end though, as if we later regretted giving him the opportunity, there would of course be no second chance.

I have no idea how much time passed, but soon we found ourselves back in ICU, this time to say a final farewell to our baby boy. Ruth was still there of course, keeping a close eye on the monitors attached to Harry. We were introduced to a man called Kevin, who was the head of the ICU. To me, Kevin seemed to have been almost genetically engineered specifically to run and control such an environment, due to appearing so perfect for it. He was professional, compassionate, and appeared to command an incredible amount of respect from the staff. Though there was a tangibly intense atmosphere within the room, there were no raised voices, and the team appeared to work in perfect clockwork, moving as one like a flock of birds.

I glanced around the room, taking in all of the tiny, helpless children being cared for within the unit. Superbly advanced and technical machinery covered the room, each one of which must have cost millions of pounds. And yet none of it was of the slightest help to Harry. Had Richard Branson, or anyone of such wealth, walked into the room and offered every penny they had, the gesture would have been futile in assisting our son. He was beyond all medical help. This fact formed the basis of the decision we'd made: If nothing could be done, medially, we would care for him and love him as much as possible, but we would do that naturally, without trying to artificially eke out every last heartbeat. If nature deemed that Harry could not breathe without aid, then at least we would all be there with him when he died.

I don't want to pretend for one second that this was an easy decision. Certainly it was made that much less painful by the fact that we were both in agreement about it, and also by the knowledge that the hospital staff all thought that it was the kindest decision. But making that choice, being asked how to proceed in such a case and being expected to provide an answer, well that is not a situation that I would wish on anyone else.

Harry was quietly wheeled, along with all of his currently attached machines, to a private room within ICU. As I looked around the room I noticed that it was decorated like a child's bedroom. The walls had been painted to depict the sea, with fish, crabs and starfish inhabiting the ocean. The small room had some windows that looked out onto the main ICU, with dolphins on the curtains that were now drawn closed to give us complete privacy.

Ruth produced a small ink pad, and as we watched she took prints of Harry's tiny feet and hands. She presented them to us, and as we stood there with tear-filled eyes, she used a small digital camera to take a photo of us standing next to Harry. The only sounds in the room were the occasions sniff from one of the nans, and the slow and regular rhythmic sound of the ventilator.

'Are you ready?' Kevin asked. The question was as much, 'Are you sure?'

We both gave an affirmative answer, and one of the nans let out a small involuntary groan. Nothing else remained to be said.

Kevin moved to the back of the room. Ruth positioned herself next to the ventilator. Without further pause for torture, she switched it off.

Silence invaded the room, and it was loud.

Harry lay motionless. His chest, which had previously been moving slightly as the ventilator inflated and deflated his tiny lungs, now ceased to move. Gradually, he turned a horrifying greyish-blue

colour. Nothing happened for the longest time.
    And then to the shock of everyone in the room, medical staff included, Harry took a huge lungful of air and began to wail.

Acorns

Some little while later, though I confess I have no idea exactly how long, we found ourselves upstairs on ward 11. By some miracle, we had been given a room to ourselves, with a small cot for Harry, and beds for Esta and I.

By all odds, Harry was not expected to survive the withdrawal of artificial life support. Even when he'd arisen Lazarus-like from his third death, the staff had asked us to wait a while: They expected the revival to be very short-lived. Eventually, they too had to concede that Harry was putting up a courageous fight, and they arranged for us to be moved out of ICU. The brutal reality was that we were now all waiting for Harry to die.

It's important to clarify though, that we were not *wanting* our son to die. It was not an inconvenience that he was battling so hard and surviving. But we had already agreed that we were not pro-life activists, and that machines would not be employed to keep Harry alive when they could be helping other children who stood a better chance at life. We had been told that no-one in the hospital could give our boy much above a zero percent chance of lasting the day. Most thought that his survival time was better measured in minutes. Consequently, we were steeling ourselves for an imminent and inevitable event.

In the truest sense of the word, it had been an incredible day. Within a matter of hours we'd moved from a situation of anticipated heart surgery, to a terminal degree of brain damage. We had then made the heart-rending decision to remove life support, and subsequently we witnessed our son return from the dead. Now we were back to waiting, and everything was up to Harry.

Gill, the nurse, poked her head around the door.
'Have you guys eaten at all today?'
Esta and I looked at each other. We could not remember if we had eaten or not. The day had seemed to consist of endless cups of tea, but we could not remember swallowing anything other than liquid.
'Go out. Get some air and some food. You both need it.'
'But what if...' Esta began.
'Give me your mobile number. I'll call you immediately if

anything happens.'

Harry had been put on a special, highly sensitive mat within his cot. The mat detected the smallest of movements, such as a baby breathing. If all movement stopped, an alarm went off. As we had placed a 'no resuscitation' order on Harry, this alarm was solely for our benefit so that we did not check on the cot, only to find an unexpectedly dead occupant.

I'm not being deliberately harsh when I use the words 'dead' and 'died'. This was literally a matter of life and death, and it needed to be faced accordingly. This was not a driving test, and Harry was not a lightbulb, so terms like 'passed' and 'expired', well intended though they are, came across as condescending.

Reluctantly, but in agreement with Gill that we needed to get out for a while, we went to a nearby pub. We began to talk about all of the things Harry would miss. We had a planned family holiday to Egypt over Christmas. We'd even already taken delivery of Harry's passport. The thought that he would never use it now brought us to tears.

'Got any change, mate?' We looked up with tear-stained faces to see a man standing in front of us, expectantly holding his hand out for money. We just wanted to be left alone in our grief, so we mumbled some dismissive apology.

'You got no idea of the day I've had, you two. It's alright for you, but things is tough for me,' the man continued. I stared at him in disbelief, sure beyond doubt that our day had been infinitely worse than his. He moved away, cursing us, and we decided we should get back. We bought some chicken and chips from a takeaway outlet, and shut ourselves in the room for the night.

We woke up to the warbling of an alarm. For a few moments we struggled to work out where we were, and what the noise was. The realisation hit us full on.

We rushed across the room, getting to Harry's cot at the same instance as a nurse arrived into the room. We stared into the cot at the motionless form, and then Harry opened his eyes at the commotion and cried. He had in fact become so utterly still in his sleep that even the sensitive mat had been unable to detect any movement. As programmed, the alarm had gone off. There can hardly be a less pleasant way to be woken up.

The morning passed. Theresa, thoroughly conversant with

our plight, suggested we take Harry out for a walk. We were at first horrified at the suggestion, until she asked, quite openly, 'What's the worst that can happen?' She was right, or course. Harry was going to die at some point. If it were whilst we were out with him, the result would make little difference to it happening whilst we sat in our room.

    Theresa found an old, heavy pram, and ensuring Harry was fully wired up to his drip, she transferred his tiny figure across from the cot.

    Esta and I were both incredibly nervous. We seemed to feel that the slightest jolt may be the ultimate cause of his death. Though that ultimate event was fully expected, we did not want to be the ones to have initiated it. We walked around for an hour, but we saw nothing. Our eyes had been continually glued to where the pram wheels were going, and to the boy who rode inside it.

    Another day somehow passed.

    Like Groundhog Day, we again woke up to the motion alarm, and again Harry woke up shortly after. Things began to get awkward at this point. Between us, we were taking up much-needed space and vital provisions such as a room and beds. Hospitals, after all, are where people go to get better, and there was a backlog of patients waiting to be admitted. When nothing more can be done for a patient, other avenues have to be pursued. Theresa came to speak to us and mentioned a hospice called Acorns. They were expertly positioned to help Harry, and us, as Acorns was a hospice for life-limited children. More specifically, they provided support for the child and for the family, including the bereavement support that would be needed for us and for Lewis. Theresa asked if we would like her to contact the hospice on our behalf, and a day or so later a lovely lady called Jan Large, whom we'd subsequently get to know very well indeed, came to meet us all.

    I liken Acorns to the most exclusive club in the world: The facilities and staff are second to none - but you don't ever want to meet the entrance criteria of this club!

    The only complication with us moving to the hospice was that Harry was still on an IV drip. Jan told the nurse that if our son could be put onto a Gastro-Nasal (GN) feed, then this would remove the problem, as her nurses were allowed to remove and replace GN tubes, but drips were more complicated. This would all require some administration, and we were told that the transfer to the hospice would therefore take place the following day.

Suddenly, it felt as if we had some traction in our lives again, a plan. Until this point, we had been marking time, waiting for the inevitable, but we now found that we had come to terms with that final outcome. The thing to do from this point was to ensure some positivity. We knew we had to work to build some happy memories, rather than skulking around waiting for death, and this realisation was a turning point for us. That evening, on a freezing cold night in November, we decided to take Harry out in the pram again whilst we wandered around the world-famous German Christmas market in Birmingham. We stopped at one of the large wooden bars and ordered some hot mulled wine. Harry was wrapped up to the eyes in blankets and clothes, with a hat pulled down over his head. His newly installed GN tube was discretely hidden from sight. Esta and I stood there shivering in the bitter cold when a businessman standing next to us indicated our boy, wrapped up warmly in the pram.

'I wish I was him right now,' he said.

He meant well, and he was obviously totally unaware of Harry's condition, but without thinking Esta and I both simultaneously replied, 'Oh no you don't!' The poor man didn't know where to look. He finished his drink quickly, and left without another word.

The next day, an ambulance was arranged to take us to Acorns. The hospice itself was located just a few miles from our house, and ironic though it was, I remembered I had even run a charity race in support of completing the building several years before. The close proximity to home was a huge bonus for us, as life would have to continue as normal with regards to school for Lewis, and at some point I would have to return to work.

Esta carried Harry down from the ward in her arms. Theresa came with us and when we arrived at the ambulance we saw that they'd strapped a car seat to a stretcher. Harry was travelling from the hospital in style.

In my notes, I mention my first impression of our arrival at the hospice: 'Acorns is AMAZING.' There were so many happy, smiling faces that we were dazzled. We were introduced to a host of people, and there were too many names to even begin to remember.

We actually felt overawed by the welcome because until this point we'd been so self-centred that we had genuinely seen our ordeal as unique. We'd thought that no-one could possibly know exactly how we felt, because, after all, our seven week-old son had been pronounced terminally ill. Suddenly, we found ourselves in a micro-environment where this was perfectly the norm.

We were escorted to a beautiful room that had been allocated to Harry, with an adjoining room being set aside for us. With Harry happily asleep in his new room, we were given a guided tour of the facilities.

Close to Harry's room, along the same corridor, there was a special bathroom. The bath within this room came equipped with a hoist to help the staff and parents get some of the children in and out, and the shape of the tub had been designed to accommodate two people, for when a parent wanted to bathe with their child. Further down the corridor was the 'teenage' room, equipped with DVD players, gaming stations and a stereo. At first, I was slightly confused by the requirement for this room. Harry would never be able to use any of this equipment, and at the time, my knowledge and understanding of the range of hospice residents was almost nil. We later learnt that many of the children requiring the use of Acorns suffered from Muscular Dystrophy. This horrendous condition only affects boys, but as treatment for MD progresses, so does the life expectancy of the sufferer. Many of the boys at Acorns with this condition would actually outlive the age range that could be dealt with by the hospice.

Close by the entrance doors was the main 'hub' of the hospice. Here, families and children gathered in a communal fashion, watching TV, playing games, laughing. It was the latter part that was at first so hard to comprehend. Our naive impression had been that a hospice was a place you were sent to be cared for until you died. Yet Acorns wanted to turn that concept around. This was a place for living, laughing and making the most out of life, for after all, we're all going to die at some point. This approach, surprising as it was, matched our earlier decision to build happy memories.

My favourite room in the hospice was the sensory room. Though fairly small, this room was crammed with tall, water filled tubes within which bubbles would rise and pop. Bells and crinkly paper and other touch-stimulating material adorned the walls. A heated water mattress lay on the floor, and the warm liquid within it sloshed around comfortably when you lay on it. Fibre-optic cables that constantly changed colour lay across the floor, and a disco glitter-ball hung from the ceiling reflecting millions of tiny shards of light around the walls of the room.

Upstairs, along with some administration rooms, there were two en-suite 'family rooms' which shared a kitchen and private lounge. These rooms could be booked out to allow families to remain close to their children for a few days at a time.

We were told of additional facilities that we would be shown the following day. For now, we felt like we needed some time alone. Everyone was incredibly friendly, and they were all doing their upmost for us. But we felt unprepared for this after the days of trauma and tension. We needed to retreat.

It was quite late at night by this point and a huge man called Paul, a night porter who could only ever be found in a pair of shorts, no matter what the month or weather, set about making up some beds for Esta and I in the room that had been allocated to us.

In the seclusion of our room that night, I told Esta that I didn't feel ready to socialise with everyone in the communal area. We were in the same boat as them, except that I didn't expect to be in the hospice more than a day or so. I couldn't put my finger on how I actually felt, but I was convinced we would be short-term residents, and that it made little sense to build up relationships with the other families.

That ridiculous attitude quickly changed the following morning.

As opposed to the motion alarm that had woken us every morning for several days, we rose to a gentle tap at the door. A nurse on the day staff asked if we'd like to join everyone for breakfast whilst she saw to Harry. Esta said that she'd like to show the nurse how Harry liked to be changed, so I had a shave for the first time in over a week whilst this demonstration took place. Whilst Esta subsequently took a leisurely shower, I took Harry along to the sensory room for the first time. I lay him down gently on the water bed, and though Harry never issued one smile his whole life, a strange look of comfort and satisfaction crossed his face when he felt the warmth of the water penetrate his back through the rubber mattress. As staff and family passed the room, they'd pop their heads in to see us and say hi. It was impossible not to instantly begin to associate and engage with these individuals who were so well-meaning, and my initial notion of staying aloft from people the night before was soon forgotten. When Esta found us, she saw our boy contentedly staring at the lights on the ceiling as he gently swayed about on the water bed. We spent many happy hours in the sensory room with our son during his time at Acorns, and it was at one of these times that we became aware how Harry was particularly soothed by the sound of the bubbles in the tube. One of the nurses suggested we try out a sound machine when putting Harry to sleep, and by trial and error we eventually found that he quickly became calm and relaxed when he could hear the gentle and rhythmic sound of waves crashing on a shore. Little discoveries like this about our boy having his own personality, despite any expectations of this being possible, were memories to be cherished.

Due to Harry's thorough dislike of being fussed, his pit-stop style changes had generally restricted him to the bare minimum use of a cleansing wipe or a warm flannel. But as I saw how happy he was with feeling the warmth of the water bed beneath him on that first visit, I suggested to Esta that we give him a bath in the special room. As Harry liked to feel secure by being tucked in tightly in bed, or wrapped up firmly in a blanket when he was awake, I proposed getting in the water with him to hold him close and safe. A nurse assisted us with running the bath, and clad only in my underwear, I climbed in whilst the nurse then passed our boy to me. Whilst ever quick to voice his indignation at any discomfort or unwanted attention, Harry had no means of showing his appreciation other than by the absence of crying. We were fairly sure our son was almost totally blind, and as he had never witnessed a smile, he was unable to mirror the expression. But seeing him content, with a relaxed look on his face and a lack of tension in his muscles, brought an incredible amount of joy to us. As I bent my knees, Harry lay back on my legs, submerged up to his chest in warm water as I held his arms firmly, the way he liked.

'I'm sure Harry will enjoy the hydro-pool just as much as the bath,' Jan Large told us later.

'You have a pool?' We asked. Our guided tour continued whilst Harry slept contentedly after his bath.

The Acorns building had been designed and built from the

ground upwards with the sole intention of being a hospice for children. Everything in it, including the pool, had been specially designed to deal with less-able people. The pool had a ramp down which dedicated wheelchairs could safely descend, and a hoist to lift children in and out of the water. It was a fantastic on-site facility that allowed residents and families to enjoy a swim without the requirement to try and use public pools. Lewis couldn't wait to try the pool out, and as Jan had predicted, Harry absolutely loved it every time we took him for a swim. Between the water bed and the pool, it was hard to decide where he was happiest. All in all, Acorns was a Utopia for us and our boy.

The tour culminated in a facility that Jan paused outside of. She needed to prepare us for what lay beyond the next set of doors.

'These are our "cold" rooms. When.... the inevitable happens, children are laid to rest here, until the funeral or cremation. I find it better that parents see these rooms now, rather than only laying their eyes on them later. This facility is much more private and personal, not to mention on-site, than a funeral parlour.' We agreed that the concept was great, but we did could stay long in the rooms and we moved on quickly.

Following on from this was the most awkward and unsettling meeting we had yet endured. AV Band, a local funeral director, had been asked to come and see us. We were to make preliminary arrangements for Harry's funeral. The only omission was the actual date of the event, as 'when' was the only unknown at this point.

It was deeply disturbing and difficult to be sitting there selecting a 'casket' and discussing travel arrangements whilst our son was still alive and asleep in his room. We were leafing through a brochure, and though the funeral director seemed to wince when I used the term coffin instead of casket, he was amazingly professional. He informed us that all services would be provided by AV Band without charge. Funerals for children were tragic for all involved, he explained, and the company could not bring themselves to subsequently invoice the parents. The kind consideration brought tears to our eyes.

A semblance of routine began to return to our lives. After a few weeks of not earning a wage, I eventually had to return to London during the week. Monday to Thursday, Esta would take Lewis to school before then heading over to the hospice for the day.

She would then return to pick Lewis up, spend some time with him until he went to bed, and then would leave him with her mum Pat whilst Esta stayed with Harry overnight, arriving home early in the morning so that Lewis never knew she had not slept at home. On a Friday, when I returned from London, we'd all move into one of the family rooms upstairs in Acorns. Our weekends would then all be spent together, with the other families, at the hospice.

We were not solely confined to the hospice building itself, however, and would often venture out. Sometimes we would take Harry with us, or very occasionally we would take the staff up on their kind offer of letting us spend some time with Lewis. When Harry came along it was only the presence of the GN tube that told anyone that anything was at all amiss. We had gradually become accustomed to our situation, and we rarely felt like a sub-normal family. In truth, few people would have known or suspected that we were pushing a terminally ill child around in a pram. For his part, Lewis was taking everything in his stride. He was making friends with lots of the children at Acorns, unaware that there was indeed anything wrong with them whatsoever. Many of the boys with MD would race their wheelchairs up and down their corridor, and Lewis loved to run alongside them. It was amazing to see the natural absence of any prejudice - Lewis saw the child long before he saw the wheelchair.

We made some amazing friends amongst the staff. Harry, at just over eight weeks old, was the youngest user of the hospice at the time. As such he was doted after by many of the female staff, and chief amongst these were Jane, Andrea and Claire. The latter two were senior nurses in charge of our boy. Jane, a very buxom lady, absolutely loved to cuddle Harry, and for his part, our boy appeared to be in bliss when sleeping snuggled into her bosom.

Jan Large, in charge of the overall facility, was always on hand and available for advice or support. Nothing ever seemed too much to ask of anyone at the hospice.

The caretaker/handyman at Acorns was a man called Tony. I don't think it is possible to meet a happier, more cheerful guy in the world. Tony had a perpetual and huge grin on his face as wide as a canyon, and he was positively effervescent whenever we met him. Tony would work happily in the garden, and to keep themselves amused the staff would shoot water at him using large spare syringes. Whenever they scored a hit, Tony would stop on his ride-on lawn mower and wave a theatrical fist at them whilst roaring with laughter at his own misfortune. During that winter, Lewis and I built a snowman in the gardens, and had many a snowball fight with Tony. How the man managed to get any work done is a mystery to me.

Christmas was approaching, and with it came a problem: We had booked a family holiday to Egypt, and clearly it was not possible to take Harry with us. We'd made no changes to the dates or flights, as we had all firmly believed that the inevitable would have happened long before we set off, and that the holiday would be a recuperation period we would all be in need of.

And yet weeks later, we somehow found ourselves still waiting for the inevitable.

'You'll have to go with Lewis,' Esta told me. 'I can't leave Harry. Honestly I can't. I'd never forgive myself if something happened whilst I was away after all of this. But Lewis needs his holiday, so please, will you take him?'

I agreed that Lewis needed some time away. His life, like ours, revolved around the hospice. He had toys at home he hardly ever saw, and for three nights out of seven he slept upstairs in the family apartment at Acorns. He would wake in the morning and make his way down to the main hub, where we'd find him later playing with some other children, or being read to by a nurse. With the hospice being such a secure and safe environment, with access only provided to appropriate areas, Lewis was always safe. But we have always loved going abroad. Lewis had already been to several different countries around the world, and he could happily play on a beach for hours. I really did have to take him away.

I began to look into the possibility of flying Esta out to stay with us for a short while, even if it was just two or three days, but she was adamant that she could not leave Harry. So Lewis and I jumped into our car and set off towards Manchester one night in December. The flight to Sharm El Sheik was early in the morning. Lewis was six and a half at the time, and I knew it was going to be a long day for him. Consequently, I booked us into a hotel close to the airport the night before the flight in order to break the journey up. It was only during the drive north that the reality of the situation hit me. I'd only ever been alone with Lewis for a few hours at a time. I was now solely responsible for him for two weeks. Abroad. Children need to be fed, and I was bad enough at remembering to feed myself. I didn't really know what his favourite food was, what he didn't eat, or what on earth I'd do with him day after day. He was my son, and I suddenly realised how little I knew him.

'Why isn't mummy coming with us?' He asked from the back of the car.

'She has to stay and look after Harry.'

'Why? Can't the nurses do that?'

'Yes, but mummy wants to be there too.'

'Is Harry getting better?'

'No. The doctors can't make Harry better, unfortunately.'

'So will he always be poorly? Forever?'

Lewis had been assigned a child bereavement councillor called Sarah. Sarah had spent some time playing with him to gain his trust, but he'd thus far been very uncommunicative about what he understood and thought about Harry.

'Children process this information in their own time,' she told us. 'You might think he isn't aware, but he is. His mind will only allow him to deal with a certain amount of detail at any one time. So you'll find he'll ask questions when he's ready, and then he'll go away and process your answer. It's important you don't lie to him. Tell him what he needs to know. Children deal with it better than adults, to be honest.' Her words and advice were astonishingly accurate, as we found out on a few occasions. It was with Sarah's advice that we came up with a little stress-relieving game prior to letting Lewis go to sleep: Each of us would take it in turn to tell the others of one favourite thing that we had done or seen during that day. We included Harry in this game of course, and one of us would begin that part by saying, 'Harry's favourite thing today was...' Sometimes this would be that Harry had been for a swim, or had spent much of the day snuggled into Jane's bosom, but generally it was the sound of the waves on his sound machine that had soothed him and sent him off to sleep.

Lewis and I checked into our hotel near Manchester airport that night. To him, this was all a big adventure. I told him that without mummy being there, he'd have to be a big boy and help me as much as possible. He readily agreed, and showed me how he could get into his pyjamas on his own, and that he could go to bed without a fuss. We played our 'favourite things' game, saying that Harry would have liked the hotel room we were in, and Lewis rolled over to go to sleep. It was around 19:00. I realised that I was going to get lots of reading done over the next two weeks, as by the same time each night I'd be alone, but unable to go out anywhere.

We'd set an alarm for early the next morning, ready to catch the flight. Lewis jumped out of bed, eager to carry on with his display of grown up behaviour. He got dressed and made his bed on his own.

As we approached the airport car park a little while later, Lewis said, 'Dad, where's blankie?'

'Isn't it in the back with you?'

'No.'

'Well did you pack it with your pyjamas this morning?'

'No.'

'Did you even bring it from Acorns?'

'Yes. I had it in bed with me last night.'

I paused. 'Lewis, did you take blankie out of bed before making it this morning?'

'Er. No.'

Great! So we were about to head off for two weeks to Egypt, and we'd already lost his comfort blanket. It was not a good start.

I distracted him on the plane by giving him a present. We don't do a huge round of presents on Christmas day, but as we go away most years, we had got into the habit of giving Lewis a small present every day or so throughout the holiday, such as a DVD to watch or a small toy to play with. He unwrapped the small parcel I gave him, and looked at me quizzically. He'd never played Top Trumps, so I had to explain how the game worked. It was a dinosaur set, for like most boys his age, Lewis was fascinated by the giant lizards. From that moment on, we played dinosaur Top Trumps almost incessantly for the next two weeks. Lewis could not get enough, and when I said I needed a break, he would sort them into categories in ascending or descending order, would invent games whereby he could play on his own, and he memorised the values attributed to each dinosaur. When we played the game together, if I inadvertently gave away which card I had next, Lewis would know what category he had to play in order to beat me. I presented him with another two packs during the holiday, but they were all-but discarded after one game. Nothing could diminish his love for the dinosaur pack.

The self-catering accommodation we'd booked was around two miles outside the main town of Sharm El Sheik. The owner collected us from the airport and took us to the apartment in the gated community, and we staying in a lovely two bedroom apartment complete with lounge and kitchen. Lewis's suitcase, packed by Esta, had a clean change of clothes for every day. In the end, as most days were spent in trunks and a tee shirt, we took most of the items home unworn. In addition to this, we had a washing machine anyway.

Days were spent on the beach. Sharm only has a few 'public' beaches, and you have to pay for sun loungers on these. One of the strange phenomenon about kids and beaches is that they always want to play in the patch of sand which is at least 20 or more meters away from the lounger you pick. If you move closer to them, they suddenly want to play somewhere else. And then, after a while, they get bored with that beach, and they want to walk along so that you have to pay for another sun lounger a hundred meters up the same beach. This was costing me a fortune in sun beds alone.

Unlike in Greece, where hotels are happy to have non-staying guests use their facilities if they purchase food and drinks, only guests of hotels are allowed on the hotel beaches in Egypt. These hotels are typically located on the best parts of the sand, with the public beaches being noticeably inferior. I noticed that the security guards appeared to know who was and was not a guest, and after a spell of people watching I figured out why: The guests all had the same hotel towels.

The next day, wrong though it probably was, I borrowed two towels that some guest had used to 'reserve' some loungers. Equipped with these items, which I washed daily, Lewis and I began to use the very best beach in Sharm. I reconciled any qualms I had by ensuring that I bought ice creams and beers from the overpriced bar at the hotel, thereby giving them our custom, as opposed to patronising the cheaper shops along the promenade. And of course at the end of the two weeks, I left the clean towels behind.

Despite my initial worries, our holiday passed without a single cross word between us. I won the occasional game of dinosaur Top Trumps, and we enjoyed sharing ice cream whilst I had a beer. More importantly, we shared dad and son time together in the sun. We spoke with Esta almost daily, but aside from everyday events within the hub at Acorns, there was nothing to report.

When Lewis and I returned home, the world had moved into 2007.

And Harry was getting by, day by day.

A Normal Life

Days turned into weeks, and though Harry had never been given any life expectancy estimate, he was actually beginning to steadily grow and put on weight. By now, our boy had developed his own personality, and it was often possible to predict what was going to happen next. Unfortunately, one of the many side effects of his cerebral palsy was reflux. With very little warning, Harry would vomit. But it wasn't always totally unexpected, as he would at first show some signs of visible discomfort, then he would issue a slight cough, and if you were quick, you could cover him in a tea towel seconds before his milk was brought back up. The signature cough was very distinctive, and we would see Andrea, Claire or Jane suddenly leap into action upon hearing it.

Harry also learnt a surprising trick that often caught us all off guard. Whilst he generally had little to no motor control over his limbs, he did have an uncanny ability to use his hands at times. His GN tube seemed to irritate him, and whilst one minute he would be sitting in his chair motionless, it seemed that the moment nobody was looking Harry was able to whip the tube out of his nose and stomach, only to be found holding the end with a 'It wasn't me' look on his face. Whilst on the one hand this was funny, it did cause issues. Reinserting the tube was a delicate and potentially dangerous task. The nurse doing this had to be completely sure that the tube had slid down into our son's stomach and not into his lung, as obviously the latter would cause him to drown when he was next fed. Placing a small sock over his hands made his removal of the tube slightly less easy, but it was still nevertheless a regular occurrence.

Harry's combination of heart problems and cerebral palsy meant that he had a whole team of specialists assigned to him, from the neurologist to the cardiologist, but also a very senior GP and even a speech and language therapist. The latter, despite the title, actually also specialised in the issue of the reflux, and could advise us on what developments we could expect as Harry grew. Having never seen him express any positive emotions, it was one day decided that we would try Harry with a tiny piece of chocolate to see his reaction to tasting something so sweet. The speech and language therapist could not be sure how well Harry's taste buds were functioning, or if the associated part of the brain would even respond, so it was with a high level of anticipation that a small crowd gathered around Harry for this tasting experiment. Esta took a tiny piece of chocolate and placed it in Harry's mouth. Instinct kicked in when he felt food in his mouth, and his gums worked away at the chocolate whilst all eyes remained glued to Harry's expression. To our disappointment, he did not even blink. Of all the pleasures in life, poor Harry was not even able to enjoy the taste and sensation of chocolate.

Effectively, Harry was suffering from four conditions: Cerebral palsy brought on by two or three massive strokes; a blockage in his main artery; large cataracts in both eyes; and sever reflux. We knew that nothing could be done about the palsy, and as he grew, the heart blockage was actually becoming less of an issue, for the arteries were growing but the blockage (whatever it was) was not. The doctors were unsure if Harry would be able to see any better if the cataracts were removed, so discussions were being had as to whether or not to operate. The reflux, however, was deeply unpleasant for Harry. It was decided that an operation could be performed on his tiny stomach, effectively tying it at the top and somewhat alleviating the issue. We were led to believe this was not a small operation, and we were torn between putting Harry through this ordeal, or leaving him to suffer the reflux. Our son was too young at this point however, so our decision could wait a while. The indignations to Harry seemed never ending.

We became very much a part of the fabric at Acorns, having been such regular visitors for so many months. By springtime, Harry had been a full-time resident for over four months. Everyone knew both Harry and us very well indeed, so at one point Andrea asked me if there was anything I could do towards organising a visit for some of the older children at the hospice. Andrea knew I was a season ticket holder at our local premiership rugby club, Worcester Warriors, and she suggested I get in touch with someone to see if any of the players would come to the hospice to meet the kids.

Sir Cecil Duckworth, founder of the Worcester Engineering Company (later sold on to Bosch Group) was the original inventor of the combi-boiler. Shortly after retiring from Bosch in 1996, Sir Cecil became executive chairman to Worcester Warriors (who were very much struggling at the time). He also contributed a very hefty sum towards the initial building of the Acorns hospice in Worcester, so links between the club and the hospice already existed prior to me getting in touch. At no more expense than sending a simple email, the Warrior's public relations officer at the time, Ben Mottram, arranged for the visit to go ahead. The hospice was already the local charity supported by the club, but Ben admitted that most of the focus that season had been on retaining Premiership status within the rugby world. The visit to the hospice would be a welcome break for some of the players.

The children at the club were enormously excited on the day, and I think Esta and I felt the same way. The players are very much local celebrities, though this never seems to go to their heads. Not one of them I've ever met has been anything other than an absolute gentleman. Many of the players who came along that day have now moved on or have even retired, such as Pat Sanderson, Shane Drahm, Tony Window and the Fortey brothers. I still chat regularly to the huge second row, Craig Gillies, whom I often see at David Lloyd's (more about that later), and he also volunteered to help me out with a mini challenge later too. I was asked to speak to the players about the vital services the hospice provided us, and I gave them a bit of a guided tour of the building. We all crowded into to see Harry, and when I explained his condition, two of the huge rugby players began to quietly cry. They may have been big men, but they were all very human too.

The Warriors had brought along a photographer by the name of Mike Henley. It was the first time we had met Mike, and he asked our names once, and has never forgotten them since. We see him regularly at rugby matches and other charity events, and he takes the time to say hello, takes a photograph, and emails it to us for free. Mike is another real gentleman.

For his part, Harry became a bit of a mascot. Months later, knowing the links between us and the hospice, the Warriors invited us along to a shirt launch prior to the start of the next rugby season. The shirts were the bright orange corporate colours of the Acorns logo, so Esta, Harry and I all donned a shirt and joined Craig Gillies and some other players for a promotional photograph, taken of course, by Mike Henley. Within the hospice they had begun to put these photos on the wall, referring to it as the Warrior's Wall. Harry featured heavily on this wall.

It was also whilst we were at the hospice that a new CEO for Acorns arrived, David Strudley. David was ex-military, as was instantly recognisable in his stance, bearing and manner. He and I hit it off immediately, and to the shock of every staff member, David showed how a real leader earns respect in a new environment: He literally donned rubber gloves and joined in with the basic hands-on work of scrubbing the hospice top to bottom. It was a tactic that worked, and David was very much loved from that point onwards.

We were hit with a major problem at one point, however. Whilst saying upstairs in the family rooms one weekend, Lewis woke up saying he didn't feel very well. He was also itching, and kept scratching all over. We quickly discovered that he had chicken pox. The worst thing about this was the potential risk to many of the children downstairs. Catching chicken pox could easily be fatal to them, so we had no choice but to quarantine Lewis upstairs whilst dividing our time between him and his terminally ill brother downstairs. It was a particularly awkward time that involved ensuring we were as sanitised as possible for every visit made to Harry, and though Lewis recovered in around a week or so, it was a long few days of isolation for him.

As summer loomed, the better weather brought with it impending operations for Harry, together with an event we'd secretly acknowledged, but tried to ignore: It was time to leave the hospice and take Harry home.

Though he would always be under the care of Acorns, Harry no longer needed 24/7 monitoring. He could comfortably be left in his specially adapted chair so that he could sit upright, and Esta knew how to change the feed bags on his slow drip feed machine. This all meant that we could take Harry back to our house, and now use the hospice more as a means of respite.

We were terrified.

Packing our stuff from Harry's room was quite traumatic. He'd been moved to another corridor from his original room, as we no longer needed the adjoining room to sleep in. Still, every one of Harry's clothes, his pictures and other trinkets, all resided at the hospice. The car seemed loaded with an inordinate amount of stuff as we drove away and took Harry to our house for the first night since rushing him to the hospital the previous winter.

I don't think either Esta nor I slept a wink that night. Esta wanted Harry in the room with us, and it was the first time we'd slept with him near us since the early days of arriving at Acorns. The regular rhythmic turning of his continual-feed machine could be heard every few seconds, together with Harry's murmuring. Everything felt very unfamiliar all over again.

But it's incredible how quickly you get used to a new way of life. Before we knew it, having a terminally ill child in the house became perfectly normal. Lewis missed seeing the children at the hospice as much as he was used to, but we returned regularly, as much to see our friends there as out of any necessity for Harry. Our son was always taken away from us for cuddles as soon as we arrived, usually by Jane, and we would sit with Andrea and Jan and have tea whilst eating homemade cakes from the kitchen.

Without having a full-time nurse on hand, we too had to learn to read Harry's little signs. A jutting-out bottom lip generally told us he was uncomfortable or unhappy about something. We had moments to work out what was wrong and rectify it before he would begin to wail. Such crying fits were, and always would be, very dangerous to Harry, as they would lead on to larger seizures which resulted in our son's breathing to stop, so we always had to keep a close eye on him. Esta recalls one time when she was upstairs in the bathroom. I was at work in London, and she heard Harry give his distinctive little cough, meaning he was going to be sick very soon. She called down to Lewis to cover Harry, and when she arrived on the scene a few moments later, the child was smothered in around ten tea towels, with only his face showing. Lewis had taken her at her word.

One thing we could not do alone, and which always necessitated a return trip to the hospice, as reinsert Harry's GN tube if he pulled it out. He'd continued to perfect this little trick, and on a few occasions either Esta or I would have to drive all the way across town in the small hours of the night to ask an Acorns nurse to help us out. They would often take Harry off us for the remainder of the evening whilst we'd crash out on the settee in the hub for a few hours, returning home with him later in the morning.

And then, at the point where we'd almost stopped expecting it, the inevitable happened. Harry died.

Our biggest worry at this point, with Harry now living back

at home, was that this might happen whilst I was in London and Esta was alone with him. Her mum, Pat would stay over as often as she could, which was a massive moral support for Esta, but that wasn't the same as having me there to help her.

It was on a Friday night that it happened. I had returned from London, and Lewis had been put to bed. We were deciding what to have for dinner, and whether to order in a takeaway, when Esta said she needed to change Harry first. This was still the delicate operation it had always been, but Esta could all-but do this in her sleep now. Harry would always complain, no matter how quick it was, and the lip would come out and the tears would start.

Except that on this particular night, Harry did not calm down. He seemed to get himself more and more wound up. As we watched, his eyes began to flicker, and we knew he was having a fit. He didn't often go as rigid as we'd experienced when he was much younger, so when he arched his back this time and thrust all his limbs out in a star shape, we looked at each other with startled and worried expressions. It had been around eight months since we'd issued the no resuscitation order on our son at BCH, and the staff at Acorns had been made aware of our wishes too. On both occasions we'd had to sign forms as proof of our ascent. But now, as Harry began to gurgle and hold his breath, we realised how issuing the order and sitting there passively (albeit horrified and in utter torment) were worlds apart in thought and deed. Every fibre in each of us screamed that we should do something. As a parent, a human being, instinct urged us to help. Many times in the past, before we knew the reason behind Harry's fits, we had gently puffed into his mouth, causing our boy to quickly resume breathing. Though we both very much wanted to do the same again at that point, we somehow resisted. Instead, as horrific and cruel as it sounds, we sat there, much as we'd instructed the medical staff to do in such an event.

I cannot adequately describe how difficult it was to restrain ourselves, and how truly devastating it was to witness our son die in front of our eyes. We fully expected the life instinct that had kept Harry alive until this point would once more cause him to take a huge gulp of air at any second, much as we'd seen him do in the ICU when his ventilator had been switched off. I gently scooped Harry up off the floor, unable to just abandon him. I held his arms tightly, the way he liked to be restrained, but I resisted the incredible temptation to start him breathing again. And as we continued to watch, Esta clinging tightly to me, Harry's body gradually relaxed. As we saw the tension easing from his taught muscles, Harry released a gentle sigh. For a while, I wondered if he'd worn himself into a deep sleep, but though I'd never held a dead body, I can assure you that there is a certain stillness to a corpse that brooks no argument.

    Though it had appeared at one point that Harry would continue to indefinitely defy all the experts, on that night in August, at home in our house in Worcester, Harry finally succumbed to the cerebral palsy that had dogged him his entire life.

    He died in my arms, aged 10 months.

After Harry

We sat in motionless silence for some time. The occasional car passed our house outside, but there was no other sound to disturb our solitude. I sat with Harry, motionless and peaceful at last, in my arms. There was no urgency to do anything. Indeed, nothing could be done for Harry, and we were aware that a storm of activity awaited us - an unpleasant flurry of necessary tasks, appointments, meetings and interviews. This little slice of peace could be stretched out whilst we had the opportunity to simply sit together and grieve alone. For a long time, long after it was at all possible, we still expected Harry to start crying at any moment.

In times of such emotion, the brain and memory plays tricks. There are many things I find myself recalling vividly, and yet other facts escape my remembrance at all. One of us must have broken the spell and spoken first, suggesting that we phone Acorns. One of us must have acknowledged the need to phone our respective mothers and allow them to be the very first people to know. Under pain of death I could not tell who that person was. I do know that I called my mother, managing only a single, strangled word: 'Harry.' Nothing more needed saying. My mother and step-father told me they were on their way immediately. In the meantime, one of us called Acorns - Possibly it was me. They professionally assured us that they would contact a doctor and ensure we had someone on site at the earliest opportunity - legally, we needed someone qualified to confirm and record the death. (Years later, whilst conducting research for a novel I was writing, I discovered that ambulance paramedics are actually also qualified to pronounce someone dead. It's a myth that only a doctor can do this).

How much time passed whilst waiting for the doctor I have no way of knowing. When he did arrive, confusion and anxiety were his unwelcome travelling companions.

'What has happened to the child?' he asked, brusquely. He was checking Harry for signs of life, and clearly he was concerned to find our baby lifeless.

We explained that Harry had simply stopped breathing. He'd held his breath, and finally he'd expired.

'Why?'

We were baffled. How could we answer such a question? Surely the doctor was in a better position to know why a severely brain damaged child would suddenly die than we were.

'This is highly unusual,' he continued. 'I don't know why a child would die like this. What was the child doing before the accident occurred?'

Having his nappy changed.

'Why would a child stop breathing just because it was having its nappy changed?'

It finally dawned on us that the doctor was not in complete possession of the facts of the situation. He thought he was attending the death of a perfectly healthy child, not a terminally ill one. As though we had not already been through enough tragedy, we were now forced to explain the heart condition, the cerebral palsy, and the fact that Harry was in the care of Acorns.

The doctor looked at us with suspicion. 'I will have to confirm what you are saying.' He told us abruptly, and promptly left the room to do just that, leaving us alone and angry at the obvious breakdown in communication.

I cannot remember the time, but I'm sure it was dark by the time my mother arrived, tearful and grieving. We told her we would be taking Harry to Acorns... as soon as a slight misunderstanding had been cleared up. When she asked how she could help, we asked if she could possibly stay and look after Lewis until the morning?

The doctor returned, matter-of-factly informing us (as though we needed such corroboration) that our story was true. There was no offer of apology, and if anything he seemed to think we should have appraised him of the situation first. He filled in some paperwork, told us we could continue with whatever our plans were, and left.

Somehow we got to Acorns. I had our lifeless son cradled in my arms, and we carried him towards the main entrance. The doors opened in anticipation, though I cannot recall who greeted us. We were quietly and efficiently escorted to one of the two dedicated 'cold rooms' we'd been shown on our guided tour. We gently placed Harry into bed. He looked perfectly at rest, as though finally sleeping a drug-free sleep at last.

Esta slept little that night. The rational and logical side of her mind assured her Harry was dead. We'd seen him breathe his last, we'd held him for ages whilst he lay there lifeless, and a doctor had confirmed he had passed away. And yet there was an uncontrollable urge inside her to go downstairs and check on our boy. Having spent almost every minute of her life for the last 10 months in thinking about Harry, caring for him, dealing with him, it seemed utterly unreal that she could now simply stop doing so. She knew he was just downstairs, and that he was alone in that secluded room. She had an irrational worry that he was cold.

    We'd asked our mothers to inform the other family members of what had happened. A death is not the sort of news to feel comfortable about in the continual retelling. It's not the happy news of an engagement or a birth. It's totally the opposite, and we'd already told as many people as we felt emotionally capable of.

    Messages and texts began to flood in. People were offering their condolences, asking if they could come and see us to offer moral support. We weren't ready for this. It was too soon. There would be a lifetime of sympathy, and we were in no rush to begin the process just yet. Acorns once more came to our rescue, and Jan informed us that we were now safely ensconced behind fortress walls. No one, at all, would breach the defences unless we gave explicit permission for them to do so. We duly passed this information on to friends and family, ensuring they did not waste a journey only to be turned away at the doors. Everyone would be informed when the funeral would take place, but for the present we requested that everyone respected our privacy.

    Of course I had to inform work of the fact that I would not be back for a few days. I sent a text to my boss, Amanda, and to Guy, her second in command. I learnt much later that Guy had been in the changing room of the gym, having just worked out on weights when he read the message. He went from physical euphoria to a state of stunned and shocked disbelief in a split second, slumping down heavily onto a bench as he absorbed the news.

    That first day after Harry had died, the atmosphere within the hospice was noticeably subdued. The staff still played games with the children, films were still shown and meals were still enjoyed, but everything was done with respect to our plight. Parents of children eyed us with sympathy, knowing that ultimately they too would be in our position at some point in the near future. The staff, all of whom had become close friends, came over personally to hug us and whisper words of warmth. It became shockingly apparent how human these helpers all were, and how attached to Harry they'd become, when many of the staff were reduced to tears upon hearing the news of his death.

For a while we pondered over the hospice's means of communicating the events amongst staff. We watched as they all arrived into the communal area with visages of doubt and concern - faces that utterly contrasted with the normal smiles and joviality they would wear upon arrival to work. Clearly they knew something had happened, but they didn't know what. We watched Jane arrive into work that first day, slightly wild-eyed and worried. Her eyes fell upon us, alone without Harry and red-eyed from tears. She put two and two together and burst into floods of tears herself.

It was Esta who eventually stumbled upon the subtle and considerate code. A bookmark in the shape of an Acorn had been placed in the signing-in book. All staff entering the building encountered the secret symbol telling them a child had passed away. Though they did not know who, the code pre-empted any of them bounding joyfully into a roomful of grieving relatives.

We spent a week secured behind the walls of the hospice, venturing out only for such necessities as to procure a death certificate from the registrar. During our stay we arranged the funeral, contacted friends and family with invites and instructions, but otherwise shut ourselves off, once again, from society. Sarah, the child bereavement councillor, again turned out to be right with her earlier advice. Sometime over the previous months, Lewis had kept a pet beetle in a box. Inevitably it died at some point, and we had used the event to discuss the circle of life. We'd told him that Harry was going to die too, and that it would probably be a lot sooner than with most children. We then asked Lewis what he was going to do with the beetle. He could bury it, or he could cremate it.

'What's "cremate"?'

'Well, instead of being buried, some people wish their bodies to be burned, or cremated, and have their ashes scattered somewhere they love. We are going to cremate Harry when he dies.'

Lewis said nothing more about it at the time, as Sarah had told us. He simply went away and processed the information. However, his timing could not have been much worse. Esta was standing at the till in Next, buying a new dress for the funeral, when Lewis suddenly asked, 'Mummy, why are we going to burn Harry?'

Apparently the shop assistant could not have been more alarmed.

I personally conducted Harry's funeral. Aside from some of the Acorns staff, of whom it would not have been fair to even request such a task, there was no one else who knew him well enough to do the job. Even had we documented the ideas, memories and thoughts we wanted to be recounted, having a stranger read such a eulogy felt unpalatable, distasteful even. We were highly conscious that there would be no second run at this. The first time would be the only time, and we wanted it to be as perfect as any funeral could be. Harry deserved that.

Strange as it may sound to some, we also did not view the actual funeral as a sad occasion. Certainly our son had died, we were only too aware of that, but in many ways we had undergone a massive period of grieving those eight months previously when we had been informed of Harry's condition. Accordingly, with everyone expecting him to pass away within a matter of hours or days, the months we had spent with him had each been a blessing. They had been bonus days in his company we'd never have dared to hope for. So though he was now gone, we could look back and say with confidence that the very best that could be done for Harry, had been done. Our son was now resting peacefully, without the dark clouds of looming operations, and finally free from the discomfort of reflux. As befitting our outlook, we requested that friends and family attending the funeral avoided wearing black, and if anything, suggested they come attired in something bright. To our delight, some attended wearing the bright orange Worcester rugby shirts which Harry had been photographed wearing at the promotional launch. We were sure that this would have been Harry's favourite thing that day.

The event itself was a simple one. As previously promised, local funeral directors A.V. Band arranged a casket for Harry and supplied cars to transport us to and from the crematorium - all free of charge.

We had always known that there was only one way Harry would be leaving the hospice. There are few, if any true miracles, and no happy endings can realistically be expected for residents at such venues. Yet despite all of this, it was unbelievably moving to see how much consideration Jan Large had put into arranging for Harry's final departure.

Being mindful of the anxiety it would cause other parents to see a hearse draw up to the main entrance of the hospice, and to subsequently witness a casket make its solemn journey through the doors, we had been anticipating a quiet exit through the rear of the hospice. Jan would hear none of it.

'Harry was a VIP. VIPs do not sneak out the back,' she told us with genuine passion. Parents were discreetly warned of the date and time of the proceedings in order to alleviate any discomfort caused by accidentally stumbling upon the scene, and staff lined the route from the cold room to the front door as Harry bade goodbye to the hospice once and for all. Esta, Lewis and I followed the hearse in a shiny black Limousine provided by AV Band, and slowly and sedately we made our way towards the crematorium. The short journey was responsible for delivering a mental image I will never forget: A lady stood by the side of the road, looking sadly at the hearse and bending her head in respect. Suddenly her head shot back up. Her sub-consciousness had noticed something that her conscious brain had only just registered. Her eyes took in the size of the tiny coffin, her mouth formed a small 'o' shape as her hand came up to her face in grief, and then we were past her, leaving her to stare on in her solitary sadness.

At the crematorium we were met by an old friend, Carl. He and I have since gone our own ways, but on that day Carl had agreed to a vital role: he would assist me in carrying Harry's casket inside the crematorium.

The box was small, and incredibly light. I could probably have carried it alone, were it not for the mortal dread of possibly dropping it.

I was not naive enough to believe that we were not on a conveyor belt. I knew that one funeral party would only have left moments before we arrived, and that another would be gathering outside the front door as we in turn held our little service inside. But for a short time the facilities were ours alone. I conducted a simple service, offering personal family memories of Harry, mentioning his few mannerisms, his likes and dislikes. I delivered a comic recount of Harry's one trip to a Warrior's rugby match when he'd woken up to the roar of the crowd, drawing involuntary laughs from guests who were not entirely sure whether or not they should be so jovial at a child's funeral; I read a child's poem entitled 'This Much Love'; and

I allowed everyone two minutes of personal reflection or prayer whilst the casket disappeared from sight.

It was then my genuinely solemn duty to press the button which would draw the curtains around the casket and to roll the small box forwards towards the waiting gas and flames.

Harry was gone.

It was 'Closure'.

We'd purchased a lovely lidded wooden box which had been placed by the exit door. I requested that everyone dig deep and donate whatever they could afford, as the proceeds would be given directly to Acorns in memory of our little boy.

And with that, I closed the proceedings.

As we filtered out, we noticed that even the weather had listened to our requests to avoid gloom. It was an unbelievably hot and sunny August day. The guests all took time to speak to Esta and I, and to admire the flowers which had been sent in memory of Harry. After a suitably respectful period of time the guests took to their cars and returned to our house for refreshments. With the weather being so good, the kids ending up playing and splashing in the inflatable pool on the decking outside. No one cried, that I'm aware of. We'd simply said a final farewell to poor Harry. Our brave son had fought a hard fight, surprising even the experts with his vigour, but finally the inevitable had happened, and now it was all over.

It was time for the next chapter of our lives.

Part Two

The Challenge

Prelude to an Idea

Understandably, having lived at the hospice for so long, and having gone through such a traumatic time with them, we remained in close contact with Acorns. We'd spent a disproportionate period of our lives there over the previous months when compared to anywhere else, and we had naturally forged close relationships with many of the staff. The hospice itself was a second home to us, and the idea that we no longer needed to return was overridden by the fact that we still actually wanted to.

Acorns have a remembrance garden within the main grounds of the hospice. It's a secluded, quite corner, discreetly sectioned off from the main garden by live bamboo and a hidden fence, and secured by a tall wooden gate. A unique atmosphere exists within the bounds of this space. It's an atmosphere which is tangible, almost palatable. It can be felt at a fundamentally physical level as soon as you enter the gate, and the silence, broken only by the gentle trickling of the purpose-built stream, has its own brand and depth of quiet.

A tradition began whereby newly-bereaved parents have the name of their child carved and painted into an individual stone they have collected somewhere. This symbol of remembrance is then placed along the banks of the tiny stream: a final resting place within Acorns grounds to act as a physical reminder of the child's former presence there.

I had collected our own stone for Harry from a beach called Shark's Bay in Egypt when Lewis and I had been on holiday, and Jan Large had arranged to get it engraved. She had told us that sometimes the stones shattered whilst being worked on, so in fact I'd brought back a few. One of the others turned out to be used much later, for a very different purpose.

Though we had seen the gateway to the garden many times during forays into the main grounds, the first time we entered the solitude of the remembrance garden was to place Harry's stone after he'd gone. The garden was otherwise a sacrosanct environment, silently respected by all, and without the need for any formal rules. It was a poignant time as we took our first foray into the garden, with our emotions still raw. Naturally though, once the stone had been placed, we wanted to return regularly and pay our quiet respects.

Having spent several years of my youth living on the Isle of Wight, I had adopted the RNLI as my charity of choice, though thankfully I had never needed their services. With Harry having spent such a considerable amount of time under the care of Acorns, it was understandable that my loyalties would now shift. I estimated that with running costs of approximately £550 per child per day, Harry's care would have cost in the region of £100,000. Clearly there was no way I could ever pay this back, nor realistically raise such an amount of money, but I wanted to ensure I would do everything I could, at every opportunity, to raise funds for the hospice. Consequently I found myself signing up for half marathons, mud run challenges and other organised events. Esta and I began to make regular donations to the Acorns charity shop in Worcester city centre, and I set up a direct debit to the hospice from my bank account.

For their part, the staff at Acorns also made sure they stayed in touch with us. In the period immediately following Harry's death, we were offered bereavement support, sibling support for Lewis, and access to councillors experienced in dedicated support for grandparents. In the case of the latter, this was something we had never considered. It is understandably hard for a parent to lose their child. But for a grandparent to lose a grandchild, it can sometimes appear as a disruption in the natural order of the circle of life: grandparents fully expect to die before their grandchildren, not outlive them.

Esta and I were also granted invites to special fundraising events, including some for the rugby team, which the Acorns team knew we'd be particularly interested in. 18 months after we lost Harry, we received a phone call asking if we would like to be included with two other couples as guests of honour at a dedicated Acorns charity evening. The event was organised by Halls solicitors, was held every two years, and was comically named, 'Halls Balls'. Halls put an incredible amount of time and energy into arranging marquees, food, wine, and canvasing for prizes which could be auctioned on the evening. Three Acorns families were invited to fill a table, free of charge, so that they could enjoy the evening and play witness to some serious fundraising taking place.

Harry's Favourite Thing

Chauffeur-driven cars would collect and return us. All we had to do was enjoy some good food, great wine, and enjoy the spectacle. It was a fantastic opportunity for me to don a dinner jacket and black tie, and to display my military campaign medals for an evening. For Esta, it was a perfect excuse to have her hair done and to wear a beautiful shimmering purple evening gown. She looked gorgeous. We were both picked up and driven to the event in a £130,000 BMW donated for the night by local car dealers and long-term Acorns benefactors, Rybrook.

On arrival at Spechley Hall, a beautiful local venue with stunning and expansive gardens, we were greeted once more by professional local photographer Mike Henley. Though it's only a slight exaggeration to say that he must have photographed a million people, Mike remembers everyone by name and he was genuinely pleased to see us. He duly took our photo (and later promptly emailed it to us for free), and we joined the throng to partake in a champagne reception.

The pure stroke of genius by Halls in organising this fundraiser was to invite local rival solicitor firms to attend the function - at a cost, naturally. These solicitors, cheerfully loaded with excellent wine and delicious food, then loudly attempted to out-bid each other for the prizes generously donated by local firms and businesses during a professionally run auction. The bidding was nothing if not furious, with the auctioneer pushed to his limits to keep up. These bi-annual events generated a staggering contribution towards the millions that Acorns required each year to keep its three hospices fully operational, and though there were undoubtedly some sore heads and depleted bank accounts the next day, Halls Balls feature highly on calendar appointments.

As if having rival local solicitors play 'look how big my wallet is' in aid of charity was not worthy of a standing ovation in its own right, a second master stroke was brought in to play. And that was where the three Acorns families came in. Not only were we there to present a very physical reminder of who was directly benefiting from such contributions, but also one of the parents had been invited to tell their story of what the hospice, its facilities and its support, meant to them as a family. The first year of Esta and I attending the Halls Ball saw us watching a very brave mother stand up and deliver a speech about their daughter. Aside from the speaker, you would have been forgiven for thinking that the marquee was empty. Not a sound could otherwise be heard. As the lady described the gradual demise of their beloved child, there was barely a dry eye in the house. Our own pain over losing Harry was still very raw, and the other couple on our table were close to distraught. Their own loss was so recent that they could not yet speak about it.

 Once the mother had finished recounting the tale of the incalculable support she and her husband Dave had received from Acorns, she went on to tell how Dave had recently completed a large fundraising event in memory of their daughter. As his wife explained that Dave had cycled from Land's End to John O'Groats, all eyes turned to him in admiration, and not a little wonder. Dave will no doubt have expected such surprise. He is not a small guy. Indeed, when he initially told his wife of his intentions, she herself was dumbfounded. She recalls her first words: 'You don't own a bike, Dave.'

 Undaunted by this mere technicality, Dave went out, bought a bike, and subsequently recruited two fellow fundraisers for the trip. Collectively they went by the name of 'three fat blokes on bikes'.

 As Dave's wife rounded off her speech, and as the bidding commenced in earnest (for a large, live, highland cow, to be butchered or saved, depending upon the preferences of the winner) I was nothing short of awed. For Dave's part, he was ambivalent, if not slightly embarrassed by the attention as I quizzed him about it. With just three month's training, he and his fellow cyclists had set off, averaging 100 miles per day, and completed the trek in just nine days. He hardly claimed to have enjoyed it, but the event had been about fundraising, not about enjoyment.

 During the chauffeur-driven ride home, I chatted to Dale, the male member of the third Acorns family. He and I were inspired by Dave's feat and, somewhat fuelled with drink ourselves, were raring to begin organising our own awe-inspiring event.

 A seed had been sown that night for me. It lay germinating for some time, but I have little doubt that the Halls Ball, and Dave's success at cycling the length of the UK, all ultimately lead to my own personal challenge.

An Idea

The germination period for my particular seed was several years. We remained close to Acorns, still participating in organised sponsored events, generally raising around £1,000 pounds each time. Every now and then I would find myself pondering on what sort of outlandish fundraising event I might be able to participate in that would generate some serious sponsorship, but nothing seemed to strike me with the right sort of passion. I wanted to hit upon an idea which I would immediately be smitten with, and one that would make friends and family gape with incredulity at the hearing. The trouble was, strangely enough, my military background. I had a reputation as someone who could turn my mind to anything and then doggedly complete it. One of the half marathons for Acorns had been undertaken and completed whilst I was suffering from a serious chest infection. I crossed the line more dead than alive, but Esta simply shrugged at the result. 'I knew you'd complete it if you started it. You don't quit.'

It's nice to have such a reputation, but it consequently made things extremely difficult when deciding upon a challenging physical event. I also had to consider how to raise serious money whilst still holding down a full time job and not abandoning my family for weeks or months on end. I couldn't emulate anything along the lines of Ed Stafford's Amazon walk, or Jason Lewis's human powered circumnavigation of the globe. Any fundraising activity had to be something affordable and geographically local. Yet juxtaposed with this it had to be jaw dropping. It was hardly surprising that it took me a few years to come up with an idea.

Since we'd lost Harry, I had changed job contracts several times. My roles had been based in London, Birmingham and Glasgow, and somehow I'd managed to migrate from government-based roles into the sphere of banking on two contractual occasions. This exposure to the banking industry subsequently led to me being offered an interview as a Training Manager for Dovetail, a small and private software engineering company who specialise in the production of a payments platform. I was given less than 24 hours to prepare for the interview, and was only able to attend it at all due to coincidentally being currently engaged on a contract just a few minute's stroll from the Dovetail offices. During the interview process I was required to deliver a presentation on Dovetail's product to one of its Senior Vice Presidents, David Chance. The idea was to see how much information I could gather and comprehend in a very short space of time, and how well I could then present the information back. It was quite a daunting task, especially given that the information and language on the company web site was specifically aimed at banks and other financial organisations who would immediately understand what the product was aiming to achieve.

Before I could confidently talk about a 'Payment Services Hub', I first had to find out just what one was.

An hour of searching through various web sites and blogs finally led me to a definition which actually made sense to me. I copied the quote, crediting the citation to the author, and set about polishing up my 10 minute delivery.

During my presentation to David Chance the next day, I showed the definition of a Payment Services Hub which I'd found, stating that this was the clearest description I could find on the Internet. David, whom I'd only met minutes before, burst out laughing. Unsure whether this was a good or bad sign during the opening minutes of a job interview, I did the only thing I thought best and continued with my delivery. When I'd finished, I discovered two things: Firstly, my requested 10 minute presentation had in fact lasted nine minutes and 57 seconds; and secondly, the genuine author of the Payment Services Hub definition was sitting in front of me conducting my interview.

Early the next day I was pleased, but hardly surprised, to be offered the role with Dovetail.

In June 2013 I found myself in Parsippany, New Jersey, visiting our US offices. This was something I did every two to three months in order to maintain a close working relationship with my only US employee. On this particular occasion however, the Hilton across from the Dovetail offices was fully booked, so I opted to try a motel a little further outside of Parsippany. This motel too was busy, with families and even pets lounging around with the room doors wide open. I later discovered that these families had tragically become displaced due to hurricane Sandy hitting New York around five months previously in October 2012. Many of them had lost everything but their lives when the storm had hit, and the motel was their new home for the foreseeable future.

For no reason that I can understand, on 11th June I woke with a fully-formed question in my head: 'How does one go about swimming the English Channel?' I have no idea where the thought of the Channel originated from. At the time, I had absolutely no concept whether such a challenge was a regular undertaking, who such a swim may be restricted to, or what logistics would be involved. My knowledge gap was so huge that I could not even conceive of all the questions that I later realised I'd need answers to.

Before even stopping to consider whether I was seriously considering such a venture, I logged onto the Internet and simply Googled 'Swim English Channel'. There were over 26 million results, though I of course did what everyone does and opened the first four or five links, arranging a selection of tabs in my browser to work through.

One thing I quickly realised was that there was a dedicated body called The Channel Swimming Association, or CSA, which had page after page of relevant information on their web site, including a bullet-point list of steps requiring completion whilst arranging your swim. (It was not until many months later that I was made aware of a second 'rival' governing body - The Channel Swimming and Pilot Federation, or CSPF. More about them later.) From the CSA site I quickly learnt that anyone can arrange a Channel swim attempt, and that dedicated safety pilot boats must be hired to accompany and guide the swimmer across the water to France. For safety reasons, the hiring of such services is mandatory, for though it's possible to see France from the English coast, it's not a sensible idea to simply jump into the sea and try and swim across the world's busiest shipping lane unaccompanied.

The CSA web site was crammed with useful facts and notes. The site had obviously been expanding on an almost daily basis since its inception, and at the time I first encountered it there were only the remains of any organised structure. In the summer of 2014 the CSA conducted an entire site overhaul, rationalising the organisation of content and removing all instances of duplication. On that day in June 2013 I had to be content with patiently sorting through the rather jumbled collection of pages. With my body clock very much on British Summer Time, I had awoken around 04:00

Eastern Seaboard Time. This gave me three hours to do my initial research into Channel swimming, and by the end of that short time I'd gleaned answers to questions I'd never have even thought of asking.

Over the coming months I found myself repeating this information almost as a stock set of Frequently Asked Questions to anyone new to the concept of swimming to France:

- The English Channel extends from the obvious Dover/Calais region all the way down to Land's End and across to Brest in France. Beyond these points the waters become the North Sea and the Atlantic Ocean respectively.
- The shortest span between England and France is from Dover to Cap Gris Nez, an area known as the Straight of Dover. Point to point the distance is 21 miles (34km). However, what needs to be immediately understood is that it is simply not possible to swim in a direct line from start to finish. The Straight of Dover is a choke point within the Channel. As the tide changes, an incredible volume of water moves North or South, depending on the direction of the tide. Everything in or on the water gets affected by this strong current, ultimately resulting in a swim path resembling an 's' or 'z' shape. The typical distance covered during a Channel swim is more likely to be in the region of 26 miles (42km) - a full marathon in the water.
- For a swim to be 'officially' recognised, the only attire that a swimmer may wear is a standard swimming costume (one that does not cover the legs at all, nor the arms for women), one (non-thermal) swimming hat, and a pair of goggles. Ear plugs and nose clips are allowed, but clearly wet suits are not permitted as they provide thermal protection and plenty of additional buoyancy.
- There are twelve qualified pilots who are licensed to escort swimmers during their swim. In order to secure the best tide times, a 'swim slot' needs to be booked a considerable time in advance - from one to three years! Neap tides are when the difference between high and low tides is at the minimum, and naturally such tides are favoured by all first-time Channel

swimmers. Spring tides see far greater changes in height difference, meaning a much stronger flow of tide to battle against. All safety pilots register the scheduled crossing with the Coast Guard, and between them they communicate with the shipping traffic negotiating the waters of the Channel. Contrary to what some think, the shipping traffic does not have to give way to a swimmer, though they may occasionally be asked to deviate course slightly. The cost of hiring a pilot is between £2,500 and £3,000 for a single attempt at a one-way crossing, and the contract which is consequently arranged is strictly between the swimmer and the pilot, with no input from the CSA or CSPF. Typically, a non-refundable deposit of £1,000 will be required to secure a pilot for the dates you want.

- Official, independent observers are required to ratify the crossing, costing in the region of £400. The observer will first ensure that the swimmer is wearing only regulation attire, and is attempting the crossing without the use of aids such as an MP3 player. Other responsibilities include confirming that the swim begins from above the waterline in England, and that the swimmer finishes above the waterline in France. Throughout the entire time, the swimmer must receive no aid apart from being passed food and drink, and receiving important moral encouragement. Touching the support vessel in any way during the attempt is not allowed. It is not unknown for cross-Channel attempts to fail just meters from shore, sometimes because the swimmer simply does not have the energy to drag their tired body up and out of the water. Channel swimming rules can be brutal and unforgiving.

- As weather and sea conditions will ultimately govern the commencement of a swim, most pilots operate a slot 'rotation' scheme, with up to four swimmers booked on any given day. Swimmer A may be told they have first refusal for day one, with swimmer B next in line should swimmer A decline for any reason. If the conditions are not favourable on day one, swimmer B will be first in line for day two, with swimmer A now relegated to a lower position. Should several days pass without any attempt being possible, the backlog can quickly stack up. It is quite common for a swimmer not to be granted the opportunity even to commence an attempt, due solely to unfavourable swimming conditions. The possibility of being unable to begin a Channel swim, after months or even years of waiting and training, is very high up on the long list of nightmare scenarios a swimmer has to accept from the outset.

- There is a swim 'season' for the Channel, loosely governed by the weather and by the willingness of a pilot to undertake a crossing with a swimmer. Typically the first swim will not commence before mid-June, and the last one will be sometime in September, possibly even October, depending on the sort of summer the UK has been subjected to. A pilot's reputation relies strongly on the amount of recent successes they have had, so it's not simply a case of a pilot taking your money and hoping for a success. If they do not think a swim is possible before or after the traditional seasonal window, they will not offer a contract.
- Depending upon the source against which statistics may be checked, only around 1,200 people have ever successfully swum the Channel, meaning that far more individuals have successfully climbed Mount Everest! Reasons for not completing the full swim are not collated for public consumption as far as I could ascertain, but a little research will allow a person to effectively boil down the facts to just a few points;
    - Hypothermia is probably top of the list. The temperature in the Channel will typically range from as cold as 14 degrees centigrade to possibly as warm as 18.5 degrees. Unless the swimmer has put a considerable amount of serious focus into acclimatisation training, hour upon hour of submersion in the waters of the Channel will result in the cold seeping into their body, into their muscles and ultimately into their mind. Hypothermia is serious. It kills. The effects are so subtle that the victim is often unaware of what is occurring. Death can sneak upon them like a gentle sleep if unobserved. Understandably, hypothermia is one of

the key things that the official observer must be on the lookout for.
- Injury can affect even world class swimmers, as I later discovered. With the constant requirement to keep moving, shoulders and knees can suffer from an incredible amount of over use. A swimmer may well decide to forge on and suffer the effects later, or they may decide that the prospect of a longer, more serious injury is simply not worth the effort of continuing any further. Jellyfish stings could potentially also put an abrupt end to an otherwise promising swim.
- Strength of mind plays an enormous part in any Channel swim. The CSA site claimed as much as 50% of a successful swim could be put down to mental attitude. I later spoke to other swimmers who claimed that figure was actually around 80%. The boredom factor is not be underestimated. I expect that few challengers will ever admit to giving up simply because they were bored out of their minds - but I utterly refuse to believe that it has never happened.
- Bad luck. This is something totally outside of the control of any swimmer. One of a host of events could occur which would result in the swim being aborted either by the pilot (who has the very final say in any safety decision) or by the swimmer themselves. Bad luck is something that it is impossible to mitigate against, or to train for. It is something that simply has to be accepted as one part of the vast challenge that makes up the English Channel swim.

- Another common question is whether swimmers still cover themselves in goose fat. The first person to ever swim the Channel, a merchant sea captain by the name of Mathew Webb, actually used porpoise oil. What he must not have considered is how on earth his safety team would have been able to pull him out of the water should that eventuality have been necessary. Assuming that a swimmer will envisage not terminating the attempt unless they are physically incapable

of proceeding any further, they will need assistance boarding the boat. Being covered in slippery fat is not conducive to affording a rescuer a good grip. Consequently, what most swimmers now do is apply some form of lubricant only in areas where chaffing may occur, such as under the arms and between the legs.
- Eating, drinking, resting and answering the calls of nature all seem to be lower down on the list of obvious questions. All of them need to be done whilst in the water on any Channel attempt. Once the swim has commenced, the swimmer is forbidden to touch the boat again until the end of the swim. This means that every other aspect, especially eating and drinking, needs to be practised during the training regime. The swimmer needs to learn what they can comfortably eat, and what will stay down. Vomiting has to be avoided at all costs - it's a waste of vital energy.
- Despite the Channel extending all the way down to Brest, there are strict rules governing a swim attempt. All swims disrupt shipping to a certain extent, but if a swimmer could simply land anywhere in France this would make the issue of safety almost uncontrollable for the both the English and the French Coastguard. Accordingly, the job of the pilot is to keep the swimmer within the permitted swimming zone whilst also getting them to France via the shortest and safest route. Straying outside of the zone means the swim must be abandoned.
- The final three miles of the water from England to France is the most notoriously difficult. Not only will the swimmer be tiring by this point, but the current here is at its strongest, pushing the sea and anything in it away from the French coast. Swimming from France to England is factually acknowledged as being far easier than attempting the crossing the other way, but the French banned such an activity in 1997. In fact, there are regular calls from the French authorities to ban Channel swimming altogether, as reported on in The Independent newspaper on 13th November 2014.

All in all, there was an incredible amount of information to take on board and to absorb. I make no pretence of my ability to fully appreciate everything I'd read immediately. Much of it would take a long time to properly sink in. But what was instantly apparent was that swimming the Channel was an extreme challenge - yet it was also one that was undeniably achievable. It appeared to take extraordinary mental strength and plenty of long-term preparation and dedication. I realised immediately that the earliest realistic opportunity for me to attempt this event would be the following season. The current season was just about to begin, and I would need a year's worth of training at the least if I was to give full justice to the scale of the challenge.

In my naivety, sitting in a warm room on a June morning in New Jersey, I anticipated that one thing I had going in my favour was my natural resistance to the cold. My internal thermostat seems to be set slightly above average, and generally I do not appear to suffer from the cold as much as others. I don't, however, pretend to compare with Lewis Pugh, who famously swam one kilometer through the sea in the North Pole at temperatures below zero. But I was contemplating waters of around 16 degrees. And whilst this was still cold enough to induce hypothermia in many swimmers, I was confident that with proper acclimatisation and my own reasonable tolerance to the cold, I could manage this.

With further consideration of a possible date for my attempt, I understood that the temperature of the Channel would rise throughout the summer. Allowing for the fact that I'd probably have to arrange to be located in the Dover area for a week, I'd have to plan and book the attempt for sometime within the school summer holidays. In which case, August seemed like a good month, allowing even more time for the water to heat up. Suddenly I had a rough commencement date in mind, immediately giving me a training time-frame of 14 months. That training needed to start as soon as possible.

Other aspects needed serious consideration, however. Living in Worcester, I'm about as far from the sea as it's possible to get within the UK. That meant my plan was akin to the formation of a Jamaican bobsleigh team. The logistics of getting to the coast would have to be considered, and I would also have to be mindful of how much impact the required training would have upon family time.

The CSA website spoke of the number of people who could regularly be found training within the enclosed waters of Dover harbour. It appeared that a whole Channel swimming community could be called upon to train with, ask questions of, and generally socialise with. The idea was attractive - a host of fellow swimmers, some of whom would be hopeful Channel swimmers and some who had already achieved it, ready and willing to share their experiences and advice. All I'd have to do is arrange regular trips down to Dover. It wasn't far by train from London, and I could take days off during the week so as to travel there without disrupting the weekend. The plan was slowly forming.

I'd come a long way in just a few hours. The previous night I'd had no concept of swimming the Channel, and before setting off for work on 11th June I was already wondering what would actually prevent me from giving it a serious go. I appreciated that in reality 14 months was not actually a very long way away. I would need to begin to make enquires regarding pilot availability immediately if I expected to get a neap tide swim slot in August the following year. Countering that urgency was the fact that I wanted to let the idea mature for just a little while before I even broached the subject to Esta and the family. With such a big challenge as this, it had to be a family decision as to whether I proceeded much further.

This would normally be the point at which I would go for a run, or to the gym, and let ideas and plans mature of their own accord as I was exercising. However: the motel did not have a gym; and New Jersey is famously anti-pedestrian. Everyone drives, or takes a taxi. Everywhere. Crossing a road in Parsippany is all-but impossible. Pavements (or sidewalks as the Americans call them) simply do not exist. Pedestrians or joggers literally have to walk or run on the busy roads. Doing so involves taking your life in your hands as you negotiate glass-strewn tarmac whilst dodging irate drivers, all of whom are unable to comprehend why someone would volunteer *not* to take a car. I was consequently restricted to my room for any exercise.

With few other options available to me, I eventually decided that I would do a series of press-ups. As boring and repetitive it sounds, I quickly realised that this could actually be the start of my training for the Channel. Boredom would be a real challenge to overcome, and being able to deal with it and mentally occupy my mind would be critical. What sooner opportunity than right now? The next logical step in my rapidly-forming plan was to commit myself to a set exercise period. An hour sounded good. One thought led quickly on to another. I was on a roll. I could use mini challenges as milestones along my route to preparing for the Channel. One of those milestones could be to complete 1,000 press-ups in public within one hour, collecting money for Acorns as I did so. Much like the figure of 50 eggs to Paul Newman's character in *Cool Hand Luke*, 1,000 press-ups sounded like a nice round number - a figure which struck as impressive, and would take some practise to build up to.

I had no idea how many press-ups I was currently capable of doing within an hour, but 600 sounded like it was achievable straight off. That was 'just' 10 per minute for 60 minutes, after all. And if I did one press-up per second, that actually left 50 seconds per minute to rest. A work/rest ratio of 1:5 seemed almost lazy. I began that instant.

After 20 minutes of this new regime I discovered that muscles begin to ache sooner than expected. My rest period was soon being eaten into by the need to stretch out the build-up of lactic acid. My biceps, shoulders and chest were growing tired. 30 minutes in, and the ache had become a pain. I exercise often, and was hardly new to press-ups, but this was a sudden and unprepared-for venture. My muscles were voicing their indignation. After 40 minutes the sweat of exertion was dripping off me. I'd given up standing upright between bouts of press-ups, as I'd found myself nervously pacing the room, expending energy which I knew I'd soon need. Instead I now knelt with my back straight in a prayer-like position.

I don't remember at what point my muscles stopped aching, or rather at what point my brain stopped acknowledging the signs of ache sent from those muscles. I do know that once I was within the final 20 minutes I became certain that I was going to achieve my first milestone of 600 press-ups in an hour. As with the final stretch of a long run, when the end is in finally in sight, the adrenaline formed from the anticipation of success nulled any pain I'd been feeling. Though I was hot and tired at the end, the effort was rewarded with the first success of my new challenge. However unrelated to swimming press-ups might be, I felt I had taken the first steps into a new stage of my life. I was going to begin to formally train for a serious attempt at swimming the English Channel.

All I required first was buy-in from the family.

My day had begun with a question formed in my dream-befuddled mind. As I prepared for work that morning, my mind abuzz with thoughts and ideas relating to swimming the Channel, neither my family nor I had any idea just how much difference that waking question would make to the next 14 months of our lives.

A Potted History

To set the scene of who I am, and what type of character I possess, it's worth briefly outlining my younger years.

Though I hardly claim to 'come from' London, I was born in the North-West of the city in the late 1960s, the middle one of three sons. My parents were young, and my dad had to hold down no fewer than three jobs in order to see that we had a roof over our head and food on the table. You never appreciate that sort of thing when you're young of course, so my older brother and I only saw a tired man who seemed irritated by our screaming and shouting. He genuinely loved taking us out for the day when he was able though, and I remember days at Battersea Fun Fair and walking through the tree-top walkway with him before it was all closed down years later.

My grandad owned and ran a building firm which he was in the process of handing over to my dad. Grandad had moved to the Isle of Wight in semi-retirement, leaving us all in the great big house he'd bought in Kensal Rise. The only way we could afford to pay for such a property was to let out some of the rooms upstairs, and consequently my brother Chris and I seemed to know a lot of adults when we were young, being either surrounded by tenants or builders.

My dad always had our best interests at heart, even under the worst of circumstances. I was running barefoot in the long grass of our little garden in Kensal Rise one day when I trod on a piece of glass. This was no mere fragment, however. It was an entire end of a bottle which had been smashed over our wall and now lay upright. My whole heel was hanging off in one ugly lump of flesh, attached to my body by no more than a thin shred of skin. My dad wrapped my foot in a towel and bundled me into the car. The towel was soaked with blood in no time, and we rushed to the hospital.

The doctor wanted to immediately sew the heel back on. My dad, instinctively realising that this would cause a huge scar and make walking difficult, insisted they bind the wound and let it heal without a scar. I'm not entirely sure how they managed this, but I do know that there is now not the slightest sign of the seriousness of that accident, and given the fact that half of my foot had been chopped off, that's quite an achievement.

Chris was very ill when I was young, and he missed a great

deal of school. Coupled with this, he suffered from dyslexia which, despite being diagnosed as far back as 1887, few people seemed to understand in the 1960s. Our parents arranged for one of the tenants, Pam, who was a teacher, to give Chris private reading lessons in the hope that he would catch up with others in his year. Though it had not been formally arranged, I hung around for these lessons, eager not to be left out.

I'm left only with vague memories of those days, most of which I'm sure have been augmented by stories told to me by my parents. Apparently though, when I was still just four years old, Pam pleaded with my mum that I stop attending the reading classes. My mum was horrified, assuming that I was disrupting the lessons with poor behaviour. Pam stipulated the reverse: I'd already picked up everything she'd been trying to teach poor Chris, and as a result, I could now read fluently. To prove it to my astounded parents, she handed me a newspaper and bade me read. I duly did exactly as I was told, subsequently finding myself excluded from the private lessons.

It seemed that in those days I could pick things up and learn them very quickly. My uncles Geoff and Steve both had a love of chess. I can't remember who taught me, but I found the game fascinating and enjoyable. My dad's friend Dennis came round one day, and I asked him if he could play. He reluctantly agreed, paying only a small amount of attention as he chatted to my parents. When he glanced back at one point, he was horrified to see the dominant position I commanded on the board. He promptly stopped his conversation mid-flow and concentrated fully on the game. He finally won, beating a five year-old, albeit through sweat and clenched teeth.

But I was a small, slight child, who was intelligent and easily prone to tears. In short, I was every bully's dream. I was a magnet for every boy who wanted to lash out through spite or anger, and I regularly came home in tears, with ripped trousers and grazed knees and hands. I hated school with a passion, and I have to confess that this feeling lasted until I finally left school, many years later, at age 16. For me, my schooldays were miserable, unfriendly, and torturous. I rarely recall them, and I certainly do not miss them. To this day I find it incredulous that some people look at their schooling as the best days of their lives.

We moved house several times in those first years of my life. This was partly due to the fact that my little brother, Phil, had arrived on the scene and we consequently needed more space, and partly to escape the bullying I was suffering at school. But running away from bullies never works. There are always more waiting for a new victim at the next location.

We eventually ended up in a house which was on the cusp of Kingsbury and Neasden. A short walk took us to the greenery of The Welsh Harp, and school was only a short bus journey away. In those days it was perfectly acceptable for young kids to travel around London safely and alone, and by the age of eight I knew the London tube map by heart. I could catch a bus through to Dollis Hill, board the Jubilee line, and gradually make my way into and around London for the day, unaccompanied. I often spent hours at Heathrow on my own, standing on the viewing platform they had back then, watching the planes taking off and landing.

With our grandad living on the Isle of Wight, our holidays were pre-destined, and we'd happily be left behind for a week or two whilst mum and dad returned to work in London. As the social situation around the Wembley area began to deteriorate, along with the continued bullying at school, my parents began to consider moving again. The decision was confirmed when a friend of ours across the road was mugged in broad daylight, having his new bicycle stolen from him. Before us three children knew it, we been relocated to the Isle of Wight.

I know that Bear Grylls has nothing but good things to say about the Island. I happen to be on the opposite end of the spectrum to Bear in that regard. Though I may have had few friends in London, I enjoyed a multi-cultured environment, and had absolutely no concept of racism at that time. In our move it seemed that we'd not only stepped back in time with regards to infrastructure and facilities, but also with regards to social concepts, bigotry and baseless phobias.

We'd moved to a tiny village called Gurnard on the outskirts of Cowes, the latter of which is world famous for its sailing races. And whilst the Island may seem idyllic to visitors, I was a city boy who had now been deposited into the countryside, not just for a holiday, but to live.

Within days my brother Chris and I were into an altercation

with some local bullies. The kids were all within our age ranges, and had been picking on a younger boy who had an unfortunate and very pronounced stutter. The poor lad was half the age and half the size of the thugs, so Chris voiced up on behalf of the victim. The entire episode could easily have been the scene of a classic Hollywood film-style set up. Two of the locals faced up to Chris, whilst the third appeared to run away. Moments later he was back.... armed with a thuggish uncle who must have been in his mid-twenties, eager and spoiling for a fight.

For an island that survives on the income predominantly provided by tourism, an especially derogative term is reserved for those very tourists who keep the economy running: Grockle. As our family were not just visiting, but had moved to the island, we were considered one level above the parasitic grockle. But we were still outsiders, and hence we were extremely fair game.

That particular situation was halted at the last moment when my mum arrived on the scene. The bullies left, chastised, having been outnumbering us by four to two after recruiting an adult to bolster their numbers.

Only two days later, Phil and I were walking back from Cowes to Gurnard along the sea front. Two of the bullies arrived, dragging along a third and admittedly unwilling friend. There was plenty of jeering and swaggering when they found my little brother and I alone, and I knew we were in serious trouble.

Maybe it was because I was used to be picked on. Maybe it was because I already hated the place and could not see it ever getting any better for me. Whatever the reason, I whispered to Phil to jump down onto the beach and not stop running until he got home. Then I feigned an escape to the left, knowing that the bullies would block my path and unwittingly allow sufficient room for Phil to slip through. As a result, I faced them at odds of 3:1.

Until that point I had only ever thrown one real punch in my life. I'd been in an argument with a kid from across the road regarding a go cart I'd built. Somehow his two front teeth fell out, though I cannot remember actually intending to hurt him. If anything, I probably swung my arm wildly whilst running away. When his father came to our house to complain, my dad could hardly contain his surprise, and hidden delight, that his weakling son had hurt anyone at all, let alone knocked out some teeth, because until that point I'd always been on the receiving end.

This situation was going to be very different. If I ran, I was sure to be chased down. I knew I was destined to take a beating either way, but something in me became determined that I would not be the only one to walk away injured in this particular instance. As the three squared up in front of me, the unfortunate tag-along was square to my front. My first punch broke his nose. There was an incredible flood of blood, and the poor lad's knees instantly gave way. He had been told I was a pushover, and the punch had come from nowhere. As blows began to rain down on me from both sides, I must have realised I'd lost any chance of surprise with the other two. I pushed over the injured boy and hammered away at his already broken nose a few more times before I finally got kicked over the sea wall and onto the beach. As the two uninjured boys stood in awe at the amount of blood and wailing emanating from their friend, I took advantage of the distraction and ran for home, covered in blood. My mother's later level of distress upon seeing the state of me was only abated when I finally managed to explain that it was not my own blood I was covered in.

I never looked back from that fight, and I despise bullies to this day. I've met them even in the workplace in adult life, and though standing up to them has cost me my job on two occasions, I refuse to back down to someone who hides behind their rank, their job title, or violent threats.

My dad continued to work hard, and from our humble beginnings we eventually moved into a vast house in Cowes, complete with its own indoor swimming pool. For one reason and another, my parents split up when I was 15. I'd reached a very rebellious age by then, and they probably secretly wished I was still the meek and mild victim of a few years earlier. My dad had converted the attached garage into my own self-contained part of the house, so before I was even 16 I was all-but living alone. When my mother left home, late one night, I was unaccountably in the wrong area of the house. I remember her walking past me with a sad smile, and I had no doubt that she was leaving for good.

Still hating school, and everything that happened there, I left at the earliest opportunity. I'd gained just three O levels, which was undoubtedly a waste of the potential I'd shown so many years ago. But it was the environment I blame, and even if I could turn the clock back, I would not. School days were the very worst days of my life.

My obstinacy and aggression, two things that had been denied any voice through so many years of bullying, came out in force when I was around 15. My school-leaving report reads, 'When Alan forgets to adopt his abrasive manner, he can be a pleasant young man.'

The drinking laws were not strictly enforced back in those days, and no-one seemed to know exactly what and 18 year-old was supposed to look like anyway. I celebrated my 16th, 17th and 18th birthday in a pub called the Harbour Lights, hanging out with friends my elder brother's age, and drinking heavily.

My attitude and behaviour led to my father and I falling out in a major way one night when I was just 16, and I subsequently left home at around midnight one night. It was an unpleasant situation, but I look back on it as part of growing up, a transition to manhood.

For two years I wasted my life. I drifted aimlessly, sometimes working, sometimes signing on and claiming social. I got into regular fights, spent every penny I had on drink, and never gave a thought to the future. I must have been a disgrace to my parents.

But eventually I realised that I had little to no education, no money, no job, no decent clothes and no food. My friends were all employed full time, and I was quickly becoming an anachronism. My dad landed me an apprenticeship with an electrician, but I had little heart for it. I found myself standing in the garden of a house staring out to sea one day, when I was supposed to be working inside laying some cables. I was looking towards what the islanders call 'the mainland', wondering how I was still on the island, and how I could escape. I suddenly knew the time had come to grow up and pull myself together.

A few days later I stood in the army recruiting office. At no point had I ever considered the navy or the air force, and I have no idea where the thought of the army had come from either. But as I listened to what the sergeant told me, I realised that not only would I potentially get an education, but that I'd also get clothes, food, and money, and most importantly, I'd have to leave the island.

The first part of the process was to do an IQ assessment, known at the time as a 'domino test'. Four of us, all hopeful recruits, sat through a never-ending series of paper tests aimed at establishing our potential suitability for various trades within the army. Two of the candidates were told that they were ideal infantry material, the third was told he should be a Royal Engineer, and I was told I should become an engineer of a different sort and join a corps known as the Royal Electrical and Mechanical Engineers.

On 28th October 1986, having spent two further days with a host of others at Sutton Coldfield in Birmingham to confirm our fitness and suitability to enlist, I took the oath of allegiance in the small office in Newport on the Isle of Wight.

My basic training started a short while later, at Arborfield near Reading. None of my family expected me to last longer than a few days of course, given my bad attitude and reluctance to conform. But I had unwittingly found an environment in which I thrived. Basic training was far from pleasant, but neither was it unbearable. I kept thinking that I was fully capable of taking more than they could give, and in many ways those days were merely an extension of the outrageous life I'd been living as a teenager. Certainly there was discipline, and in the jockeying to establish identity and a pecking order within our platoon there was some initial bullying. But the latter was soon superseded by the mutual respect and camaraderie which predominates military life. We built a team, we formed as a unit, and we gelled as a platoon. Some, but very few, fell by the wayside, and genuine bonds of friendship were formed.

My army career lasted 14 years. My exploits during that time, including many promotions, two near cases of being court-martialed, travels, adventures and a spinal injury that finally made me decide between my health and a continued military career, could all provide enough content for subsequent book.

One of those experiences was a thoroughly disastrous attempt at SAS selection. The notorious selection course is famed for a success rate of just 1% or 2%. It's not unknown for every single applicant on one intake to fail. But it's not failure itself which is so bad, so much as the nature of that failure. My own end came very quickly and very suddenly due to the highest level of ignorance possible: failure to research and prepare properly.

Consequently, many years later, and planning to take on another infamous challenge in the form of the English Channel, I was determined to maximise on my ill-gained experience. I wanted to ensure that I went into this challenge open eyed, fully informed,

and with a complete understanding of the scale of the event.
As they say: Fail to prepare = prepare to fail.
It was important that I did not make the same mistake twice.

First Strokes

I must admit to some nerves at the prospect of broaching my new idea to the family. Once I was back home from the US I waited until Will, our four year-old, was in bed, then I told Esta and Lewis that I had something I wanted to talk about. Those words are always something that brings people to an immediate stop, worry etched over their faces, so I wanted to get into the meat of my proposal as quickly as possible. This was not intended to be bad news, though I admit I had no idea how it would be received.

I began by recalling the incredible achievement of Dave, cycling the length of the country in nine days. I reminded Esta how inspired I'd been at the time, saying that I too wanted to do something which would make people sit up and think, and which would subsequently enable me to set a high fundraising goal.

'How high?' Esta asked.

'£10,000!'

Esta looked at me. There was a mixture of apprehension and doubt in her eyes. Our prior events had raised in the order of £2,000 - and that was in total. For me to surpass that figure by such a magnitude would take a very serious challenge. Yet Esta was worried about discovering exactly what that challenge was. Finally, she relented.

'Go on then, tell me: What are you thinking of doing?'

'I want to swim the English Channel.'

Nothing like this had ever been broached in family discussions before. Lewis had little if any concept of what I was proposing, but that was hardly surprising - I'd had no idea myself until a few days ago. He consequently lost interest in the conversation very quickly. My news had been an anticlimax to a 12 year-old.

Esta though, was pensive.

'Can you do it?'

'I have absolutely no idea. I know it's possible, and it'll take a long time to train. That's the challenge.'

'When are you thinking?' She asked.

'August next year, if I can book it for that month.'

I then had to explain the logistics of a Channel swim,

describing the necessity of booking a pilot well in advance. I explained the swim slots, the part the CSA played in ratifying the swim, and the requirement to acclimatise whenever possible.

'How much will this cost?'

'The logistics will be around £3,000. But I don't intend to pay anything. I'll be doing the training and the event itself. I want to find corporate sponsorship to pay for the logistics... except that I have no idea how to do that, or how to separate the corporate money from the funds pledged to Acorns. I want to put my proposal to the hospice and get their help and advice. What do you think?'

'Will it make any difference if I say no?' Esta asked.

'Of course. We'll all need to play our part in this. I want us to all agree.'

Lewis just shrugged. Our conversation was dragging on and keeping him from watching TV.

'How are you going to find the time to train? I don't want it disrupting the weekend. You're already away four nights a week.'

I outlined my sketchy plans about getting to the coast during the weekdays, and of doing the majority of my training during the working week. 'I'll still have to train at weekends, but we should only see any real impact as of March or so next year. That's nine months away. I want to do this, but I want it to be a family decision.'

Esta looked at me steadily, wondering how I'd take it if she said no. She could tell I was already sold on the idea, and in truth, she would have hated to say no to anything I was planning on doing for Acorns.

With a resigned sigh, she said, 'Make a will!'

Those three words were my green light.

With Esta, Lewis and Will all aware of my plans, I began to tell other members of the family. As is happened, my eldest son, Sean, was having his stag weekend down in Bournemouth the weekend of 21st June. Meeting them down there gave me the opportunity to explain to him and his younger brother, Connagh, what their crazy dad had in mind. I'd actually planned on getting them alone in order to break it to them in private, but as chance would have it we ended up on the same train into Bournemouth, me coming from London, and them joining at Southampton. Naturally, as soon as they saw me they wanted me to join them in celebrating with a beer. An ex-soldier like me, never one to say no without a very good reason, was suddenly on the spot in front of all the stag weekend guests. I had no choice but to tell them of the challenge in front of their friends, as I had one important last test before I fully committed myself to the Channel: I wanted to go for a swim in the sea as soon as we got to Bournemouth.

The CSA website had mentioned that some indoor swimmers were not suited to open water swimming - especially sea swimming. They could often find the sheer expanse of water intimidating, or the waves off-putting, or simply not like the salt water. I had spent many hours in the sea as a teenager on the Isle of Wight. But that had been many years ago, and I'd never strayed far from shore whilst swimming, always being mindful of the tides. To venture out alone with the sole intent of swimming up and down was entirely new to me. I wanted to ensure I would be comfortable with a small sample before plunging ahead with an endeavour which would see me in the brine for hour upon hour.

Once we'd checked into our extremely basic accommodation, Sean took his brother and friends to the nearest pub whilst I grabbed my swimming shorts and goggles and headed for the beach. It was my first trip to Bournemouth, and I must admit I was impressed with the huge expanse of sandy beach stretching left towards Southampton and right towards Poole harbour. I had no idea of currents or tides in the area, so I was still somewhat nervous as I stripped down into my swimwear, leaving my jeans, top and shoes in a carrier bag on the beach. I'd left my wallet back at the accommodation, just to be safe, and Connagh had the key to the room we were sharing. I'd meet up with them at the pub in an hour or so.

I waded in for my first sea swim for the Channel. As I got to chest height the waves crashed into me and sprayed sea water into my face, that familiar saltiness of the ocean brining back memories of scuba diving and sailing adventures. But this time I had no wetsuit, no boat, and no diving equipment. I took a breath and plunged beneath the waves.

It took a few seconds for the cold to hit me. The water must have been relatively warm in all honesty, but I was quickly made aware of just how much acclimatisation I would need to do. The Channel in June seemed freezing to me that day. My forehead felt tight, and my face felt as if I'd been slapped. This actually transpired to be nothing in comparison to what I'd later experience, but at the time it was a perfect early indicator of everything I could expect to experience.

I began to swim towards the pier on my left. It wasn't far away, as this was not intended as any kind of physical test. I wanted to know how my body and mind reacted to the experience of actually swimming in the sea, as opposed to just playing with the kids and bobbing around. Most importantly, I wanted to know if I would enjoy it. After all, there were many hours of training to look forward to.

The sea was murky due to the sand stirred up from the waves, and pieces of seaweed kept bumping me in the face unexpectedly. The waves came in from my right as I swam towards the pier, so I had to ensure I did not swallow any water as I turned my head to breathe. But I was making progress. I felt out of my element, but I was gradually relaxing and beginning to enjoy it. Most importantly, my primeval fear of being swept out to sea was proving to be unfounded. If anything, once I'd turned around and begun to swim back towards my clothing, I realised that the current was actually lateral to the beach, not away from it, meaning I was either swimming with it, or against it.

I'll be honest and admit I did tire quickly. I don't think I fully relaxed on that first swim, even though it served perfectly to alleviate many of my fears. Swimming with any tension in your muscles is not conducive to an efficient swim. Yet the main thing was that I emerged from the water with an increased level of determination. That test swim had confirmed many important points to me: I was not afraid of the sea, despite my deep respect for it; the waves had not made me sick; and nor had the salt water taste put me off. Certainly I had a long way to go in swimming fitness and cold water acclimatisation, but there too the swim had proven to be effective, as there's nothing like a wake-up call to show you how much improvement is required in order to attain a goal.

All in all, I was now convinced I could proceed with my intention to swim the Channel, and I made my way back to join my sons for the stag weekend. My planning would commence on the following Monday.

The CSA website had a bullet-point list of steps that must be taken in order to swim the Channel. The list seemed simple enough, but I soon discovered that bullet points belie complexity. On reflection, anything could be boiled down to a set of steps, such as becoming a self-made millionaire. Step one: hit upon a unique money-making idea. Step two: exploit and market it. Except that most of us remain stuck at step one.

Something that was missing from the list, due to not being a mandatory requirement for everyone, was the securing of corporate sponsorship. For me, this was crucial. My primary reason for swimming the Channel was as a means to raise funds. The swim would also be a huge personal challenge, but I could not afford to spend £3,000 of my own money in order to be able to raise £10,000 - all whilst also training hard for 14 months. Essentially, if I could not secure corporate sponsorship to cover the costs, the challenge would be over before it had even begun.

Being ignorant of such things, I was completely unconscious of any legal requirements or considerations with regards to raising such funds. Would I need a dedicated bank account? Would I need to keep formal records? What about an accountant? The unknown side of this seemed daunting. To help with all of these issues, I contacted Carole Crowe, community fundraising manager of Acorns. We arranged to meet for a drink in order for me to formally present my idea, and to get some guidance on the management of corporate sponsorship.

Esta and I had met Carole on numerous Acorns events of course. She arrived with her husband, Steve, who we'd also met at the Halls Balls. To show that this was a family effort, we also took Lewis along with us for the presentation.

It was a beautiful summer's evening, and we sat around a picnic bench outside a country pub in Worcestershire. After a friendly catch up, I fired up my laptop and launched the presentation. I set the scene, restating that I estimated Harry's care to be in the region of £100,000, and then boldly delivered my anticipated fundraising target for my challenge. Both Carole and Steve raised their eyebrows, patiently waiting in anticipation for me to deliver an explanation of how I'd actually achieve this. When I told them I intended to swim the Channel, they were silent for a moment.

'Can I just ask,' Steve began. 'What's the furthest you've ever swum?'

'Around two kilometres. Just over a mile or so.'

'And you now propose to swim 26 miles? How many kilometres is that?'

'42.'

They both looked at me as though I were utterly insane. It wasn't a look of admiration, but more of pity and worry.

'And how long do you anticipate the swim taking you?' Carole enquired.

Needing to know the answer to this myself, I had been doing some rough calculations prior to our meeting. The world's slowest one-way swim was 28 hours, set by a lady called Jackie Cobell, whilst the world record was just over seven hours. The average time for a successful crossing was 12 hours. I saw no reason that I could not achieve an average time, so I gave them this figure.

'12 hours in the English Channel? In the cold water? Without a rest?' Carole was incredulous. 'And I assume you'll have to deal with passing ships too?'

'Not just ships. Potentially oil and fuel spills, jellyfish, sewerage, flotsam - possibly even shark sightings.'

'Can't you think of something less... dangerous? Less dramatic?'

I confessed I'd love to canoe the Amazon or trek through the rain forest for a week or two. But nothing of this ilk came across as challenging enough to raise £10,000, and all would involve a large amount of time from home. Furthermore, any such option would be prohibitively expensive, and would sound as if I were going on an adventure holiday at corporate expense.

'And how much will a Channel swim cost?'

I told them both the figure, stating that this was the point where Acorns came in. 'I'm going to need help securing that funding. I can't afford to do it. If I could, I'd just give the money directly to the hospice and save myself 14 months of training and acclimatisation.'

'We can't give sponsorship,' Carole pointed out.

'That's not what I'm after. I need access to companies and individuals who would fund a venture of this sort. Without that, I can't get it off the ground.'

Being very naive at the time, what I'd actually anticipated was Acorns taking over all fundraising activities, allowing me to concentrate exclusively on the training. I had envisaged being allocated some sort of fundraising expert who could also act as a project manager for the venture. This was, perhaps, totally unrealistic. So when we left Carole and Steve, having been told that they would give the idea some thought and get back to me, I was utterly deflated. I'd expected a level of enthusiasm equal to my own, and instead it felt as I'd walked away empty-handed.

'Don't be despondent,' Esta told me. 'Let's wait and see what happens. Carry on training and planning as before. If you want it badly enough, it'll all come together, somehow.'

To make matters worse, a tragedy struck the very next day. Susan Taylor, swimming the Channel to raise funds for another Children's hospice, Rainbows, sadly died during her attempt. My mother, Carole and several others all called to ask if I was still serious about my own attempt. And yet tragic as it was, I decided to do further research into the dangers and history of Channel swimming. It transpired that there had been eighth fatalities since the first successful swim back in 1875. The first recorded death was Rodriguez de Lara of Spain in 1926. (A further tragedy struck in 2016, after my swim, bringing the current total to nine). By comparison, roughly one or two people die every year during the London marathon. Whilst no undertaking of the Channel could ever be considered 100% safe, and whilst I had every sympathy for Susan's family, I did not want to let this sad news sway my own determination.

Esta had known better than to even ask. All she insisted on was adequate insurance, should the worst ever happen.

Knowing that I would require freedom and flexibility to train for extended hours once we hit 2014, I told my boss, David Chance of my plans. David was immediately impressed, and was fully sympathetic to my reasons for wanting to undertake such a task. 'Rather you than me, though,' he said.

Though I sometimes have the luxury of working from home, when I am in the office I tend to be one of the first people into the building. Martin Coen, the CEO, also arrives early, so I sometimes use this opportunity to have a catch up with any work issues before our day fully gets going. I decided I wanted to send a company-wide communication out once things got off the ground, so I approached Martin with my idea, telling him about Harry, and of all the help Acorns had afforded us. Martin was under no illusions as to how tough the Channel attempt would be. When I explained that more people had successfully climbed Everest, he was completely unsurprised. He wished me luck, and told me to keep him up to date with progress.

One of my first tasks from on the CSA bullet point list for any Channel attempt was to arrange a safety pilot escort. I set about contacting the six pilots affiliated to the CSA. I did not appreciate at the time that another other six registered boat operators were affiliated to another governing body. Over the next couple of weeks I began to collate the replies as they came in. Some pilots were already fully booked for the following August, others had availability as the fourth swimmer on certain days, and one pilot, Kevin Sherman, had a 'slot one' availability for the period 18-20 August 2014. This was perfect. All I needed to reserve this slot was funding in the order of £1,000, non-refundable. Not having yet secured any corporate funding meant I'd immediately hit snag one. Kevin said he'd reserve the spot for me for a week, pending me getting hold of the money. An immediate deadline had already been imposed. The pressure seemed to be on me already, and I felt no further enlightened or empowered regarding fundraising than before I'd spoken to Carole.

Regardless of Esta's words of encouragement, I felt despondency closing in. I felt like I'd made no progress other than some initial enquiries into availability. Everything seemed so passive, and it was not in my nature to be so unassertive. Carole promised me she was looking into corporate funding, but anticipated that it would be eight to 10 weeks before I heard anything. I believed that I needed to do something active, and to feel that I was actually making a committed effort to realise my intention of swimming the Channel.

On 15th July, just over one month after waking up with my fundraising idea, I had no real progress to show other than a presentation demonstrating some basic fact-finding around swimming the Channel. I sat at my desk at work and decided I needed to make a decisive move. Having mulled the situation over for a short while, I eventually penned an email to the CEO, Martin Coen, giving details of the financial requirements necessary to secure the pilot boat. Kevin Sherman, pilot of a boat called Connemara, had further stated that if I could send him £250 as an initial deposit, he'd be happy to wait a few months for the remaining £750 deposit. But I'd need to act quickly. I asked Martin if Dovetail would be interested in sponsoring me, even if it was 'just' the initial £250.

I paused briefly over the completed draft of the email. Then I hit send. All I could do now was patiently wait for Acorns or Dovetail to get back to me.

In the meantime, I began focusing on my swimming training in earnest. My basic level of fitness was already very high, especially for a 45 year-old. I could work hard in the gym for an hour, or run hard around London with some old running friends. What I now needed to do was begin to transfer that fitness and stamina into the pool. I knew it would require different muscles, and that this adjustment would take some time. More importantly, I knew from my army days that trying to do too much too soon would be disastrous. As well as physically injuring myself that way, I would cause a huge self-imposed mental block. What I needed to do was establish what level I was currently at in terms of distance and endurance, and build steadily from there.

I started off simply, in the council pool in Worcester, swimming a kilometer and a half. Obviously, that's a long way off the 42km I'd need to build up to, and I had just over a year to make that improvement. All of this was what made the challenge such a huge one. I was not an established runner undertaking a marathon. Neither was I a top-flight swimmer taking on the Channel. And though I was physically fit and could swim with average ability, I'd never swum any real distance in open water. I was pushing myself well outside my comfort zone with this task, and my belief was that this factor would directly contribute to larger donations.

The next step was to locate an open water venue. Luckily, working in London proved to be a huge advantage. Though they are not located centrally, both Hampstead and Tooting have large open-air lidos, and I quickly learnt that Hampstead was 60 meters long, with Tooting Bec being 90 meters.

With the length of most UK pools being given in metric measurements, I found it easier to constantly refer to the Channel in terms of a 42km swim. This meant that one kilometer of a standard 25m pool was 40 lengths. By the same token, the equivalent distance of my swim would be 1,680 lengths. The distance was truly daunting, but it was something that I had to clearly understand and fully acknowledge if I was to stand any chance of building myself up mentally and physically for a successful attempt.

Another consideration was the fact that I was effectively only swimming one width of the Channel. This meant I'd be ploughing away, stroke after stroke, without turning round and pushing off from the side. In a 25m pool, the edge looms up fairly quickly. What I needed was to be able to swim further without the necessity, dare I say the relative luxury, of turning round.

At this time I had been staying with my uncle whilst working in London. He lived in Ickenham, at the end of the Metropolitan tube line, towards Uxbridge. A quick glance at the tube network map showed that the most accessible outdoor venue for me was the Parliament Hills lido at Hampstead, a huge steel-lined pool measuring 27m by 61m. During the summer it was open all day, with additional evening swims on a Monday, and early morning swims every day.

I found the pool to be fantastic. The minute I plunged into the water I knew I was going to enjoy swimming here. The water felt cool and clean, the lining of the pool was gleaming, and it felt a pleasure to be swimming outdoors. Of course, this was July. I did not appreciate at the time that the water was not in fact 'cool' - it was actually quite hot compared to what I would later face. But I enjoyed my naivety and began to churn out my first few lengths.

For someone who had only ever experienced a 25m pool, 60m seemed endless. I found myself glancing up regularly on my first visit, wondering where on earth the end of the pool was. And though I kept telling myself that it was irrelevant, and that I would not be able to do such a thing in the Channel, during my initial swims there it took a long time to adjust to such a comparatively long pool.

The one problem I encountered was that the lido was hardly a secret. Even during evening swims, when the pool was open from 18:45 until 20:30, I found that there was congestion in the swim lanes. I was still trying to find a pace which I could endure for hour upon hour, and the necessity to speed up to overtake someone who was swimming fractionally too slow made this awkward. Signs around the pool suggested that endurance swimming was best practised during cold and wet weather. It seemed criminal to be enjoying a hot summer in the UK, yet wishing for worse weather.

Within those first few weeks I focussed on building up my stamina in order to swim continually for however long the pool session lasted. In the mornings I could stay from 07:00 until 09:30, and on a Monday evening the session lasted an hour and three quarters. I quickly progressed to being able to endure the length of an evening swim, though two and a half hours of sustained morning swimming would take longer to acquire.

What I did discover was that after around an hour my neck began to ache from continually turning to the right to breathe. This highlighted the fact that my swimming technique was bad, as I should actually be rolling more to my side, breathing in the space created as I rotate my right shoulder. But until I could work on a better swimming style, I had to make do with swimming the occasional length breast stroke in order to stretch my neck muscles by looking to the left for a few minutes. Try as I might, I found it impossible to swim front crawl whilst breathing to the left. I simply swallowed too much water. I wondered if I was too old and long in the tooth to learn to swim any differently. I was essentially self-taught, and I knew from taking Lewis to swimming lessons that my technique was dreadfully poor and inefficient. Yet after only one length of trying to imitate the way I'd seen Lewis instructed to swim, my muscles would protest, and they'd soon revert to my old, clumsy style. The challenge seemed to be growing in scale on a daily basis.

The closest I'd ever come to being a member of a swimming club was during my first years of being in the army, whilst I was based at the School of Electronic Engineering in Arborfield, undergoing my trade training. We had a regular Monday morning parade run by the Regimental Sergeant Major (RSM), which was dreaded by everyone except the RSM himself. Having hair slightly too long, having missed a patch of stubble whilst shaving, or having a face that didn't fit on any particular Monday, were all guaranteed ways of earning an 'extra' - an additional entry onto the hated guard duty roster. Guard duty resulted in little sleep, and deprived you of either a weekday, or of a Saturday or Sunday.

Noticing that a friend of mine never attended RSM's parade, I eventually heard of a way out of this miserable event - attend swim practise at 06:00 instead. The only caveat was that if you attended on Monday morning, you also had to attend on Wednesday morning.

The sessions were run by a Warrant Officer called Garry Mitchell. I remember them being very physical and challenging, with regular army-style 'beastings' ensuring that the number of attendees was kept to a manageable size. Many people actually preferred to take their chance on an RSM's parade rather than have Garry push them to the point of vomiting in the pool.

Garry was actually the Army Swim Coach, a position he went on to hold for over 20 years. Though we had both retired from the army when I was beginning my Channel training, I contacted him via Facebook to ask if there was any advice he would give me. It struck home just how much I was out of my own area of expertise when Garry replied that he felt unqualified to advise me. He trained people for indoor swimming events. Open water swimming, and especially The Channel, were both areas he felt that I should speak to an expert about. He did tell me that he had coincidentally been contacted by another ex-army colleague, Ian Davies, who was currently training to join in on a Channel swim relay. He suggested that I contact Ian to see how he could help with any questions or training suggestions.

A Channel swim relay was something I had considered, and quickly dismissed, at the very beginning of my planning. Although it would arguably have made better business sense to have several swimmers all raising funds towards Acorns, my decision was actually based on the rules governing how a relay swim is conducted, and had nothing to do with me believing I'd rather complete the full distance alone. With a relay swim, the team has to decide on a strict rotation order. If it transpires that during the swim one of the members cannot get back into the water when their turn is due, the swim is automatically officially over - a substitute swimmer is not allowed to take the place of the allotted person. For me this was absolutely key in my decision making. I read stories of relay swimmers who were so sick on the boat during their rest period that they were utterly incapacitated by their illness, making it impossible for them to even contemplate swimming. Others had not put in the physical or acclimatisation training required, and subsequently let their team down. For my part, I would rather be the sole reason for a failed Channel swim than forever end up blaming someone else. It was an easy decision, regardless of the fact that opting for a solo swim made the venture vastly more challenging.

Harry's Favourite Thing

With no news received from either Acorns nor Dovetail, things were looking bleak. I took Esta and the boys to Stratford-upon-Avon for the day in July sometime, and we talked about the statistics of swimming the Channel as I drove. Whilst I'd got more and more mentally prepared for the swim, Esta had been somewhat left out. There had been nothing to really update her with in terms of progress, so I wanted to use this opportunity to reinforce the family commitment to the swim.

'So what percentage of swims is actually successful?' Esta asked, once I brought the conversation round to the subject.

From what I could gather, it appeared that only around 10% of attempts made it across to France. That was a staggeringly low success rate, I had to concede.

'So what makes you think you can do it?'

We wound our way along the country roads, through Inkberrow and on towards Stratford as I considered the answer.

The truth was that I could not answer for the 90% who didn't make it. I had no idea what they did wrong, or why they had to stop. But I did know that a huge part of the challenge was going to be psychological. I knew I'd have to focus, and I would have to train correctly. In the army, to train for war, you train harder than war. In rugby, you train with the same level of intensity you expect to take into a match. I needed that same mentality, that same resolve, in everything I was going to do towards the Channel.

'Are you going to give up drinking then?' Asked Esta.

I've always been quite a drinker. It's very much a part of army life, and it continued to be so once I'd become a civilian again. I'm fully aware that alcohol is a poison to the body, but far from feeling bad about it, having a beer or two is my only real vice. I give up now and again, but without a solid reason it's hard to maintain abstinence. Well the Channel was a undoubtedly very solid reason. More than that, I believed that a serious attempt at a successful crossing required a change in lifestyle. I told Esta that I would quit the booze a few months before the swim, when I was in the final build up stages.

'I really believe that if I put my mind to this, I can do it. I can barely swim for two hours at this stage, but I have over 12 months left. It's got to be steady, sensible progression. I can do it.'

Esta looked at me. 'I know you can. I just hope we don't get forgotten about in the process.'

I think that deep down inside we both knew that this was almost inevitable to a degree. The level of commitment required for a serious attempt on the Channel is staggering. Add to that work and travel requirements, and something simply has to give. In order to attempt to raise the £10,000, there were going to be a sacrifices made at many levels.

Yet the weeks ticked by, and the dream seemed to fade, little by little. No news was forthcoming from Acorns, and I began to doubt that my email had ever been seen by Martin. The financial backing I so desperately needed was simply not there. It began to appear that I would be one of the many who had considered swimming the Channel, only to find that the financial logistics had barred me long before the water ever got to take its toll.

Without any indication that any discussion had been taking place, I arrived into work on 30th July to find an email from the CEO:

If you have not already found someone, Dovetail would be up for sponsoring you the £1,000 pilot fee. It is a very significant challenge you are taking on for very sincere and personnel reasons. Dovetail will fund £250 upfront for down payment and then the balance (£750) payable in December. We would expect you to reimburse us should you not go through with the attempt.

The email went on to recommend that I spoke to the HR manager to discuss a communications strategy, and that I liaise directly with the Chief Financial Officer to ascertain how to access the pledged funds.

Without warning, my biggest obstacle had abruptly been swept aside. A commitment of this sort made an unbelievable difference to the entire situation, and to find out that the Executive Management Team at work had such faith in me was tremendous. There were still problems to overcome, including somehow raising the other £2,000 corporate sponsorship that I would require to fund the challenge. Yet I firmly believed that subsequent funds would be easier to come by now that I could say I *was* going to swim the Channel, as opposed to saying that I *hoped* to do so.

Six weeks after the initial conception of the idea, the swim had suddenly and delightedly become a very real possibility!

Wading In

My list of priorities that I'd created about the swim seemed to be never-ending. As fast as I was ticking one item off, others were being added. Now that I had secured a pledge for one third of the total necessary funding, it was time to re-evaluate my situation.

    A mandatory requirement for any crossing was of course the pilot boat. Some weeks had now passed since I'd first requested availability from each of the 12 licensed pilots, so I now had to contact them again, albeit this time with the knowledge that I could put down a deposit immediately.

    Kevin Sherman, owner and captain of Connemara was my first choice, as he had previously stated that a slot was available for the period 18-20 August. This date tied in nicely with the anniversary of Harry's death, making the swim seem all that more poignant for all of us. I envisaged that the significance of undertaking the challenge so close to the anniversary may also give me that tiny mental edge when things began to feel tough. I knew I would benefit from all the psychological help I could get.

    I emailed Kevin again to check that date was still available. I was worried that all available slots may now have been taken, and I did not want to contemplate the possibility that the challenge may have to be set for not just one, but two years ahead.

    During the summer months communication with the pilots can be very sporadic. Whilst the weather is good the men (the pilots are currently all male) will be out plying their trade, sometimes working back to back shifts in order to cater for the demand of services by the many swimmers. It's a mutually beneficial arrangement. The pilots earn (or at least supplement) their living in this way, and all Channel swimmers require a safety escort. The swim season may appear to be brief, but working long, slow, back to back shifts can be exhausting for the boat crews.

    I was quickly to learn that the weather I was experiencing in central London often bore no relation at all to the conditions being experienced 75 miles away in Dover. The Straight has a micro-climate of its own, meaning that the pilots have to be experts in understanding and gauging the local climatic conditions as they change and unfold. It's not uncommon for a swimmer to stand on the beach and stare at the calm inshore sea, wondering why their pilot recommended against an attempt that day, whilst all the time being unaware that just two or three miles out at sea there may be a force five wind blowing. Certainly, a calm day in London meant absolutely nothing with regards to attempting a Channel swim.

To my incredible relief, Kevin replied to my email less than three hours later that same day, confirming my hoped-for slot was still available. I acknowledged that I had the deposit, that I wished to confirm booking of the swim window of 18-20 August 2014, and that I would forward the money immediately.

I was now actively working my way down the CSA bullet list, and the next step was to formally register my Channel swim with them. I had to apply for a registration/information pack via the web site, doing so by contacting a lady called Julie who acted as the CSA secretary. There was a fee of £35 registration costs to bear. My original intention was to fully fund the swim from corporate sponsorship, but I now concluded that there may well be fees that I would have to bear out of my own wallet if I was to maintain momentum. This registration fee was the first such cost.

Now that things were formally underway, the next stage was to begin to plan a communications strategy. Having Dovetail sponsor me was incredible, but they were doing so out of respect for the scale of my challenge, not because they wanted anything back from their financial offerings in terms of media coverage. And as Acorns was a local midlands charity, what I really needed was some Worcester-based businesses to get on board and back the challenge. This way, we could then get the local press involved and begin to build a wider awareness of the challenge. I hoped that securing one local sponsor would mean that others would subsequently want to jump on board.

My first step was to begin a blog. I wanted to ensure there was some history to it by the time I began to canvas for funds, as I could imagine a board of executives discussing how realistic my attempt would be, and wanting to gauge just how committed I was to the training requirements. A blog would enable all interested parties, including my family of course, to have an insight into my training schedule, my experiences, and even to my doubts. An added bonus was that the blog subsequently acted as a source of accurate dates, times and distances when I needed to reflect on my progress.

Next I set up a Twitter account, linking it to my personal web site so that all new blog postings would automatically send a corresponding Tweet. I did the same with Facebook and LinkedIn, before then beginning to contact friends and acquaintances through each of these social media sites, aiming to expand my network as much as possible.

My blog quickly gathered a fairly significant and regular following. It was strange at first to bump into people who would say how impressed they were with the scale of the challenge. They'd read my latest blog, and would comment how the training commitments seemed daunting. It was great to know that someone other than Esta and my mother were getting to read my postings.

But communication breakdowns still occurred. The Acorns media and relations team picked up on my progress, and they subsequently spoke to Free Radio, asking if they would like to cover the event. Free Radio contacted me, and we exchanged some emails whilst trying to arrive at a good date for an interview. However, the station then asked me to confirm the actual date of the challenge. When they realised that the event was not imminent, but was in fact to take place the following year, they promptly dropping me like a hot rock. I followed up the brusque one-line email they'd sent me which suggested I had deliberately misled them about the commencement date, and suggested that it could make a good on-going story to cover throughout the year. Apparently my email did not deign a reply.

Regardless of what Free Radio thought, August 2013 was a busy time for me. I quickly found myself blogging the fact that there was exactly one year to go, and I ensured I was conducting swimming training whenever possible. In Worcester, this was restricted to the council pool in Sansome Walk (which has since closed), and in London I continued frequenting the Parliament Hills lido, gradually increasing the amount of time I could swim for. The lido was a fantastic facility, but this fact also meant that it tended to get incredibly busy. Like everyone else swimming there, I longed to have more space. Bumping in to people and being swum over by the triathletes in their wetsuits was a huge frustration for me. I was probably as much of a hindrance to others, of course, but I knew that of all the things that I may miss during a 12 hour swim, other people getting in my way would not be one of them.

due to the shortening daylight hours as we moved towards autumn. It became apparent that I would soon have to start taking half day holidays from work in order to achieve the required swim durations that I would need. My aim was to achieve a four hour swim prior to the cold weather beginning to set in.

In order to swim for such a duration, however, I knew I would have to begin practising taking fuel on board during the exercise. Feeding during the Channel swim was an important part of the challenge, and the CSA website advised experimenting to ascertain what food could comfortably be consumed. With this aspect of the challenge being very personal, there was no direct advice as to what was best. If anything, it was possible to receive a host of conflicting suggestions, especially with regards to electrolytic drinks. (Incidentally, the CSA website also refused to give advice on swimming practice. Though at first this may seem utterly ironic, the CSA staff do not want to give any suggestions which may conflict with other professional advice a swimmer may be paying for, or any training techniques that may be practised within a club. In this way, as a completely individual swimmer, I was left in a void with regards to understanding what I should be aiming for in the water.)

Prior to the end of August my swimming sessions had simply comprised me swimming non-stop, bar the occasional re-application of lubricant. One evening at the Men's pond in Hampstead was my first experiment with taking fuel and water on board during the swim. I had bought some energy sachets, and practised treading water whilst eating some of the gel, firstly after an hour of swimming, and then after another 40 minutes. I didn't notice a huge energy boost, but the idea was to sustain a suitable energy level required to keep going, as well as to get used to keeping the food down. Being able to eat and drink during the challenge without vomiting is crucial to success. The physical act of being sick is an energy drain in its own right, and coupled together with the loss of food and liquid, it's something that needs to be avoided at all costs. As with everything on this challenge, feeding whilst in the water was something that had to be practised and rehearsed.

It needs to be pointed out that the discomfort caused by chaffing is insanely irritating. As with the formation of a blister, the sensation makes itself known gradually. But once your conscious mind is aware of the rubbing, it's next to impossible to ignore, especially considering there is almost nothing else to focus your attention on whilst you are swimming. And with the shoulders rotating constantly the areas under the arms are particularly prone to this rubbing. Other potential areas for chaffing include between the thighs and around the neck, though luckily I appeared to be spared such discomfort in those regions. So another lesson I learnt from that long session at the pond was that if I used the Body Glide substance and Vaseline together, I didn't chaff. Quite how long this mixture would last before being washed off needed to be discovered, but certainly I was still coated in the mixture at the end of my session, and there had been no rubbing at all under the arms.

    It was not always possible to access a pool, of course, so I was mixing the swimming in with other physical activities. My army days had always revolved around keeping fit, usually by running or by circuit training, so this was arguably an area where I was more in my element anyway. I intended to keep up the high level of overall fitness at the same time as working on my swimming endurance.

    I'm generally very good at pushing myself physically. When I work out, I tend to work out hard. Even on days when I envisage a 'gentle' gym session, I generally come away puffing and sweating profusely. This is probably because the army never, ever, took us out on a gentle run, or gave us an easy PT session. Consequently, even now it always seems like cheating to me if I ever do take it easy, like there is little point in exercising if it's not in an attempt to push myself a whole lot further than may feel comfortable.

    Despite this ability to highly motivate myself, occasionally it requires someone else to encourage you to push that little bit harder still, and to go that little bit further. Even Sir Ranulph Fiennes makes use of a personal trainer for events like the Marathon de Sables. I knew one of the personal trainers at the small London gym I frequented at lunchtimes. I'd spoken to 'JJ' Hewitt a few times, and though there were a range of personal trainers at the gym, I suspected from what I'd seen that JJ would truly be able to put me through my paces. I informed him in no uncertain terms that I was training for an extreme endurance event, and that I expected a proper military-style beasting. JJ duly delivered!

    High Impact Training (HIT, or what the army used to refer to as circuit training) hurts at the best of times, if such an oxymoron exists. But when you have someone pushing you, urging you on, encouraging you to go further - then it really, really hurts. JJ constructed an excruciating workout comprising several sets, with each set consisting of six types of exercise. Each exercise was an extreme variant of a more basic form, so instead of a standard press-up, JJ had me using a balance board between my hands and bouncing up off the ground with each upward thrust. Shuttle runs up and down the gym floor were conducted with 20kg weights in each hand, and lunges were performed with heavy dumbbells held at shoulder height. By the end of the third and final set, I was literally curled up on the exercise mat, gasping for breath and dripping with sweat.

    The adrenaline was still coursing through me several hours afterwards. I worked on the fifth floor of our London building at the time, before Dovetail moved to larger premises. When I left for my train later that day, my legs were still so unsteady beneath me that I almost had to stop on the second floor and call the lift to get me to the ground floor. There was no question around the fact that JJ had delivered what I'd asked (and paid) for!

    My last few years in the army had seen me posted at the base of the Malvern Hills in Worcestershire. A good friend of mine, an army captain by the name of Bill McDougall, had often pointed out to me the irony of people exercising on a step machine at a local gym when the world-famous hills were just outside the window. I've loved running over the Malverns for years, and at one point they formed a huge part of my physical rehabilitation following a massive disc prolapse which almost saw me wheelchair-bound.

    Ideally, I like being dropped at the southern end of hills and making my way across the whole range, going from the base to the tip of each hill, and finally ending up at the clock tower at the foot of North Hill. The distance is around seven miles as the crow flies, but this does not take into account the elevation gained and lost along the route. My personal best time to complete the entire length was one hour and 20 minutes.

    Unlike when I was in the army, I no longer have the opportunity to run the course at lunchtime, and I now have to take the family into account when planning the logistics of a hill run. I occasionally get Esta to drop me off at the far end still, and then meet her and the kids in Malvern town. Even this is far from ideal though, as I have to leave them to find something to do whilst I'm off running.

To really test my fitness level during my swim training, I decided to try something different.

From Malvern town, up past St Anne's Well to the main path leading to the Beacon, is steep. VERY steep. I estimate it ranges between a 1/8 and a 1/4 gradient. It also starts with a killer set of steps, almost purposely designed to knock the wind out of you right at the beginning. One Saturday I got Esta to drop me off at the base of the steps. I set off at a brisk march up the steps, then began to run up the steep, pebble-strewn path. I was out of breath almost immediately due to the severe gradient. My legs muscles were screaming at me, and my lungs felt fit to burst after around five minutes, but I kept urging myself on to the next bend in the winding track. I found myself overtaking ramblers and forging further on up the hill. With every step I wanted to stop and walk, and yet each step also brought me closer to the summit of the path. Somehow, without fully intending to, I managed to run all of the way up the steep path and over the hill to the clock tower to meet up with Esta and the boys.

Esta had not anticipated my arrival so quickly, and I somehow managed to get to them not long after they'd arrived at the clock tower. They had only just parked the car and were putting their hiking boots on when I ran up to them. From there we could all enjoy a far more sedate hill walk together, with me already getting my workout out of the way. I found it a great way to integrate the family into my training, without the necessity of having them endure it with me, nor sitting and watch me swim.

As the year moved into September I realised that I needed to start raising the publicity of the swim. This was necessary both to attract more corporate sponsorship, and to begin to climb towards my target of £10,000 for Acorns. I'd set up a JustGiving page as soon as the event was confirmed, and close friends and family had already begun to donate, but I wanted to accelerate the process and heighten awareness beyond my immediate network of contacts.

Realising that a challenge which was due to take place in the somewhat distant future may not have the media beating a path to my door, I had also loosely planned some mini-fundraising activities. The first of those was due to be the 1000 press-up challenge. News from the Acorns media team had been scarce until this point, so I contacted them to ask if a high profile and public venue within Worcester city centre could be booked for the event. A date of 16th November was confirmed, with Crowngate shopping centre plaza to be shared between me and a large festive Christmas tree. I also contacted Craig Gillies, the huge 6 foot 8 inch second row rugby player from Worcester Warriors, and arranged for him to pop along at some point during the hour of the challenge to act as a local celebrity.

It occurred to me, however, that people walking through Crowngate doing their Christmas shopping may be somewhat bemused at the sight of a man doing apparently random press-ups in the middle of the plaza. We would need some flyers to hand out, detailing what the event was in aid of. Ideally we'd also need a large banner which did the same thing, as whilst some people instinctively accept something that is handed to them on the street, many others will refuse the offering without even knowing what it is. Flyers alone were insufficient.

I began to contact some of the local businesses in Worcester who produced such advertising material. Initially I began to ask if these companies would produce the banners as part of them sponsoring the Channel swim. I suggested that they could advertise their own part in the venture on the posters and flyers, thereby making the cost of production free for me but relatively cheap for them. It seemed like a sensible idea at the time, but the negotiations seemed to continually break down for some reason. With company bosses being away, messages not getting passed on, and me working in London, dealing with this whilst also holding down a full time job, commuting and training was simply too much. I should also mention that Esta and I moved house during this time too, which was far from a stress-free process. I eventually asked the banner company what the cost would be if I were to pay for the merchandise myself, and having received the quote it looked as though I would have no choice but to once more self-fund this part of the venture.

Prior to embarking on what I was beginning to consider as an increasingly stupid idea of swimming the Channel, I had spent Sunday mornings during the winter assisting in coaching Lewis and other children of his age at rugby practise. For my part I mostly supplied an extra pair of hands, bags of encouragement and the occasional loud voice in lieu of any actually useful coaching skills. The parents and kids seemed to appreciate my input though, so that was reward enough for two or three hours of running around in shorts in the cold and wet winter months, usually on a field that was invariably fully open to the biting wind. But as my training regime for the swim began to increase, I gradually took a step back from assisting with the coaching and instead began to focus more on my own fitness. At first I'd turn up with Lewis, ensure he was settled in, and then exercise on an empty part of the field with shuttle runs or circuits - anything to make full use of any spare minutes.

    Naturally, this invoked some questions from the parents who would normally expect me to be more closely involved with the rugby. Gradually they began to find out about the swim, and I'd use any opportunity to try and steer the subject onto my need for corporate sponsorship.

    It was in this way that Becky Widdowson, a partner in Worcester's oldest legal firm, got to talking to me about something other than our boy's respective progression in rugby. Through a series of conversations and subsequent emails, Becky suddenly delighted me by announcing that Hallmark Hulme would like to offer the money I needed to pay for the banners and flyers. This was fantastic news. Not only did it mean that I would now be exempt from funding the advertising merchandise myself, but it also signified the signing up of the first Worcester-based business. From Hallmark Hulme's point of view, this was them pronouncing their commitment both to me, and to Acorns. It was a significant step forward in my organisational plans.

    Another huge bonus was the suggestion by Becky that her husband, Simon Fall-Taylor of FT Images, take some photos of me for use within the advertising campaign material. Having made appropriate arrangements with Simon, I popped along to his home-based studio for a photo shoot prior to rugby training one Sunday. Becky joined me in some of the photos for promotional use within the local business community, and there was an bizarrely stark contrast between us as we posed next to each other. I was clad in nothing more than a skimpy pair of swimming trunks, complete with shaved head and tattoos, whilst standing next to Becky, the besuited solicitor. The images came out brilliantly of course, and Hallmark

Hulme were proud to use the shots of both of Becky and I for their own promotions, whilst I used the solo shots of me to advertise my Channel swim. The banners and flyers were subsequently commissioned, with the addition of Hallmark Hulme's logo to be used alongside Dovetail's.

Still being very naive, and very much a learner in the Channel swimming requirements, I continued to regularly visit the CSA site in order to check up on other issues I'd need to prepare for throughout the build-up year. Though it was not something which appeared on the check list, regular reference was made by swimmers to their boat support crew. Such on-board assistance was not something I'd given any serious consideration to. All my training had thus far been conducted solo. I motivated myself personally, I decided upon my own training regime, and I was the only one to answer to. So though it would be nice to have someone there to see me reach the other side, in my ignorance I'd not yet fully appreciated the necessity of having someone aboard my safety vessel. So it was more out of realisation that I *could* have someone aboard, rather than understanding that I'd *need* someone, that I contact my eldest sons Sean and Connagh to find out if they would be interested in accompanying me. Sean, newly married, had actually planned a mini-tour of Australia shortly after my swim was due, so he had to save all of his money and his holiday time for this, which was completely understandable. Connagh was due to finish his degree at Buckinghamshire University just a few months prior to the swim, so for him the timing was perfect. At this stage, I knew of nothing further that I needed to make Connagh aware of. Looking back, that's quite a frightening realisation.

With a combination of the autumn season resulting in the earlier closure of the lidos in London, and of my swimming endurance increasing, I realised I was going to need access to an indoor 25 metre pool. Another problem was that the council pool was not open to the public for periods of longer than an hour or two. I'd need access for six hours, eventually.

David Lloyd's had recently opened a brand new facility next to the Worcester Warriors stadium, Sixways. I contemplated joining as a member, but I first decided that it must surely be worth me initially enquiring about sponsored membership. With nothing to lose, and with Lewis in tow one morning, I walked into the gym reception and asked if it would be possible to speak to the duty manager. Though I had not appreciated the significance of it at the time, Acorns had sent me a certificate acknowledging the legitimacy of my event. I explained to the duty manager what I was attempting, showed him the official document, and explained that I simply required access to their pool Friday to Sunday when I was home from London.

The duty manager explained that he would not be able to authorise such access without consulting people higher up, but he took my details and asked if he could photocopy the paperwork from Acorns. I thanked him and left, wondering if this request would ever come to anything at all.

Adding to the increasing list of things I was ignorant about was the fact that the David Lloyd's group are closely affiliated with the Together for Short Lives charity, and they were consequently extremely familiar with the requirement for funding by hospices which provided palliative care for children. My request for membership most certainly did not fall upon deaf ears. Around two weeks after my visit to the club I received a phone call late one evening informing me that my membership forms were ready to sign at my convenience. It had been deemed appropriate to give me one year's full membership of all of the club facilities, as such an extreme event would require more than just swimming training alone. With an incredible spring in my step I arrived at the club the following day to sign up. I maintain even now that taking the bold decision to walk in and ask about sponsorship was one the best choices I made during this overall period of the swim. Quite how I would have done so well without access to proper facilities is impossible to say, but I do know that the hours and hours I put into training at David Lloyds undoubtedly put me on the best possible course.

From August through to October I'd been practising building up my press-up endurance, gradually extending my personal best target up to 800 press-ups in one hour. The 1,000 mark was still a long way off, but as with the Channel, that was the idea of the challenge, and mini-fundraisers such as this one were planned to highlight my dedication.

Foolishly, I took my eye off the ball with regards to the press-ups. I've no idea how it happened. Perhaps it was complacency, having got fairly close during one of my build up sessions, and then assuming I'd be ok from that point onwards. All I do know is that I had another practice two weeks before the planned fund raiser, and the results were disastrous. It was a real eye opener as to how long it can take to achieve a physical level, but how quickly the body will deteriorate from that same stage if left to stagnate. As a result of this lapse, I had to quickly initiate a training plan which would necessitate a rapid improvement. I'd almost left things too late, as Saturday 16th November came around quicker than I'd have liked.

The day dawned crisp and cold. We'd planned to hold the fundraiser at a time which would seek to capitalise on the highest level of footfall, namely at midday, the peak hour for Saturday Christmas shopping. Despite the hour, there was little warmth to be felt in the air. We'd dropped Will off with my mum for the duration of the event, though she planned to pop along and give some moral support for a few minutes, and to let Will watch his dad try and raise some money. Esta and Lewis would be employed with handing out flyers and explaining to bemused passersby what was happening and why. To add to the publicity assistance I'd amassed a small promotional team: Esta and Lewis would be ably supported by Becky Widdowson and Julian Powell from Hallmark Hulme, sponsors of the advertising material, and Carole Crowe and her husband Steve would be there to officiate the count of press-ups; Craig Gillies had promised to turn up as a local celebrity; and I'd further arranged for Simon Fall-Taylor to once again lend his photography expertise.

There was no need for a great deal of equipment, of course. I arrived with my roll-up exercise mat, my Kindle with its countdown app, a bottle of water and a towel. We erected the large banner which Hallmark Hulme had kindly sponsored, and Esta shared out flyers with Lewis, Becky and Julian. Carole set up a large flip chart to begin to record my progress, and at midday I made a start.

During my preparations I'd made a plan of attack and had gradually increased it as I improved in strength and stamina. On the day of the challenge, I had no intentions of deviating from that plan, despite the adrenaline, the audience, and the high sense of anticipation. So at the stroke of twelve, having been on my knees in a prayer-like stance, I simply adopted the appropriate position and performed six press-ups. There was a small murmur of consternation as I stopped and knelt back up. What was I playing at? Everyone naturally assumed I'd power through several hundred exercises, rest, and repeat. They weren't expecting me to stop after just six! Yet at 20 seconds past 12 I performed another six press-ups, and at 20 seconds to the minute I did another five. In this way, by performing 17 exercises per minute, I would be on target for 1020 in an hour. This all seemed mathematically easy, but the real test was of course muscular endurance - being able to maintain that per-minute count for the entire 60 minutes.

The plaza was quite busy, and I was vaguely aware of people coming and going. Becky's voice was very distinct in the background, and I could clearly hear her explaining to people the reason for this fundraiser. I heard the English Channel mentioned numerous times, and Harry's name was always somewhere within the explanation. Hearing our son's name was a fantastic reminder of exactly what all of this was about. It was sometimes easy to get caught up in the vastness of the Channel swim attempt and to forget the very reason I was putting myself and my family through all of this. Carole was loudly calling out the cumulative count, having quickly understood my strategy for pacing myself. Her tally chart was attracting plenty of attention and the sound of coins being tossed into the Acorns collection buckets was inspirational. This was what it was all about: raising funds.

Mostly my attention was focussed on the timer displayed on my Kindle. Resting 10 or so seconds to shake off aching muscles and take a sip of water may sound like a long break, but as the minutes ticked by, I had to make the choice between drinking and wiping my face with the towel, or stretching my arms. 10 seconds was not enough for both.

I heard Esta greet someone whilst I was exercising, and an unmistakable Scottish accent told me that my friend Alistair MacLeod had arrived. Ali began cheering me on loudly, encouraging the support of other bystanders, and as I moved towards 700 press-ups it suddenly occurred to me that Ali would be an excellent crew aboard the boat. I made a mental note to ask him about it sometime later.

Simon's camera was flashing, Carole was calling out the count, and my arms were aching. Craig Gillies arrived at an excellent point within the proceedings, and he posed next to me as I continued to work.

Once I'd broken the 900 mark, I knew I would successfully achieve the goal of 1000. A small crowd had now stopped to watch, as opposed to people just glancing at me as they walked by, and I could sense a growing anticipation. Unfamiliar voices were now urging me on, and people I'd had never met were calling my name in encouragement.

I stuck to my plan of 17 exercises per minute so rigorously that even when the crowd was counting loudly in unison and fully expecting me to break the 1,000 mark, I stopped at 998 for my regular rest after performing my set of six press-ups. The next set took me beyond 1,000, and during my final 20 seconds the muscles in my arms and chest managed to squeeze out an additional three. In total, I achieved 1,023 press-ups in 60 minutes, raising a total of £145.63.

What none of us had appreciated at the time was that my event took place the day after the annual Children in Need appeal. In addition to this, there had been a tragic tsunami in the Philippines just days before, and local appeals were taking place just a short distance from my own charity appeal. With all of this in mind, I was exceedingly happy with the hourly rate we'd achieved, with every penny of those funds raised going directly to Acorns, creeping me ever closer to my target.

Finally, it seemed that both the fundraising element and the publicity for the swim were beginning to gather momentum.

Training and Acclimatisation - Part 1

My basic training in the army took place within the winter months. Our platoon was detailed for duty over the Christmas period, and I remember walking around on guard duty in the middle of the cold, dark winter nights, struggling to keep warm and stay alert. Our passing out parade was in January, and in the morning prior to the proceedings the parade square was filled with trainee soldiers all scraping the ice from the concrete upon which we would later be marching, eager not to slip and fall over in front of visiting dignitaries, comrades and family. The inspecting officer took his job exceedingly seriously that month, and for two hours we all had to stand stock-still whilst he inspected the two main platoons (30 men apiece), the back-up platoons, and the entire band. Several men fainted from the lack of blood to their heads. Standing still for so long is not natural. The heart typically relies on movement of the limbs to provide capillary action, assisting the flow of blood up to areas above the heart, such as the head. Whilst we'd all been trained to wriggle our toes, tense our muscles regularly, and to slightly rock ourselves backwards and forwards onto and off our tip-toes, all of this had to be done without the slightest outward appearance of any movement. But when the cold begins to seep into your body, your mind also begins to shut down. Apathy sets in. Hypothermia is never far behind.

    Similarly, on exercise, I'd had to lay still in shell-scrapes on the frozen ground, tucked behind a rifle or a machine gun, silently watching out for the enemy. I'd stood in fire trenches with feet so cold and frozen that they had long since ceased to hurt and had now simply become numb. All in all, I was no stranger to the cold.

    But water is 1,000 times as dense as air. Once you've jumped in, you are submerged in it, engulfed in it, surrounded by it. Every exposed inch of flesh is in direct contact with the water, and your own body temperature will not make a fraction of a difference to that vast body of water in which you swim. No measuring device on the planet would be able to detect an increase in warmth accrued due to your presence - but you will be painfully aware of the water's effect on your own temperature. The only way to be able to cope with such an ordeal is through practice, gradually increasing your mental and physical endurance to resisting the cold.

Acclimatisation training is one of the biggest recommendations given on the CSA web site, next of course to actual swimming practice. Indeed, much of the time the two can be combined, should a suitable outdoor venue be available. But often, over the winter months, the swimmer will need to seek warmer, indoor waters if they are to be able to put in the required time and distance training. It's during these months that the swimming training and the acclimatisation can sometimes diverge and become separate activities.

Between the initial conception of my Channel swim idea and up until November, I'd already learnt many lessons, and had progressed a long way. I'd discovered where on my body I was prone to chaffing, and what remedies worked for me to alleviate that rubbing. I'd begun to practise feeding, and though my final food choices for the actual challenge had not been made, I knew that I could keep down liquids, energy gels and chocolate without vomiting. My stamina and endurance had increased to the point where I could comfortably swim for far in excess of two hours. This meant I was theoretically already able to qualify as a Channel relay participant by performing the required two hour continuous open water qualifier swim. As a solo challenger, however, I needed to build up to achieve a six hour qualifier.

And then there was still the small question of achieving 42km across the Channel.

In addition to all of this, I'd been following the guidelines of the CSA website, using every opportunity to acclimatise to cold water. One of the biggest problems faced by swimmers is Sudden Immersion Shock Syndrome, sometimes referred to as cold-shock. Most people will have experienced this unpleasant experience at some point, and they will know that sudden exposure to cold water induces automatic reflexes in the body which are impossible to totally overcome. The most obvious of these reflexes is the involuntary inward gasping of breath. This single act has been known to kill many an unfortunate victim who find themselves accidentally thrown into cold water. Without being able to help themselves, the natural tendency to hold their breath whilst submerged is nullified by this involuntary gasp, resulting in a huge lungful of cold water. In such instances, death can quickly follow.

Subsequent to the sudden and sharp intake of breath, uncontrollable shallow and rapid breathing follows, along with a rapid increase in heart rate and in blood pressure. All in all, cold-shock is unpleasant, and can kill.

But it's important to understand and appreciate two facts: Firstly, the effects of cold-shock only last for around the first two minutes; secondly, the human body can be conditioned to adapt to the shock, reducing (though not eliminating) the degree of effect caused by the cold.

It appears that several studies have been done, comparing those people who regularly swim in cold water to those who do not. I don't pretend to understand all of the findings, but two things were apparent from all of the literature I read. It was clearly shown that regular encounters with cold water swimming significantly reduced the effects of cold-shock - some studies even suggested the effects became pleasurable to the point of being mildly addictive. What was also shown was that the resistance which was built up did not significantly diminish through lack of repeated exposure. This meant that during the summer months, when the water may be warmer, a cold-water swimmer would not lose the tolerance they will have gained through practise over the previous winter.

The second point was of little significance to me. Had my swim been two years off, instead of the following summer, it would have been a different case. What I needed to focus on was overcoming any initial shock, and subsequent to this I had to be able to cope with prolonged exposure.

The advice given by the CSA was that to increase endurance to prolonged exposure, it was necessary to allow yourself to be cold whenever possible: start to wear thinner clothes, sleep with a blanket or even just a sheet instead of a quilt, and to take cold showers or baths instead of warm ones.

The latter part may sound easy. I can assure you that it takes some serious will power first thing in the morning to turn the dial of the shower to the cold setting, as opposed to requesting a nice warm and welcoming blast of water. This is especially true in the winter. That first splash of cold water against your skin certainly wakes you up, and sticking your head under the downpour is far from instinctive. What you do notice is that the external warmth of your skin is rapidly dissipated. Though it's not pleasant at first, once your skin has cooled down, you suddenly find there is a less eager desire to get out of the shower. You simply have to overcome the instinct to turn the water off before you are even fully soaked, and after that first couple of minutes you are able to lather up as normal. Believe it or not, this does get easier and easier to cope with and endure.

Getting in to the cold pool at Parliament Hills was easy at first. I started swimming there during the summer months, of course, and the water could not be described as cold, so much as cool. But a vast body of water quickly loses its heat once the daylight hours begin to shorten and when the strength of the sun begins to fade. By October, the experience of jumping in was becoming distinctly less pleasant. Each morning when I'd arrive, I'd glance at the digital display announcing the respective poolside and water temperatures, noting how quickly the two were being reduced, day by day.

In November of 2013, following advice I'd taken, I began to keep a detailed log of all of my physical activities, my state of mind, and of my overall progress. Despite my background, my history, my mental determination and the strength of my resolve, I am only human, and I'm far from fallible. That November was a cold month, and on Wednesday 13th I made the following entry into my log:

"Freezing this morning. Opened the door, saw ice on the cars and the road. Chickened out, closed the door and went back to bed. Felt guilty all day."

Once the sun is up and the day has a tiny amount of heat in it, or when you're sitting on a nice warm train, or are in your heated office, it's all so easy to make that promise of throwing yourself into the cold water the following day. But opening the door of your accommodation and stepping out into the dark and frost-bitten air, trudging to the train station when you're tired, and all the while knowing you have to strip off and pad across bare freezing concrete before submerging your body into ice-cold water - well the reality is not so easy, I can assure you.

And don't be fooled into thinking that the cold showers will achieve all of the resistance to cold that is required for a Channel swim either. When I hauled myself to the lido the day after my embarrassing u-turn, the digital display announced the water to be just eight degrees centigrade.

'Time to man-up', I told myself, standing on the pool-side and watching the retired regulars slip into the water as though it were the Mediterranean Sea. They made it look so easy. Their level of resistance was what I needed to achieve. That resistance would come at a price though - and an initial down-payment was due immediately.

I lasted just eight minutes before the pain in my fingers drove me out of the water. Any thought of a cold shower was instantly abandoned as I cranked the dial up to hot, trying desperately to drive the chill from out of my blood and bones. One of the locals noticed me shaking, and though I was barely able to speak, I managed to tell him I'd only endured eight minutes. He assured me I would be able to cope with around an additional five minutes per visit, if I stuck with it regularly, day in, day out.

It was at that point that I first began to seriously regret my decision to attempt the Channel.

As the autumn months continued, the lido at Parliament Hill was perfect for gradually increasing my resistance to the cold. The water temperature was dropping steadily, and the open air venue meant the that pool surroundings also failed to retain any warmth, adding to the acclimatisation process I needed. The problem was that these factors also made it harder to continue to progress my long distance swimming in the open air. At this point, my acclimatisation and my distance training began to drastically diverge.

Of course, due to the incredibly generous offer of club membership by David Lloyd's, my distance training could now be conducted in the luxury of a heated indoor pool in Worcester. By the beginning of December I had increased my endurance to the point that I was swimming 5km fairly regularly, and this was the point at which I began to face my next challenge. The problem now was that a 5km swim was taking in excess of two hours to achieve. And whilst I was ready to start to swim for longer in terms of physical ability, I would need to plan how I could manage this within my working day once the New Year came. It appeared that I would soon be having to take annual leave in order achieve the swimming hours required for a Channel challenge.

My swimming agenda covering the Christmas period was fairly simple. We were booked to spend two weeks in the Canary islands, namely on the island of Gran Canaria, and I planned use this time as an opportunity to get some proper induction to sea swimming under my belt. My plan commenced on the first full day of our holiday. The most worrying thing about this, of course, was the complete unknown with regards to currents, tides and other such hazards. I'll be the first to admit that I was rather brazen about my attitude to getting into unknown seas, but in many ways I was deliberately pushing myself in terms of fear boundaries. 'Do one thing every day that scares you,' Eleanor Roosevelt once said. Well I'd signed up to attempt the most notorious swimming route known, and I knew I had to mentally prepare for being far out to sea, well out of sight of any land. Yes, a safety boat would be alongside me with observers ensuring I was not experiencing difficulty. But I'd also heard reference to swimmers who had pulled out of the swim at every stage (even just before getting into the water) due to 'stage fright'. I figured that the more accustomed to a bit of lone sea swimming I could be, within reasonable safety margins, the better. That training was due to start right here.

    The apartment we'd hired was in a small coastal enclave slightly beyond the eastern end of Playa De Ingles. There was a small, private cove right outside our gated community, with a pebble beach sloping fairly steeply down into the dark blue waters of the Atlantic Ocean. We saw people swimming in the cove on the first day, which was a good sign that the waters were not too treacherous. On Monday 23rd Dec I went for a run along the sea front to explore the local area. I discovered a larger pebble beach several hundred meters further along the eastern coast. This second beach, which was maybe 500 meters long, led on to a lovely promenade fronted by hotels and a few small cafés. Following this to the end, I discovered that the resort abruptly stopped at a steep set of rocks roughly 1.5km - 2km from our apartment.

    I decided that as a starting point I should commence swimming from the local cove and continue along the eastern shoreline to the larger beach. I would then meet up with Esta and the boys there, and at least they would know where I had started, and where I was expecting to finish. This was not a great distance, but it would give me an initial indication of how the tide and current felt. I could always swim up and down along the larger beach if I felt comfortable with the conditions of the sea.

    Though I'd made (and kept) a resolution some years back to go swimming in the sea every Christmas, the previous 12 or so winters had seen me do little more in terms of exercise than floating around and cooling off. This holiday it would be some proper swimming, with real distances and measurable outcomes.

Now, equipped with a latex swimming hat and some ear plugs I'd been recommended to employ, I walked over the smooth, round pebbles of our small cove and into the Atlantic. The waves were quite high, crashing onto the stones and dragging them up and down the beach, eroding them gradually and smoothing them bit by bit with each new wave. The surf pounded at my legs as I waded in, driving me back to the shore, but I took a breath and dived beneath the next wave, pulling strongly with my arms to force my body out to sea.

The first thing I appreciated was the water temperature. I could tell instantly that the hat was making a small but noticeably significant difference to the heat loss via my head, meaning that the sea actually felt almost warm. This was fantastic news. In truth, and strange as it sounds, I actually did not want the water to be any warmer. This was firstly because I would have found warmer water more of an energy drain once I started to really get going, and secondly because I was convinced that the Channel would be around the same temperature as the Atlantic appeared to be in December.

For that first sea swim, the conditions seemed ideal all round. There was a reasonable swell, but the sun was shining warmly on my back. The salt water was proving immediately more buoyant than the fresh water I'd been experiencing up until now, and the lack of any bone-numbing chill was a such a welcome change after a winter of cold-water swimming. It gave a real psychological boost to not be shivering with cold for once. I set off east, heading towards the large pebble beach on the other side of our cove.

The wind was onshore, driving the waves towards the beach. I quickly discovered that this meant that the swell was also on my right - in the direction to which I turned my head to breathe. It was my first experience of having to deal with this since Bournemouth many months earlier. Normally, in the pools and ponds, the water was calm. Now, I had to be aware once more that when I came up for air, there might be a wave coming towards my face. The sensation was slightly unnerving, and it took me some time to relax my shoulders and gain a more comfortable rhythm of swimming. The natural temptation when prohibited to take a breath was to stop and lift my head. I appreciated more than ever now that this was not a race. I needed to ensure that I was not out of breath at any point, such that I could accept occasionally having to breathe on every fourth stroke, as opposed to every second one.

As with my first experience in the pond at Hampstead, the problem of navigation again became apparent, once more resulting from my unilateral breathing pattern. What I decided to do was to take a rough bearing of the sun each time I took a breath, and I tried to ensure that it remained in a constant position, confirming my course had therefore not changed, and that I was swimming parallel to the shore, not further out to sea.

The first confirmation swim went well. It lasted just 45 minutes, but it gave me the confidence to plan a longer route the following day, knowing that the tide was not likely to sweep me off to Africa or into the middle of the Atlantic.

With the wind appearing to invariably blow on-shore, and taking into account my unilateral breathing, I decided that I should make my way to the far eastern end of our little resort before entering the sea and subsequently swimming back towards our accommodation. This would mean that the shore was always in sight, and that the wind and waves would be at the back of my head as I turned to take in some air. That second sea swim, just over an hour in duration, worked well. It meant that I could get up fairly early, have a light breakfast, and head off along the coast a couple of kilometres. I then swam back towards our apartment before joining Esta and the kids for the day, with all of my training out of the way whilst the family pottered around enjoying a relaxing morning.

Generally, my swims continued in this fashion, occasionally substituted for a coastal run instead. But December and January are still the winter months in the Canaries. And the winter brought some heavy winds. As I walked along the promenade one morning towards my regular swimming departure point, holiday-makers were standing on the beach looking at the huge waves crash onto the beach. I admit to being more than a little scared that day, anticipating venturing out into those choppy waters alone.

I'd procured a high-visibility safety float to take with me on such occasions as this, and I carried it with me now. Many triathlons require such clearly visible floatation devices for the swim leg of the event, and though they would be of limited use for very long emergencies, I knew mine would certainly help keep me afloat for a while if I did get into real difficulties.

The concept of the float is simple: It's essentially a waterproof rubber bag which can hold a few small items such as a towel, keys etc, and it has an inflatable 'pocket' on one side into which air is blown. The device is attached to the swimmer via a nylon strap around the waist and is towed behind as you swim. One of the huge advantages of it is that it sits high on the water and is far easier to spot than a primarily-submerged swimmer. For areas where motorised sports take place, such as jet skiing, these floats really can save lives.

When I entered the sea at the far end of the resort, few if any people were around to observe me. I placed my flip flops into the bag, took out my goggles, hat and earplugs, and fought my way into the water before anyone had the chance to come along and prohibit me.

It was an altogether frightening experience. The waves seemed far bigger from sea level than they did from the shore. My swimming progress was being made erratic due to the huge sea swell. Sometimes I could feel myself being dragged back by a gathering wave, whilst at other times I had the experience of suddenly swimming downhill as the surge rushed forwards. Several times waves crashed over my head, and I went under the water more times than I care to remember. The presence of the float was at once welcome and annoying. Knowing it was there whilst I was battling against such conditions was a big comfort, and yet the device itself would often be tugged away from me by the waves. At such times I could feel the belt around my waist dragging me backwards as the line became taught. In such a way, the float itself was one thing more to battle against.

It was somewhat ironic that after a swim of almost two hours in those violent Atlantic sea conditions, that landing safely on the beach turned out to be the most treacherous part of the whole ordeal. I'd swum all the way along the coast, around jagged, jutting headlands to Playa Del Ingles. Here, the coastline turned, running south-west to north-east. As such, it meant that the waves were pushing me at an angle of 45 degrees to the beach. This in itself would not have represented any real problem, were it not for the vast groynes that stretched out to sea. These groynes were designed to prevent the sea stripping away all of the beautiful golden sand imported from Africa, and they were constructed from huge, jagged boulders. The angle of my approach meant that I could never clearly see the shore between these groynes until I'd over-shot my chance of landing between two of them. I was being driven directly onto the rocks that comprised these man-made sea defences. As I was taken further and further along the western shore, I realised that my only hope of avoiding being dashed against these rocks was to veer sharply right immediately after I'd passed the next groyne. I'd then have a hard battle against the waves as I struck out directly for shore. It was no easy task. Every turn of my head for a gasp of air took my face directly into a huge wave. There was no time to stop and relax either, as I was still being quickly swept directly onto the next line of man-made boulders. Any assumption that the sea would be sheltered once I'd rounded the groyne quickly proved to be unfounded. The wind was simply too strong for that.

    As I finally approached the shore I began to encounter people body-surfing in the huge waves. I rode a breaker into the shore myself, and emerged onto the beach at last. I watched as another swimmer gazed at me wide-eyed. He'd seen me climb out of the sea next to him, but clearly he had not witnessed me get in several kilometres down the coast. He was obviously bemused as to where I'd therefore suddenly appeared from.

    Overcoming and surviving that long sea swim ordeal was a huge confidence boost. In reality, I'm sure I should not have considered venturing out alone in such conditions. Yet without another strong swimmer, I only had the choice of missing the swimming opportunity, or taking the risk that I did. Rightly or wrongly, I concluded that I could not waste a single sea-swimming opportunity, and I'd headed out alone. Luckily for me the weather conditions generally improved for the remainder of our holiday, allowing me several more long swims in much more favourable sea conditions, hence allowing me to rack up some much-needed open water miles.

    Back in London once more, I found it interesting chatting to the regulars at Parliament Hill, many of whom were retired and had been coming for an early morning swim for many years. The swim formed an important part of their daily routine, and on the mornings when the pool was unexpectedly closed, perhaps due to insufficient lifeguards being available that day, the regulars were as inconvenienced as I was. Some had their routine down to such a degree that they would have finished a length or two before I was even ready to jump into the water. I change very quickly, so I've no idea how they ever achieved this. I did understand from some of them that they based their daily swim distance on the temperature of the water: they would swim as many widths (it's a 28 metre-wide pool) as there were degrees of heat in the water. During the winter they would therefore only expect to swim a maximum of around eight widths - sometimes as few as three or four. But it was never considered 'too cold' to swim.

It's worth expanding upon and detailing the feelings and sensations that are experienced during these cold water swims. Following more advice I'd been given (more of which later), I had begun to wear wetsuit boots and gloves, simply so that the excruciating pain in my extremities was not responsible for driving me out of the water before I was physically tired. In January of 2014, to explain to sponsors and supporters at the time exactly what I was doing in terms of training, I made an update to my blog. This is an actual record of what I wrote just a few hours after my cold-water swim that day:

> Few of you will have the inclination or sanity to spend any considerable period of time in waters of just five degrees. Allow me to try and articulate the experience on the body and mind:
> There is no way I can compare with the experiences of Sir Ranulph Fiennes or Lewis Pugh. Those men are both heroic. But every morning that I push my cold water resistance that bit further, I have to endure not only that which seemed impossible to achieve the previous day, but also a little bit more.
> This morning I aimed for 2km in the outdoor pool - some 600 meters more than I had achieved last week. On arrival to the lido, however, I discovered that the water temperature had dropped another degree.
> Simply getting into water that cold requires a huge degree of mental strength, not to mention considerable practice. Sudden Immersion Shock Syndrome can kill. But

believe it or not, you get used to it. At first, the contact of the liquid against your bare flesh confuses your senses, even though your mind is 100% aware of the actual temperature. Initially, it simply burns.

Reality sets in towards the end of the first 25m. The cold begins to penetrate your body. For me, it takes much longer to be able to keep my face in the water, so I start off by doing breast stroke. Initial submersion of my forehead feels like being hit in the face by a steel tray. All I can do is raise my head out of the water, wait for the pain to subside, then submerge again. Eventually, my face and head simply go numb. I can begin front crawl at this point, and the next thing that happens is my jaw freezes. With no-one to speak to on these glorious morning outings, I can only assume I would be unable to talk anyway. Besides, rational thought soon becomes difficult.

The latter part, that of not being able to hold a sensible thought for long, may be self-induced. After all, the one overriding logical wish is to get out of the water and get warm. Yet the main thing I have to keep telling myself is to ignore that desire to quit, and to just keep swimming. And added to this, I need to ignore the cold and pain that is slowly penetrating through my wetsuit gloves and boots, and is eating its way into my flesh like an acid.

The pain at the extremities is physical and undeniable. What creeps up on you, stealthily and subtly, is the cold to your core.

At 400m shy of my target this morning (but still 200m progress on my previous best), I realised I needed to get out. I can't say I left it too late, but neither do I think I could have left it much later.

To exit the water I had to roll onto the side of the pool. My legs could not support me properly, and though my arms could lift my body out of the water, they could not drag me to the showers. Some moments were spend on all fours, worrying that I was looking frankly ridiculous, whilst also wondering how I was going to proceed from here. I could see a lifeguard eyeing me with concern.

Determined not to look any more foolish, I somehow

managed to haul myself to my feet. Walking is sometimes referred to as controlled falling. My stumble to the showers that say was with a severe lack of any control.

I realised just how cold I was when, after two or three minutes of a hot shower, I was still completely unable to take off even one glove. A deep, uncontrollable shiver set into my entire body. Hot water was pouring over me, and though this was reviving me on the outside, my insides were not being penetrated by the heat. A flask of hot, sweet tea was available nearby, self-prepared at 05:30 for this very eventuality.... except that I would not have been able to unscrew the lid, and nor did I want to step out of the shower to go and get the flask.

It was more than ten minutes later before I could turn the water off. The shivering had subsided, but had certainly not stopped. Tea was self-administered, but my hands were shaking in the most violent way imaginable. Simply bringing the cup of hot liquid close to my face should have warranted a dedicated insurance policy.

All in all, for around a 45 minute swim, it took well over half an hour to properly warm up. Even now, some two hours later, pin-pricks of sensation still cover my skin. It's this 'invigoration' that keeps regulars going back every day. Except that they are currently only doing four or five minutes.

And the best thing about all of this: I have to do it all again tomorrow... plus a little bit more!

So, regulars were climbing out of the water and getting into the warm showers after around five widths, whilst I was building up to 80. That in itself was an excellent indication of how far I'd improved in a matter of months, for initially I'd only been capable of eight minutes. And in addition to my cold water endurance, I could feel my swimming improving week in, week out. The muscles in my shoulders were solid with the continual work they were required to do. Hours in the water were redefining and re-shaping my body. Though I'd not exactly been overweight prior to training for the challenge, I must nevertheless have been carrying a few extra kilograms. My training regime now resulted in my body beginning to shed this excess load. My clothes began to hang off my body untidily. My suit trousers were loose, my shirts looked as though they belonged to someone else, and I had to tighten my belt an extra notch. All of this was achieved without any change whatsoever to my diet, and my habit of enjoying a few beers whenever I liked had not yet changed.

All in all, my training and its effects had progressed to a level or two beyond my usual state of physical fitness. But I knew I was in no degree yet ready for the full challenge. My training log indicated that I was swimming at a rate of 3km/hr for the first little while, but that this speed then began to drop to just 2.5km/hr. This suggested that my initial estimation of crossing the Channel in 12 hours therefore had to be re-evaluated. From a psychological standpoint, I needed to have no illusions about how long I would be required to swim for. During my actual swim, if I had anticipated finishing after just 12 hours, and was subsequently to be told that there was another two or more hours to go, this would be hard to bear. It was not unrealistic to say that such news may be impossible to bear. I'd far rather expect to land in France after 16 hours and be happy with any early arrival than have to swim for far longer than estimated.

Consequently, this new figure, that of swimming non-stop in the cold waters of the English Channel for 16 hours, became my new expectation. As such, I also had to acknowledge the fact that my training regime would need to be taken several notches higher than it already was. I had to somehow find extra hours in the day, and I needed to swim longer and harder than anything I had yet trained at.

None of this was proving to be much very much fun.

Harry's Favourite Thing

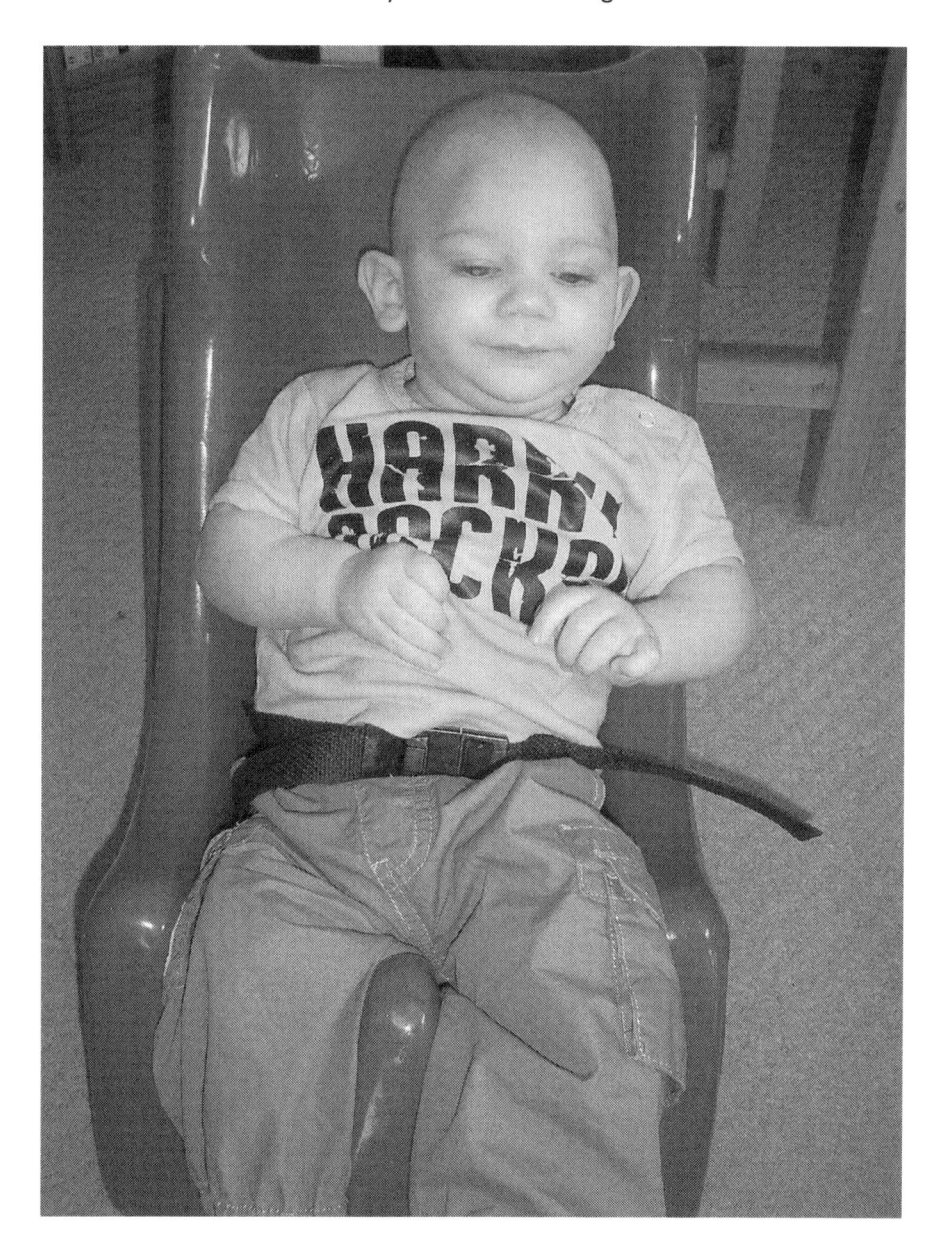

Harry

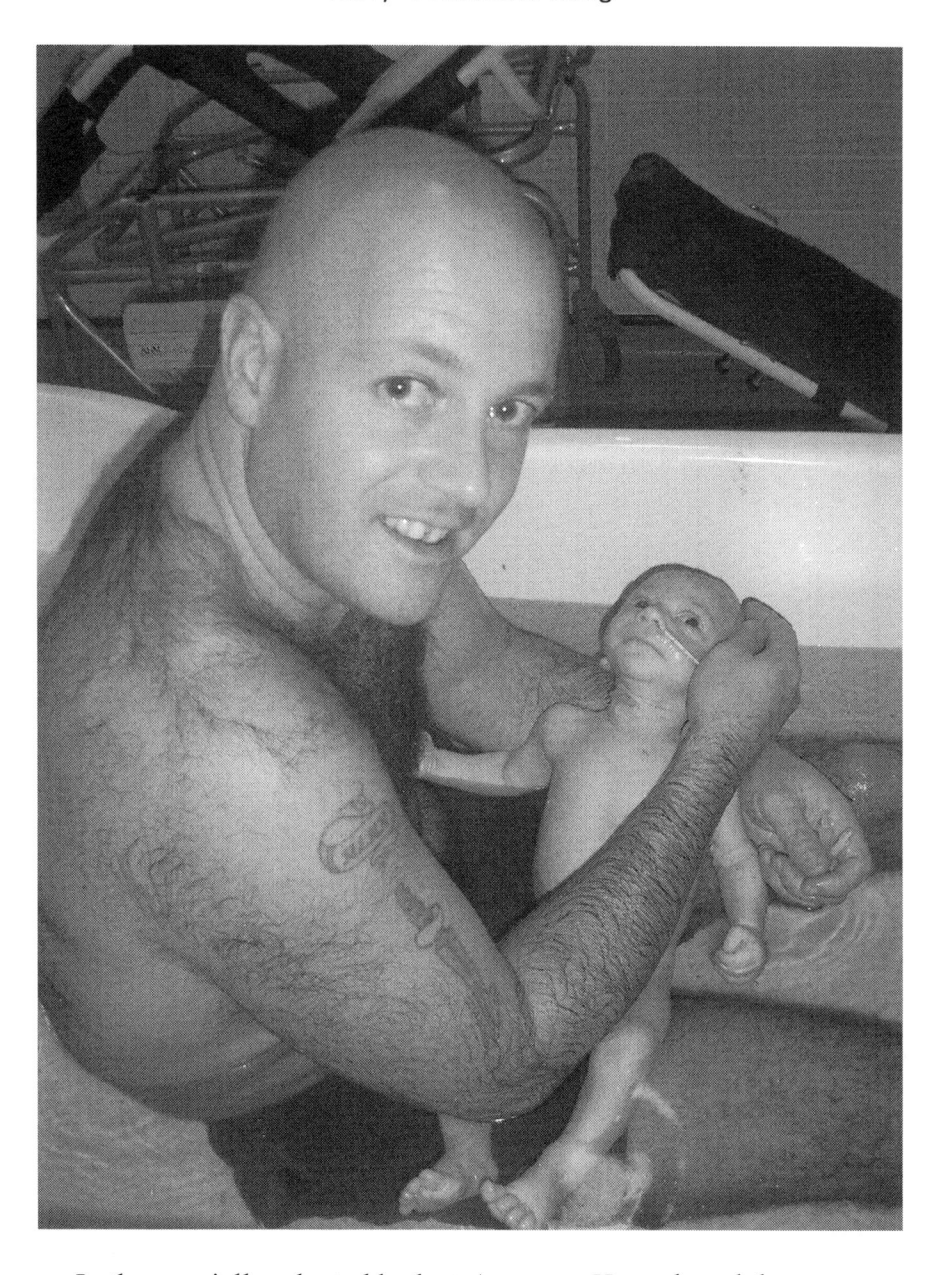

In the specially adapted bath at Acorns – Harry loved the warm water

Before I grew my hair and beard
Photo courtesy of FT Images

Parliament Hill Lido. At six just degrees centigrade, you often get the pool to yourself!

Me and Ali at Bournemouth beach
Both images courtesy of Mother Hen Films Ltd

Craig Gillies joins me for my 1000 press-up mini-challenge
Photo courtesy of FT Images

Ali and I aboard Connemara

Getting ready whilst being filmed for the documentary

Harry's Favourite Thing

Leaving Dover behind me

Mid-Channel

Giving way to a 100,000 ton Maersk container ship

Post-swim pint. According to one friend, I had aged 30 years in 11 hours

Harry's Favourite Thing

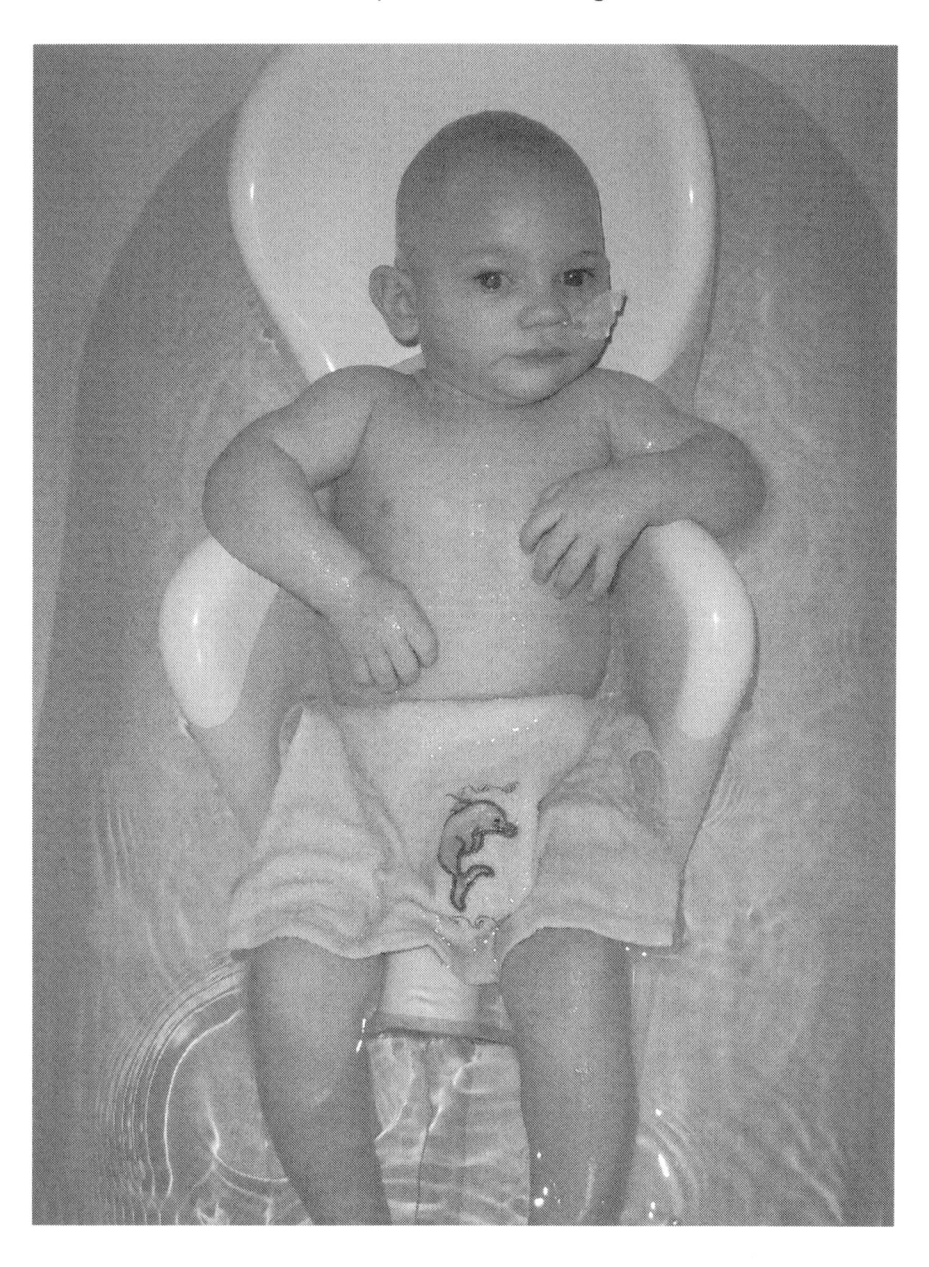

It was all for Harry. This is our last ever photo of our boy

Professional Help

In addition to out-and-out training, I devoted a lot of time to knowledge acquisition. I wanted to find out as much as I could about Channel swimming, including the many pitfalls and schoolboy errors that challengers must make year-in, year-out. The CSA website had a very useful FAQ page, but I wanted something less polished, less politically correct. I wanted, and needed, a warts-and-all depiction of what mistakes could be made, ideally giving me the ability to learn from the errors of others.

Even those professional swimming instructors I knew of, such as Garry Mitchell, had their experience limited to pool swimming. Without a doubt he would have been able to put me though aerobic and anaerobic sessions that would have left me gasping from breath and writhing in pain, but he had openly admitted to being ill-equipped to advise me on Channel swimming. Garry suggested I find someone with directly relevant experience, and though I was only a few months into my training, I capitulate that this was the only real way of getting the information I needed. I brought the subject up with Esta.

'This really is a huge challenge. It's no pun when I say I'm out of my depth on this one.'

Esta raised her eyebrows at me. 'And it's only now that you're realising this?' There was little answer to that one. Esta sighed. 'What do you propose to do, then?'

When we'd moved into our new house, one of the first things we did was have a supporting wall taken down, merging two rooms to form an open kitchen-diner. We then had the new, larger room decorated, whilst also having a brand new kitchen fitted. And though I'm happy with most DIY jobs, the extent of these renovations meant that we quite clearly required the services of contracted professionals. I told Esta of the analogy.

'If it was a run, or a hill climb, or something I was doing alongside professional and experienced people, it would be different. I really need to pick the brains of someone who has been there and done it. I need someone who can say they are truly qualified to give professional Channel swimming advice.'

'And do you know of anyone such as that?'

I did. Of course I did. I'd already been in contact and paved the way, ascertaining exactly what I would get for my money from the individual I had in mind.

The lady I chose to mentor me was Dr. Julie Bradshaw, MBE. Julie was a character of eye-popping experience.

Whilst most people make their first foray into their chosen sporting arena in a quiet and unassuming way, Julie literally burst onto the swimming scene at the age of just 15. Having booked a slot to swim the English Channel, an event which had far fewer participants in 1979 than it does now, Julie's parents accompanied her to Dover in anticipation of seeing her set off from England. Whilst waiting for the weather to settle, they spent an inordinately large part of their savings paying for accommodation, hoping that their journey down from Blackpool would be fruitful.

As the days dragged by, with conditions remaining unfavourable for a Channel attempt, things began to look dire. Money was running out, and so was time. Julie remained focussed and optimistic throughout the ordeal, and when at last the weather broke, she completed the crossing without major incident. However, what really made Julie's attempt exceptional was her swim time. Completing the challenge in 10 hours and nine minutes meant that the 15 year-old had immediately beaten the British Junior record. It's a time that remains unbeaten to this day and in the process raised much needed funds for charity, including the Fylde Hospice which began that same year.

Regardless of the Channel arguably being one of the most difficult and infamous challenges on the swimming circuit, in terms of duration it was one of Julie's shortest events. Following on from her first success, the young Miss Bradshaw was just one year older when she became the first woman to complete two demanding English Lake challenges in Cumbria, UK. The first of these was a three-way swim of Windermere; a distance of 31.5 miles which she completed in a time of 20 hours and 17 minutes. The second record was a one-day swim of three lakes: Windermere at a distance of 10.5 miles; Ullswater at 7.25 miles; and finally Coniston at another 5.25 miles. The challenge was completed in just 14 hours and 12 minutes. In the process of completing these events, Julie world records for both. As with the Channel, these records remain unbeaten to date.

Harry's Favourite Thing

Windermere was to become a favourite venue for the young swimmer, and once she had complete a three-way swim of the lake, Julie decided that such an event could only be logically topped with a four-way, 42 mile swim. The challenge took 23 hours and 17 minutes. It was another first by a woman, another world record, and another time which remains currently unbeaten.

At the age of 18, Julie was chosen to represent England at the Windermere International, a 16 mile race which she completed in a fraction over eight hours. It was at this point that Miss Bradshaw decided to re-think her swimming career. Not satisfied with simply being the first *woman* to tackle various swimming challenges, Julie decided she wanted to be the first ever *person* to do so. She consequently begin to specialise in the arduous and infamous butterfly stroke.

Commencing some nine years later, lakes Windermere, Coniston and Ullswater, previously tackled freestyle in the one-day world record, now individually succumbed to a butterfly assault, all surrendering world records which still hold true.

But Julie now had a distinct goal in mind, and it was one towards which all her energies were focussed: She aimed to swim the Channel via butterfly. The challenge had already been completed, once, by a Canadian marathon swimmer named Vicki Keith. An initial world record had consequently been set during the attempt, and Julie was convinced she could claim the title as her own. Other world records were claimed as she prepared for the Channel, such as a two-way Coniston butterfly swim, but all of these swims were mere practice sessions for the main challenge.

Yet injury can affect even world class athletes. On Julie's first attempt at crossing the Channel in this exhausting and technically challenging stroke, her shoulder began to give her pain. Her father, acting as support crew aboard the pilot boat, suggested she abandon the attempt. Whilst Julie could undoubtedly complete the crossing, her injury was slowing her down. The world record would not fall on this occasion, and her father advised her to avoid further injury and to try again another time.

Humbled, Julie recuperated before redoubling her efforts. A subsequent, successful attempt was made on 5th August 2002, resulting in an incredible nine and half hours being slashed from the world record. It was a staggering achievement which instantly shot

Julie to a wider circle of fame. Indeed, such was the scale of the record that it too, along with so many of her times, remains unbeaten.

A further host of swimming achievements from relays to solo swims were to be claimed, and in all Julie now boasts more than 20 world records to her name. She has raised thousands of pounds for charity, and in 2006 was awarded an MBE for her 'Services to Swimming and Charity.'

It was obvious to me that Julie was precisely the kind of person I was in need of. But gaining access to such a wealth of knowledge and experience would have been impossible had Ms. Bradshaw been a shy recluse who avoided all human contact. Fortunately, as well as working part-time as a Sports and Exercise Science Lecturer (specifically in swimming) at Loughborough University for 17 years, Julie now makes a living from providing the exact professional swimming services that I seeking. Various boot camp swimming weeks can be booked and arranged, along with support for swimming the length of her favoured Windermere or Loch Lomond. And of course Julie's experience means she is more than qualified to coach and advise on Channel swimming.

For our first meeting, Julie suggested I simply come to her house so that we could get to know one another professionally. I had a host of questions I wanted to ask, and for her part, Julie wanted to find out what scale of a challenge she would be taking on by agreeing to mentor me.

Like Worcester, Loughborough is in the midlands. Julie lives a short distance away from the university she lectures at, and which also holds the facilities she uses for training. The university is fiercely proud of its swimming facilities, and of the high record of excellence of which it can boast. Listed amongst those accomplishments are the facts that in 2012, 14 swimmers attended the Olympic Games and one swimmer attended the Paralympics, representing Great Britain, Ireland and Luxembourg. Loughborough University has also been the British Universities National Champions for the past 16 years.

Julie sat me down and made me a cup of tea as she sized me up. Her ever-present and faithful dog, Molly, watched us closely from her bed as we chatted about the weather and the journey time from Worcester before moving on to the business at hand. I had so many questions that I hardly knew where to start.

    Hanging on the wall in Julie's kitchen is the framed chart which marks the actual swim route she took during her world-record butterfly swim from England to France. The wavy line it traced showed me that Julie must have passed Cap Griz Nez first on her right, then on her left as the tide swept her south, before she finally landed on French soil.

    'That must have been hard, seeing the landing point a few times but not getting to it,' I ventured.

    'I knew exactly where we needed to be,' Julie replied. 'I remembered it from previous swims. When you get close to shore, a few miles out, you'll see land clearly from the water. But don't get too excited too quickly. You have to be patient and trust in the pilot. They will get you there by the shortest route they can - but that will not be direct. You have to allow for the tides, and if that means swimming parallel to the shore at some point, you do what the pilot says. Striking out and trying to land too quickly will see your swim come to nothing. The real indicator is when the pilot gets out his little dingy. The main boat will not be able to come close to shore, but the dingy can come in and bring you back with it. So when the dingy comes out, you're almost there.'

    I had to admit, I'd never even imagined how I'd get back to the boat.

    Julie paused and looked at me for a moment before asking her first question.

    'Close your eyes and picture your swim. Where do you see yourself right now?'

    I did as I was told, visualising the experience. I could picture myself in the middle of the Channel, surrounded by vast oil tankers and cruise ships, a tiny and insignificant dot amongst the waves, miles from shore on either side.

    Julie raised her eyebrows and nodded. 'That's not bad. I just wanted to ascertain your current mental state. It's a simple but effective test. Many people come to me, and they picture themselves standing on the beach in England. That means they are right at the beginning of their mental journey. I need to get them, and you, to be thinking about climbing out of the sea in France and onto dry land. But I don't just need you to think about it - I need you to believe it, to mentally be in that place, having successfully completed your swim.'

We chatted a while, and Julie told me more about her butterfly swim, including her dad being aboard the boat as support.

'Who have you got acting as boat crew?'

I told her that Connagh was coming along to witness the swim, and that I had another friend, Ali, in mind - though I'd not yet got round to speaking to him about it.

'You've got to get all of that sorted out soon. They need to know when to feed you, what your routine is, what your average stroke rate is, and they need to be able to recognise that you're tired.'

Even at this early stage, I was already sure I'd done the correct thing in taking on professional advice. None of anything Julie had just mentioned had occurred to me at all.

'Have you been practising feeding yet?'

'A little. Mainly with energy gels.'

'You need to start soon, so that you know what works for you. I used to eat canned peaches. They slip down well, and the juice helps take away the taste of the sea. You need a warm drink too. Not too hot either, or you'll burn yourself.'

Suddenly I could visualise myself in the water alongside a boat. The image of the vessel was vague, but I did know that the sides of the boat would be far higher than I could reach from the water.

'How do they pass the food to you?'

'It's probably best if they put it in a container and throw it to you. There needs to be a line attached so that they can pull it back afterwards. Don't attempt to throw it back into the boat yourself, or you'll pull a muscle. The line needs to be long enough so that they can throw it past you, and pull it back towards you. Hitting you on the head with it is not a good idea.'

'And what was that about stroke rate?' I asked.

'The CSA observer will count your stroke rate per minute every hour. It's mainly for their records, but it's also a good early indicator of fatigue or hypothermia. What is your average stroke rate?'

I admitted I had absolutely no idea. Julie said we'd try and remember to calculate it during one of our swimming sessions.

'What about speed? How long do you anticipate your swim taking?'

At that point I had not recalculate my time, so I was still expecting a swim of around 12 hours. I told Julie that I could swim 1km in just over 20 minutes.

'And how long can you keep that up for?'

I really had no idea. My training had mostly consisted of swimming round and round the men's pond, or just ploughing length after length of the pool.

'OK. There's several things we need to do next time you come up. Firstly we'll go to the pool and get you swimming. I want to take a look at your technique. There are bound to be some small but significant changes we can make that will improve your efficiency. Then I want to put you through some swim sets. The mileage is one thing, but you'll get bored doing that for the next nine months. If we mix in some drills, it'll keep your mind occupied and increase your swimming fitness. I've got some suggested stamina, aerobic and anaerobic sessions which I can print off and let you have. In the meantime, I need you to get together with your boat crew and begin to familiarise yourselves with a routine you can stick to. Aim to feed every hour, or even every 40 minutes. You need to sort out your communication between you, keeping it short and simple.'

I was already compiling a large mental list, and was reeling from all of the extra tasks I'd suddenly been made aware of. Had I really hoped to achieve success without seeking such advice?

'How's your swim log coming on?' Julie continued.

'I've been keeping a note on how long I've swum for,' I began, hopefully.

'What about recording the distance? How far are you swimming each week?'

I had absolutely no idea. I confessed as much.

'That's not good. You really need to be aiming to swim the Channel distance each week.'

Wow! That far? Weekly? 'By when?'

'Now! I still swim 30km a week, and I'm not even training for the Channel.'

Of all of the pieces of advice that put things into perspective, that one statistic really did it for me. I needed to be racking up swim distances somewhere in the region of 40km per week. That was a lot of hours in the water.

'I just don't know if I can achieve that. In London I've only got outdoor venues, and though I can access a warm pool indoors at Worcester, that's only three days a week.'

Julie shrugged. 'You'll have to work it out somehow. I used to train in one pool in the morning until it closed. Then I'd dry, change, drive to the next pool, and continue. You've simply got to get the miles under your belt if you're at all serious about any chances of success at the Channel.' There was no mistaking the undramatic and factual way that Julie intended to give advice.

For the rest of our meeting we began to put together a loose schedule of when the two of us would meet, and what we planned for those sessions. I wanted Julie to witness and verify my six hour qualifier swim, and for her part she was keen to have me swim in Windermere for three hours prior to that, so that I knew exactly what the qualifier would entail. Those open water swim meetings would take place the following spring, prior to the actual Channel challenge. Between now and then we could arrange some pool sessions at Loughborough, with on-going support available via phone and email as and when I encountered any issues or problems.

Finally, Julie asked me if I was doing the swim in aid of any charity. I explained about Harry, and of the vital support that Acorns had provided us with. It transpired that Julie was no stranger to children's hospices either. Much of her fundraising, including her famous butterfly swim of the Channel, had been done for Rainbow Children's Hospice in the east midlands, with her MBE being in recognition of such fundraising. I later found out that Julie had been firstly a mentor and later a close friend of Susan Taylor, the lady who had tragically died earlier in the year during her own Channel swim attempt. Between the three of us, there was a common link of tackling the challenge for our respective hospices.

I felt strangely daunted about the amount of work and the number of tasks that my visit to Julie had resulted in. And yet without me having made such an arrangement which allowed me to benefit from her services and experience, it looked extremely likely that my swim would have been an utter disaster, much like my SAS selection many years earlier. Thankfully, as it was, I now knew what I needed to do to get myself on the right track. And more importantly, I still had time on my side.

The first thing was to update the swim log that I had been

keeping. To date, the information it contained was very minimal. What I now needed to do was record the actual distances I swam each day, and to begin to construct an actual plan which would build me up to the required 40km per week. I was sure I was nowhere in the region of such distances at that point.

There was, however, one point upon which I was quietly confident. I had started my current training regime beginning at an already high level of personal fitness. So though my weekly cumulative swimming distance undoubtedly needed to increase, that swimming was also being supplemented by runs and gym sessions. My real challenge was now to find the extra hours in the day that would enable me to swim for longer and further. At the weekends this would mean eating into more precious family time, and during the week it would mean somehow finding a means of balancing work requirements with hours in the pool.

At the first opportunity, I asked Ali how well he could cope with being on a boat. Ali and I had been friends for around 18 years. During my army career I'd been a radar technician, responsible for the repair and maintenance of the army's guided anti-aircraft ground-to-air missile system called Rapier. To practise guiding these missiles, the Royal Artillery gunners would fire at targets towed behind another aircraft flying off the coast of Benbecula in the Outer Hebrides.

This firing range in the Hebrides provides employment for many of the locals on the Scottish islands, and Ali worked as a civil servant within the MoD, supporting the contracts for spares and servicing of the Rapier systems. As such, he was posted to Malvern sometime around 1997, working in the same team as me, assisting in the support and maintenance of the equipment. We became friends and drinking buddies, remaining so even after I'd left the army and Ali had left the MoD.

Ali is the first to admit he's not the sporting type. He drinks as hard as I do, but he smokes too. That said, he's an extremely good worker who never shies away from a hard graft. He was the first person I called upon when Esta and I needed to move house, and he willingly lent his help when I had to landscape the front garden, shifting tons of mud in ready exchange for a few beers and some company. But Ali also partook in a round-the-Island yacht race when he was in the MoD, and if there is one sport he can claim to enjoy undertaking, it's sailing. Personally, I hate being aboard a boat - I'd rather be in the water than on it - so the fact that Ali was loyal, dependable and had good sea legs, made him a perfect choice for boat crew. On top of these qualities he was local to me, so unlike Connagh who was studying for his degree in High Wycombe, Ali would be able to accompany me on some open water swimming events, in order that we could practice our communication and try out various feeding regimes. Over a few beers I explained, in my admittedly limited knowledge, what the role would entail.

'I'm going to lose track of time when I'm in the sea,' I began. 'It's not going to be like the pool, where I can judge how long I've been swimming for by the number of lengths I've done. I'll need you to let me know when it's time for a feed, somehow. Have the stuff ready, pass it to me, pull the line back in... that's about it. You can sit back and enjoy the boat trip. Just don't forget to bring your passport. The French authorities can board at any time, and if we don't have the correct documentation, they'll turn us around. That would be an embarrassing ending to my swim.'

Ali had one big concern. 'I don't know how I'll encourage you and spur you on. I've known you for years, and you've always been fit, but how do I keep you going if you begin to tire?'

I assured him there would be no requirement for such action. 'The only way I'm getting out of the water is if I'm ordered by the pilot, or when I get to France. I'll spur myself on more than you'll be able to, believe me. This is for Harry, after all. There's not much better motivation than that.'

The deal was struck. It was early days, however, and we were completely ignorant of just how naive we both were. We had a lot to learn about the close partnership that is required between the swimmer and the boat crew.

Prior to Christmas I made two more trips up to Loughborough to see Julie, this time meeting her at the swimming pool on the university campus.

'The first thing I need to see is your swimming stroke,' Julie said once I'd changed and met her on the poolside. The large 50 metre pool was split in two by a removable partition, effectively creating two 25 metre pools but also allowing for a 50 metre facility for Olympic distance events. At present a full-on training session was taking place in one of the pools, with highly skilled swimmers effortlessly gliding through the water, turning out length after length with barely a splash between them all. They were tumble-turning at each end, and their mouths appeared to barely break the surface as they took a breath. I was highly conscious of how clumsy, inefficient and amateur I was going to look in comparison.

It was not for the first time that I could compare my swimming style to the boxing skills displayed by Sylvester Stalone's character, Rocky, who simply slugged it out doggedly whilst utterly lacking in any finesse. The boxer stubbornly refused to quit, urged on only through a strength of character which knew no option other than to keep going. It was as nice mental comparison which the Channel would undoubtedly test to the limits in due course.

For the time being, I jumped into the pool and swam a 300 metre warm-up, as requested by Julie. It was unnerving knowing my 'style', such as it was, was being closely scrutinised by someone with over 20 world records to her credit. I knew too that Julie was recording my swim by video on her iPad so that she could more clearly point out my faults. This knowledge made it very difficult to relax and swim naturally, akin to trying to walk normally through the airport scanning devices at security. My limbs felt made of wood, and I knew I was producing more splash than the entire swimming squad in the adjacent pool.

'Who taught you to swim?' Julie asked when I joined her at the poolside a few minutes later.

'I did, mostly. But I also take my son Lewis to proper lessons, so I do try and imitate the instructions he's been given over the years.' I asked the question I was reluctant to hear the answer to: 'Was I that bad then?'

To my surprise, Julie shook her head. 'No, not too bad at all. There are some immediate adjustments I'd like you to try and implement, but overall it's not something that I'm unable to work with. I once had one person come to me wanting to swim the Channel, and they stopped for a rest after one length. That sort of thing makes a mentoring job very, very difficult.'

One of the technical adjustments Julie wanted me to make was in contradiction to the very style I'd seen Lewis taught. I could immediately understand why the CSA adamantly refused to give any advice on coaching: Should their advice conflict with any other that the swimmer had sought, an instant problem would arise. My decision at this point was simple: either listen closely to the suggestions passed on by the world-record holding Channel swimmer I had commissioned as my mentor, or pay her fees and ignore what she said.

'Your hand is entering the water next to your head, and you're then reaching forward whilst your arm is submerged. That action is actually slowing you down, minutely, due to the drag of the water. Multiply that by the number of strokes you will take during your crossing, and you have added an unnecessary resistance to an already difficult swim. What I want you to practice next is to reach all the way forward *before* your hand enters the water. It will be tricky at first. Our muscles need to practice something over 400 times before it begins to become instinctive, but even then, your current style is burned deep into your muscle memory. Learning a different technique is difficult, and will take time. Give it a go.'

If my first 12 lengths had felt wooden, the next few were even more so. I knew immediately that I was forgetting to kick my legs, as all of my concentration was focussed on my arms, ensuring that I fought the natural instinct bring my hands into the water whilst they were next to my head.

'Much better,' Julie confirmed, even though I found it hard to believe. Such focus had made eight lengths feel more like 40, as my muscles had been tense the entire time.

'It felt very exaggerated,' I told my mentor.

'It will at first. You're having to fight against the natural tenancy to slip into your normal style. The exaggeration is good. Now, the next thing you need to do is to ensure your arms are not reaching across your body. Imagine a line down your centre, going through your nose and down your body. When you're lying in the water, your arm should not reach across that line, or again you'll be introducing drag. If anything, I want you to exaggerate again, pulling your hand so that it's to the side of your head, well away from the centre line. It will feel very odd, but when I show you the video, you'll actually see that your arms will be nowhere near as wide apart as they feel. Don't forget to reach forward too, but this time, more so to the side.'

When you see a child first move from doggy-paddle to an attempt at front crawl, their arms flap at the side of their body looking awkward and clumsy. My next 12 lengths felt as if I had regressed to that exact stage myself. With every few strokes I could feel my arms beginning to come inwards, towards or past that imaginary centerline down my body, and I forced myself to push them out wide, towards my shoulders. Already, with only two fairly minor changes to my technique, I felt like I was trying something utterly new, such as learning to ride a uni-cycle, as opposed to still swimming front crawl. Yet Julie was please.

'You did that very well. It didn't look awkward at all.'

'Really?'

'Yes. I know how it will have felt, but you need to stick at it. Once that becomes natural to you, you will have removed a huge element of drag from any long swim. Your efficiency will actually have improved, just by some minor adjustment. Now, let's add a little speed, whilst still trying to maintain the new style.'

The remainder of the first session was spent in interval training, fast-swimming 75 meters and 'recovering' over the next 25, all the time ensuring I was applying the techniques Julie had advised.

Afterwards, back at Julie's house, we discussed dates for the six hour qualifier swim that was a mandatory part of being allowed to begin a Channel attempt. I initially suggested May as a good month, as I was planning on building up my training distance from that point onwards.

'I'm not sure you'll be able to cope with six hours in the open water in May. There's a good chance it will still be too cold. Let's plan for a three hour swim in May, and then book the qualifier in for June, a few weeks later.' Again, I capitulated to my mentor's experience and advice. Julie told me she would ideally like to conduct both swims up in Windermere, and though the distance would provide some slight logistical problems for me, it turned out to be the more realistic option when compared to otherwise having to pay for Julie's travelling time were she to come down somewhere closer to Worcester.

'Have you been doing much open water swimming?'

I confessed that aside from the ponds at Hampstead, the rest of my training had been in pools.

'Do you plan to go down to Dover and mix with the crowd down there?'

For some reason, my initial enthusiasm for doing this very thing had waned. I knew, and Julie confirmed, that I'd be inundated with a host of 'helpful' advice, some from seasoned professionals, and some from well-meaning novices such as myself. Now that I had a dedicated mentor, I felt somewhat reluctant to visit Dover prior to my swim.

'That's entirely up to you. But you need to get some sea swimming in. You need to learn to predict when the waves will be in your face, and to find out if you may suffer and sea-sickness after a longer swim. Some people suddenly find that on the day, they cannot cope if the waves come from behind them, or from one side. The more sea-swimming experience you can get, the better.'

At this point, I had not yet been across to the Canaries for Christmas, so I told Julie of my plans for swimming over there. After hearing her advice on the use of a safety/visual float, I purchased one from her and subsequently used it whilst on holiday later in the year.

'What other training are you doing besides swimming?'

I told her that I did everything from circuits to weight-training to running.

'Ease off on the heavy weights,' Julie told me. 'I noticed in the pool, your shoulders are very muscular, and clearly defined. Drop the weights and go for stamina as opposed to bulk. There's plenty of muscle on you, but not much fat.'

The latter issue was something I would fight with quite seriously later in my training.

As part of my support package arranged with Julie, I was able to email or phone her for advice and support. During the winter months, when the water was so cold that it was physically painful to get into, a serious amount of doubt began to take seed in my head. If I couldn't rack up even 15km a week whilst it was so cold, how would I ever begin to reach the required 40km mark in time? Most mornings during the week I could only manage around 20 minutes in the water, achieving around 1km before the cold and the pain drove me out. I found it hard to build this cold-water endurance up to 30 minutes.

'Do you wear a swimming hat?' Julie asked me when I spoke to her.

'I've got one, but I've not really used it yet. I wouldn't have thought it would make much difference.'

'You'll be amazed. No serious Channel swimmer would

enter the water without a hat - or ear plugs! Get yourself a pair of those too. The cold water within your ear canal will sap the heat from you like you won't believe. A tiny amount of extra heat on your head will also make the world of difference, which is why the CSA rules stipulate that the swimmer is only allowed to wear one hat: two would make things a lot warmer and easier.'

From the time I'd left the army, I'd been shaving my head for several years, purely through personal preference. Wondering what difference it would make, I asked, 'Should I grow my hair too then?'

Julie gave an embarrassed pause for a second before she asked, 'Can you? If I'd have known that, I'd have told you to grow it weeks ago.'

From that point onwards, I stopped shaving my head. In fact, I stopped shaving at all, deciding to grow a beard which would protect my face not only from the cold, but also potentially from any jellyfish stings. Further to this, Julie suggested that during the winter months, in order for me to stay in the water longer, I should use wetsuit boots and gloves.

'If it's pain in the extremities which is making you get out, then for now, wear something to keep you warm. As the water begins to warm up, you can lose the other items. If it helps, you can even wear two hats for now. It's your distance you need to work on, and you'll still be acclimatizing to the cold even with these items on, trust me.'

That 'permission' to don other attire was an absolutely massive relief. I had seen other locals doing precisely this, but I had genuinely believed I would be cheating myself were I to copy them. I flatly refused to wear a full-body wetsuit, despite having all of the gear necessary for scuba diving. But gloves, boots and thermal hat would be allowed, as decreed by Dr. Julie Bradshaw.

On the next visit to see her, prior to Christmas, Julie had me concentrate on various swim sets. We started off using some hand paddles, shaped like an arrow head. They had a 'keel' on the underside, and sipped onto the middle finger of each hand via a rubber band.

'The idea is to keep your hand flat on the paddle. Don't grip the edges. If your stroke is correct, everything will feel fine, with some extra pull to each stroke. But if your angle is wrong, the paddle will give you immediate feedback in the form of vibration -

you'll feel it shudder through the water.'

I quickly found out what Julie meant. A good technique was like swimming with extra propulsion, courtesy of the increased surface area of the paddle compared to my own palm size. But if my hand entered the water at an angle, or twisted slightly in during the stroke, the paddle caught against the water and tugged at my fingers. The devices were intended to ensure a consistently correct technique, as well as focus the swimming effort onto the shoulders of the swimmer.

Next, Julie introduced a 'pullboy' float. Formed in an approximate figure of eight shape, the float can be employed in a number of ways, as my mentor explained. The first exercise was to clamp the float between my thighs, isolating my legs from the swimming process, but ensuring they floated, rather than sank. The result was a far more streamlined body, again with the focus now being on the arms and shoulders during the stoke. The pullboy could be used in conjunction with the hand paddles, or just on its own.

'Now hold the pullboy in one hand, and swim one-armed, breathing to the same side as that arm. Do two lengths, then change arm.'

This was more difficult than it sounded. The pullboy supported the weight of one arm held out straight, but doing this in my right hand meant breathing to the left. After one length of breathing in lung-fulls of chlorinated water, I had to pause for breath.

'Again, it's something you'll want to practice. A varied routine is going to help with your hours of training.'

Once she'd seen that I'd had enough of one-armed swimming, we moved onto another exercise.

'Form your hands into fists, and swim that way. Try two lengths.'

This too, sounded simple in theory, but proved far more difficult to accomplish. Without the traction generated by a wide open palm, forward movement and even staying afloat became much more difficult. A vastly greater amount of energy than normal had to be employed to complete even one length.

When we'd finished, I asked Julie about my leg technique. 'You've said nothing about my legs, and I know I don't use them the way I should when I swim.'

Julie did not disagree. 'Your kicking is sporadic, as opposed to regular. But we need to prioritise what we focus on. Legs will account for up to 10% of your swim speed. So using them properly would undoubtedly reduce your swim time. If you were not using them at all I'd be worried, as your muscles and feet would get cold due to lack of blood circulation, and cramp would set in. But a sporadic kick will keep them warm and will provide at least some extra propulsion. That's why I've been concentrating on your arms - they provide the more important 90%.' It made sense, so once more I bowed to Julie's experience and stopped worrying about my leg kick.

Of all of Julie's expert guidance, there was one piece of advice that I simply could not adhere to.

'During your acclimatization process,' she told me, 'splash yourself with the cold water before getting in to the pool. Splash your face and arms to let your mind comprehend the cold temperature you are going to expose it to. Only a complete idiot just jumps straight into the water.'

I must admit that I had seen some swimmers doing just this at the beginning of some of the races in the Olympics. I gave the technique a go the next time I went to the Hampstead lido, but rather than serve to prepare myself mentally, it gave me even stronger temptation to change my mind and call it all off. I generally find being splashed by other people intensely irritating, so voluntarily doing it to myself just seemed ridiculous. I realised after the second try at this approach that it simply was not for me. I had to admit that simply walking up the edge and immediately stepping into the water was a technique far better suited to my own temperament. In short, I was destined to be one of the 'idiots' that Julie had referred to.

All of this advice, whether I ultimately adopted the various practises or not, was information I would undoubtedly have been unaware of had I not employed a professional. The ability to tap into the experience of someone who had been there and done it all, not just in a pool, but in lakes and across the Channel, was undoubtedly money very well spent in my opinion. There was a mentor/tutor relationship between Julie and I, but we also got on very well. Julie liked my sense of humour, and I responded well to her northern, no-nonsense approach. Ms. Bradshaw was in no way afraid to say what she meant. I was paying for her advice, and she would give it to me

\- straight from the hip.

It was ultimately due to this friendship between us that something completely unexpected occurred next.

Fame

On 19th March I received an unexpected email from Julie. She had been contacted by a film crew who were making a privately-funded documentary on Channel swimming. To date, they had only been liaising with swimmers registered with the CSA's 'rival' organisation, the Channel Swimming and Pilot Federation, or CSPF. The documentary crew had suddenly discovered their oversight in not realising there was another Channel swimming governing body, and had consequently contacted the CSA secretary, who was none other than Julie, asking if she knew of anyone whom she could suggest as being suitable to appear in the film. My name was the first that sprang to mind for Julie, but she wanted to confirm with me first, before passing my details on.

Naturally, this extra opportunity to promote the good work Acorns do, and to likewise increase the chance of sponsorship for my film, were as extremely unexpected as welcome. I replied to Julie, thanking her, and got in touch with the film crew immediately.

The first thing the producers did was send me a questionnaire. Amongst other questions, the short survey asked if I were a member of a swimming club, where I lived, and what motivation I had for swimming the Channel. I gave frank, but light-hearted replies, not wanting to appear too dry in my responses, and promptly returned the form via email. I was amazed at how quickly I was contacted.

Over a phone call, Steph, joint founder of S+O Media, explained the conceptual approach of the documentary, and gave me an understanding of why they were producing it privately:

A short time previously, Steph had been training to run a marathon for charity. As with partaking in any challenge which requires a high degree of preparation, it quickly became apparent to Steph that arriving at the start-line of the event itself represents no more than a tip of the iceberg. What remains unappreciated by all but those who have been training, preparing and possibly suffering, is just how much background work goes in prior to the commencement of the actual event itself.

During her training, Steph had somehow happened upon one of the Channel swim safety boat pilots. He commented something along the lines that whilst Steph's entire marathon would take around four to five hours, the Channel swimmers in training would be doing those sort of times almost daily, merely in preparation for their event. Intrigued by such dedication, a seed was sown. Whilst continuing her running training, Steph began to appreciate, and to want to capture, the experiences and commitment necessary to stand on a beach in Dover, gazing out towards France before getting into the Channel and commencing a swim. She knew that the vast majority of the media focus to date had begun at the same time as the Channel swim attempt itself, with little if any focus on the preparatory side. With her own training regime having to fit in alongside work commitments, Steph realised that the difficulties she was facing to find sufficient time to exercise would be significantly magnified for a swimmer. Running could, she knew, be done late at night - Steph had to do this herself. But unlike the public roads, pools had closing times, and the sea would not be safe in the dark. The impact on work life, the disruption to family life, and the dedication required to stick at cold water acclimatisation, were all elements that could be captured by S+O Media in documentary format.

 From a business perspective, the company decided that they were fortunate enough to be in a position whereby they could fund the entire project. Such a decision had considerable benefits. Most significantly, the producers would be free to film, frame, edit and present the footage exactly as they saw fit. As a media company normally hired on a contractual basis, their responsibilities were usually very closely dictated to them. Even applying for funding for the Channel swim film would potentially see a shareholder wanting to become involved in the finished product, so only an internally funded project would give them complete freedom of reign. In this way, the documentary would become a feature-length showpiece reel. But to give the film the depth and scope they wanted, it meant a commitment of over a year, including all travel and expenses that would need to be borne by the company.

 The questionnaire I'd been sent was intended to quickly identify any individuals who may be of particular interest to the project. By the time I'd been confirmed as a potential subject in the film, the main project leads, Steph and her fellow producer Emma, had already selected around five other swimmers to follow. As the project and time advanced, the swimmers they would ultimately decide to focus on would be confirmed. The team were fully aware that almost anything could happen during the preparations for the swim, including injury or a complete change of heart, so they needed to ensure that they had sufficient footage to cover such eventualities. It was also highly improbable that every subject would actually complete the crossing. Ideally, they needed a mixture or personalities, and of successes.

When I spoke to them, Emma and Steph were reluctant to tell me much about the other 'stars'. All I could ascertain was that I was unique in many ways. Firstly, I was not an out-and-out swimmer, and I was the only one who was not a regular member of a swimming club. I understood that the majority of the others were looking at their crossing to be the pinnacle of their swimming careers. For me, the Channel was actually a secondary aim, with the goal of raising money for Acorns being the primary motivation. These factors offered an interesting contrast that the producers could use.

A meeting date was set up towards the end of March, and I introduced myself to Emma and Steph at the Hampstead Lido early one morning. The film crew had arranged permission to film me swimming in the cold outdoor water, so my mundane morning swim was made less usual on this occasion by the presence of cameras (both above and below the water), sound booms, lights and several members of the team watching me closely. By this time of the year, though there were yet barely any leaves on the surrounding deciduous trees, I could manage an hour in the water. Steph told me to ignore the cameras and just train as normal, for as long as I needed. I began my usual routine, acknowledging the locals I usually spoke to whilst trying to ignore the strange looks I was getting as they wondered why I'd brought a film crew with me. The camera was close on my face as I put my ear plugs in, and I was conscious of how ridiculous I must look, working my jaw round to allow the plastic plugs to more easily enter my ears. I strolled towards the edge of the pool trying to appear nonchalant, and stepped directly into the water like one of Julie's idiots.

Regardless of how closely I was being observed, and no matter how hard I tried to act normally, the cold shock on my body took my breath away as it always did in the winter months. Whilst I would normally wait a few moments to control my breathing and get my heart rate down slightly, this time I set of swimming as soon as I could, beginning to bang out the widths whilst waiting for the lido staff to tell us it was time to switch to lengths.

    The film crew seemed to be all over the venue. One minute they were one side of the pool, the next they had magically relocated to the other side. A sound boom was following me closely at times, and a waterproof Go-Pro camera suddenly made itself visible to me on an extendable pole, filming me from beneath the water. If I had been conscious of my poor swimming technique whilst being observed by Julie, that feeling was dwarfed by this close scrutiny I was currently experiencing. I knew I would be viewed by hundreds or more people when the film eventually came out, and that I would be contrasted with the other stars of the documentary, many of whom I understood to be very serious swimmers. All I could do was stop thinking and keep ploughing out length after length.

    I swam until I was borderline hypothermic, and then dragged myself out of the pool. Had Steph or Emma wanted to interview me there and then, it would simply have been impossible for me to speak. As usual, my hands were curled into claws from the cold, regardless of the wetsuit gloves I was still wearing. It would take up to 10 minutes in a warm shower before I had sufficient use of my fingers to enable me to remove the gloves. Removing the boots would take even longer. Even with these items, my digits were blue and useless for some considerable time every day. Acclimatization was undoubtedly the most painful part of the entire venture for me, regardless of my initial and naive belief that I felt the cold less than others.

    Connagh, who was in his final year of studying film and video production at Buckinghamshire University, had come to London to watch me be filmed, and to gain some experience from witnessing a live production. When I was changed and dry, if not yet warm, we made our way to the Dovetail offices where we would once more be met by the film crew. Martin Coen, the Dovetail CEO, had given permission for me to be filmed at work, so I'd booked the main board room and recruited two colleagues to act as trainees during a presentation I was giving on the use of the Dovetail software. The experience was very surreal - more like the production of a promotional work video than a documentary on

Channel swimming, but I understood how the background to who I was and what I did was important to the film. The team wanted to ensure that viewers had empathy with the swimmers, and that could only be achieved if an appreciation of their normal lives outside of swim training could be gleaned.

The last point of call on this initial day of filming was at the Union Jack Club in Waterloo. Due to a change in circumstances, I'd had to move out of my uncle's flat in Ickenham, and was now staying at the famous ex-serviceman's club several nights per week. The Club had kindly allocated us use of the private Writing room on the ground floor, so we gathered there to conduct a filmed interview.

I'd changed into casual clothes, and whilst now wearing my bright orange Worcester Warriors rugby shirt featuring the Acorns logo, and with my Hallmark Hulme banner in the background, I took a seat in front of several cameras, ready to be interviewed by Steph. The atmosphere seemed professional but relaxed. I was once more the centre of attention. The cameras were rolling, but the crew anticipated that the answers to my questions would be used as 'sound-overs' during the actual film. It could well have been a very intimidating experience, but having spent years standing in front of an audience delivering training, I actually enjoyed it. In many ways too, I'd answered these very same queries on an ad-hoc basis as friends, family and colleagues had enquired as to my progress or my reasons behind doing the swim.

Steph's questions were deliberately open, designed at giving me a steer onto a topic and giving me free reign to expand and reply as I saw fit. The one requirement was that I fit the wording of the question into my answer in order to give my reply a proper context. Having spent four years on a literature degree where the prerequisites for assignments ran along these exact lines, I was once more equipped with sufficient experience to deal with this demand relatively easily. If anything, I may have answered so openly that I was pre-empting other questions Steph had. Regardless of whether or not this was the case, the crew seemed very satisfied with the performance I gave on that initial meeting.

I must confess that at that point I had not fully appreciated how closely the documentary was going to be charting my progress. Accordingly, I was very pleased when Emma got in touch shortly after the first meeting and asked if they could come up to Worcester to interview me further, and to speak to Esta. In addition to this they wanted to know if they could film me training at David Lloyd's, as the club was forming such a vital part of my training regime. Lastly, they were interested in capturing some footage of us at Acorns hospice. Emma asked if I could make enquiries as to what permission would be needed at each venue.

Carole Crowe, our contact with the PR side of Acorns whom I had initially told about my idea, had been on long-term sick leave with a severely bad back. Her position had been temporarily filled by a lady called Mandie Fitzgerald, whom I met at regular intervals up at David Lloyd's. Mandie had introduced me to the manager of the club, Wayne Isaac, and the two of us had struck up a friendship. Wayne had no problem granting permission for the film crew to capture footage of me swimming, and he duly posted advance notice around the club, notifying members of the date of filming.

The logistics of filming at Acorns were a bit more complex, due of course to the presence of children. The promotional prospects were too good to ignore though, and we were eager to ensure that the documentary benefited Acorns as much as possible. Esta contacted Jan Large, for whom nothing is ever too much trouble. Preparations were duly made, and the arrangements were confirmed.

When Emma and Steph arrived in Worcester it felt like we'd known each other for years. Lewis and I met the crew at the car park at David Lloyds. They greeted me warmly, with friendly smiles and a genuine hug before introducing me to Ollie, Steph's husband. I in turn introduced them to Lewis, and they made sure they included him in our casual chat to settle his nerves. Lewis had requested not to interviewed, but he was aware that the cameras would be on us as we both trained in the pool.

Regardless of the fact that the media team had asked to me to train normally and to ignore their presence, this was simply not possible. Firstly they would not have been willing to sit around for four or more hours each time they came along, and I also wanted to ensure they could interview Esta and capture some footage of Acorns. With Lewis along for the swim too, I told them we'd keep the training session down to an hour.

Lewis, having attended swimming lessons since he was around four years old, has a far better swimming technique than me. He is graceful in the water, gliding along smoothly and effortlessly.

Consequently, he is also slightly faster, producing less drag by being more streamlined. The real difference between us though, is all in the mind. Boredom quickly sets in for a 13 year-old, so whilst Lewis was perfectly capable of swimming for an hour, after that he'd clearly had enough, mentally. He was probably no more tired than I was, but he stopped because he wanted to get out and do something else. I could hardly blame him. By that point in my training, the repetition of hours in the pool was already becoming a challenge for me too.

As before, the camera was maneuvered all over the pool. I did my best to ignore it, but every now and then I'd notice that it had moved from its last position, and with little else to concentrate on, the mental distraction of wondering where Ollie had repositioned himself was a welcome relief to the boredom. Towards the end of our session Lewis decided to finish his routine with a few lengths of butterfly. He always puts everything into this stroke, finding it physically exhausting, but the muscle definition on his back and shoulders is sincerely impressive to see whilst he swims. 'Did your mentor really swim the Channel butterfly style?' he asks me on regular occasions. 'How is that even possible?'

After our swim, the film crew followed Lewis and I home to meet Esta. The whole team were so easy to get along with that Esta quickly relaxed into her normal, chatty self. She was apprehensive about being interviewed, and even more nervous about the cameras following us into the privacy of the remembrance garden at Acorns. Yet the genuine friendliness of the team did wonders for alleviating Esta's fears, and Steph ensured that there was a prolonged period of camera-free background chat to further settle Esta's nerves.

In order for the film audience to build empathy with the swimmers they had to feel that they knew the person undertaking the challenge. By inviting the cameras into our home, by letting them see us in our own kitchen and allowing them to follow us into the remembrance garden where our stone for Harry lay, we hoped that such empathy and familiarity would be possible. It was a big invasion of privacy, and not something that many people would truly feel comfortable with. Esta was only complying at all because she knew this would help promote Acorns. Had this been a paid-for fly-on-the-wall documentary, I'm convinced Esta would not have agreed to her participation at all.

'What do you do when you're home and not training, Al?' Steph asked me. 'We'd like to film you do whatever it is you do to relax at home.'

I don't often relax. We'd recently moved house, and there was some serious work still to be done. Our front garden was a jumble of hideously ugly concrete paths, with piles of earth raised over a metre high and bound by concrete blocks. The entire garden had been a local eye-sore since the late 1970s, and one of the first actions I wanted to complete was the removal of the concrete and the levelling of the earth. It was a huge project to undertake by hand.

Now that the spring had thawed out the ground, Ali and I had already made a start. I'd done many trips to the council tip, all-but ruining my car transporting the blocks to the hardcore recycling skip. The first part of the lawn was in the process of being levelled, and I quickly lost count of how many neighbours congratulated me on starting the renovation they had long awaited.

The camera crew followed me into the garden as I showed them what I did in my spare time. Armed with a pick axe, a shovel and a wheel barrow, I continued my onslaught on the heavy concrete blocks, piling them into the barrow and breaking up the surrounding soil so that it could be levelled. It was heavy, backbreaking work, but it was also a strangely welcome alternate use of my muscles. I simply had to watch out for injury whilst I transformed my hitherto wasteland into a respectable lawn.

The cameras captured some footage of me at work, and whilst I continued working on the front garden the crew went indoors to interview Esta in private.

The media team's visit to Worcester culminated in the filming at Acorns. Even after several years, Harry's photograph adorns several walls. His many visits to Worcester Warriors during charity shirt launches and other photographic opportunities means that he features highly on the Warrior's Wall display in the foyer, and a photo of his meeting with The Duchess of Gloucester at the official opening was also hung on the walls.

After meeting several of the nurses and discreetly filming some of the interior of the building (ever mindful of the children and families who still use the facilities), Ollie filmed Will and Lewis playing outside for a while, before we all moved on to the remembrance garden. This was undoubtedly the most difficult part of filming for the entire production as far as Esta and I were concerned. The solitude of the garden perfectly lends itself to quiet reflection of a lost child, and this is always a very poignant time, no matter how often the experience is repeated. It was quickly apparent to Steph that they had sufficient footage when both Esta and I became unusually withdrawn and uncommunicative, and the team respectfully left us in privacy as they made their way back to London.

Very shortly after the Worcester visit, I was commissioned to deliver Dovetail training to a Client in Bournemouth. I decided that it would be a perfect opportunity to include some sea swimming into my routine by combining work and training in one trip. I was in regular communication with both Emma and Steph by this point, so I dropped them an email giving them the date of the proposed training. As a result, I met the team again, this time at Basingstoke train station, so that they could film me working whilst en route to the Client. The combination of the cameras, sound equipment and me as the obvious focus of the production lead to much intrigue on the part of fellow travellers. Not all of it was subtle either, with one young college student so eager to be a part of the film that she kept asking Emma how she could participate. Emma was polite, but I could see that she was becoming very frustrated with the interruptions. 'We'll have to voice-over any of that footage if we use it,' she told me later. 'We won't be able to use any of the sound recording.'

We were met at Bournemouth train station by a mini van driven by another member of the media team, so after capturing some footage of me exiting the station we all piled inside and drove to the car park closest to Bournemouth pier. It was still only mid-spring, and whilst the weather had been pleasant during our train journey from London, heavy black clouds were now rapidly gathering overhead. I changed out of suit and tie and into my swimmers, leaving my clothes in the back of the van and covering up with a tracksuit for the walk down to the beach. As we made our way to the sand, the rain reached us. Visibility dropped dramatically, so whilst I pointed out to the cameras where I would be swimming to, we noticed that Boscombe pier, just one mile away, was no longer visible due to the rain.

We sheltered from the downpour beneath Bournemouth pier. Alongside us was a large group of Japanese tourists, all of whom were of course keenly interested in the fact that I was being interviewed in front of cameras on the beach. They became highly bemused when I then had to strip down to my swimmers and head towards the sea with nothing but a pair of goggles in my hand. A loud clap of thunder, which could not have come at a more theatrical time, accompanied my progress into the chilly waters of the Channel, my movements closely followed by film crew and tourists alike.

My acclimatization over the winter months served me well. I felt cold on entering the water, but it wasn't the numbing and painful cold I'd endured over the winter. I quickly began swimming, the blood pumping round my body to warm my limbs up, and I struck out in the direction of Boscombe pier, despite being unable to see very far up the coast at all due to the heavy rain.

That first sea swim of the year taught me a lot. Firstly, it proved that my acclimatization training, painful as it had been, was paying dividends, but it also confirmed I had a long way yet to go. Something that I had not thought to take into account on that day was the tides. With the water flowing up and down the Channel as the tide came in and out, it meant that on this swim (and indeed on the many others I subsequently did at Bournemouth) I made faster progress in one direction that I did in the other. Arriving at Boscombe pier, slightly cold but buoyed by my progress, I turned around and began to make my way back. I had a deadline by which I had to be out of the water and be ready to get to the Client site, and as the time ticked by I soon realised that I would be late if I tried to swim all of the way back. It was with a slight sense of failure that I had to get out of the sea and jog back along the beach in order to make it to my inaugural meeting, but the film crew were mightily relieved to see me. They had quickly lost sight of me once I was swimming, and had waited over an hour, wondering what they should do, were I not to materialise within the next few minutes.

As I approached the camera I was shaking with cold, regardless of the run along the sand. Steph handed me a warm, sweet drink of tea and began to interview me between the chattering of my teeth. The drink would not stay steady in my trembling hands, and my whole body was shaking quite violently and they passed me my warm and dry post-swim clothes. The Pro-Glide lubrication I'd been using in the Hampstead ponds had soon washed off in the sea, and the abrasive nature of the salt water had severely chaffed my underarms, leaving them raw and red. The cold had made the chaffing unnoticeable at the time, but now that I was beginning to warm up the stinging pain was quickly becoming more apparent. It was obvious that I would have to find a lubricant that would survive being washed off by the sea. If I'd chaffed so badly during a swim of less than two hours, it was a very real problem that I was facing: how to avoid such rubbing whilst in the water for up to 16 hours. Luckily, I had already secured the services of the person best suited to provide such an answer.

This was clearly a question for Dr. Julie Bradshaw.

Fundraising

Parallel to all of my training activities was the ongoing requirement to seek corporate sponsorship, and to simultaneously raise local awareness of what I was doing. My fundraising total was slowly creeping up, and in some ways this was a worry: If I could not raise the required funds to finance the cost of the event, I would either have to somehow pay for it all myself, or I would have to call off the challenge and refund those individuals who had donated. As unbelievable as it may sound, the latter option was the far more likely one, given the expense I'd already had to lay out on professional support, travel, and accommodation: I simply could not afford to outlay another £1,500.

Understandably, the necessity to acquire the funding was a constant background concern.

There were, of course, two parts to the fundraising I was required to do. The entire purpose of my swim was to attempt to raise £10,000 towards Acorns. As of November 2013 I managed to break the one £1,000 mark thanks to a generous donation from my old army friend Bill McDougall, but there was still a very long way to go. In truth, with the scale of my initial target beginning to appear unrealistic, I began to harbour secret thoughts of being content with securing just £5,000. On the corporate side of things, Hallmark Hulme had been so impressed with my press-up exploits and the local publicity the event had generated that they offered to cover the remaining official observer fees required by the CSA. In addition, after I had tentatively enquired, Hallmark Hulme further agreed to arranging a Will to be drafted, not only for me during the swim, but also for Esta, as neither of us had one in place. To have earned so much respect in so short a time was a huge encouragement, and having such local and committed support was absolutely vital to the success of any Channel attempt.

From this point onwards, having established a local and highly reputable legal firm willing to back me, the power of networking began to establish itself. By now, of course, the local papers were beginning to pick up on the story, and even though the radio station may have thought that an event in 2014 was too far away in the eyes and ears of their audience, Worcester News were happy to do a full page spread. The publicity photos that Simon Fall-Taylor had taken were gratefully accepted by the paper, and the momentum to spread the word about my sponsorship requirements really began to gather pace. Not all offers of help arrived in the form of direct funding though. At the end of November I was contacted by Hugh Thomas, UK brand manager for Vita Coco, the natural coconut drink. Hugh offered to send me a 'few' samples of his the Vita Coco product, and simply wanted to know the most convenient delivery address to dispatch the consignment to. Within days, five large boxes containing various flavours of the drink had arrived, and this meant that I was immediately able to begin to trial-drinking the juice whilst training. Having such a long lead time prior to the swim meant that I was free to experiment with the various possible flavours and quantities well in advance. And such a large initial delivery gave me the opportunity to become totally familiar with the texture and taste, as well as allow my body to adapt to the liquid in my stomach as I swam. Hugh was pleased to have been of use to me, and simply told me to get in touch when my supplies ran low.

As the end of 2014 drew to a close, there were two other significant events worthy of mention. The first, as a result of the work that the Acorns PR team were putting in, was the pledge of £400 from Rybrook of Worcester. Rybrook had been a long-term benefactor of Acorns, and they had provided the chauffeur-driven cars to the Halls Ball several years earlier when I'd heard of Dave cycling the length of Britain. This meant that there was a direct link between that previous fundraising evening and the fact that Rybrook were now also sponsoring an event which was born out from that very night.

There was still around £1,800 required to settle the balance with my pilot, Kevin, but that could be settled in cash on the day of the swim. So whilst there was still a very real necessity to obtain pledges for this sponsorship, getting my hands on the actual cash was secondary at this point.

The second notable event came once more from my employers, Dovetail. I was in the US office again, having delivered internal training to some new employees, when the HR manager asked to speak to me. Denise, touching gently on the subject of the hospice, asked if I would be in favour of Dovetail using Acorns as their 50/50 charity at the US Christmas party, which was scheduled to take place the next day. My perplexed expression obviously spoke volumes, so Denise explained how the 50/50 event worked: Essentially it was a raffle, with employees free to buy as many tickets as they wished. There was one prize, consisting of 50% of the overall takings, with the remaining 50% going to the nominated charity. If I agreed, all I would be required to do was to give an explanatory speech describing what the charity did and why we should support them. Naturally I could also lead in to more details about my swim, why I was doing it, and what preparations I was having to undergo.

Understandably, there was no hesitation in my acceptance of Denise's offer, and I began to prepare a suitable speech for the occasion.

The real challenge with this task was that I needed the audience to have a deep level of empathy with my reasons for undertaking the swim, yet at the same time I did not want to ruin the jovial mood of the Christmas party. The speech therefore had to be initially hard-hitting, and then had to move to a more up-beat tone.

On the afternoon of the Christmas party itself, everyone gathered in the hallways of the US office to listen to the CEO deliver his end of year round-up. Immediately after this the entire office emptied as staff all piled into cars to make their way to the venue for the party - the function room of a large hotel a short distance from the Dovetail offices, complete with its own private bar. In addition to the 50/50 raffle, Dovetail had laid on some prizes for a free raffle, and the draw for this was conducted amidst much cheering and whooping. It was announced that the total prize fund for the 50/50 raffle had reached $500, which would be a nice tidy Christmas bonus for the winner, so it was with great anticipation that I climbed onto a chair and began to explain why I was conducting the draw.

Even though I stopped one rank short of Warrant Office in the army, my mum still refers to my 'sergeant major's voice' whenever I speak up, and I certainly had to do so on this occasion to ensure I was heard at the back of the room. Initially, there was a fair amount of shuffling, murmuring and even inattention within the audience. But as I began to explain the extent of the injuries poor Harry had suffered, a level of utter calm and silence began to pervade the room. By the time I informed them that there are no happy endings when a loved one is submitted to a hospice, and that

Harry died in my arms when he was 10 months old, many of the women had tears rolling down their faces. They must have been wondering what I was trying to do to the mood of their party.

'But if you think a children's hospice is a place for dying, you are very wrong,' I told them. 'If you ever get a chance to visit one, I can guarantee you will experience an atmosphere and an attitude that will shock you. These places are about getting the very most out of life, despite the certainty that such life will be very limited. You'll see smiles, you'll see wheelchair races, you'll see disabled children playing games, and above all, against expectations, you'll hear laughter.' It's always a moment of satisfaction to reset the expectation level of an audience. I saw slight frowns of initial doubt, followed by the dawning recognition that such an attitude was the only logical way a children's hospice could realistically function. It becomes a comfort to people to realise that in the face of such adversity, such tragedy, there can be smiles and laughter, despite any abandonment of hope.

'But these hospices are not government funded in the UK,' I explained. 'They mostly rely upon charity, and it would have cost around $150,000 for Harry to been looked after.' I paused to let the figure sink in, watching as jaws dropped and glances were exchanged. *Did he say one hundred and fifty THOUSAND?*

'So I'm trying to raise 10% of that figure: £10,000, which equates to around $15,000. Every penny really does count, so I'd like to say a big thank you to Dovetail for allowing the other 50% of this raffle to go to Acorns. Now.... let's do the draw.'

I climbed down from the chair I was on, with every eye in the room watching me. I reached into the bucket full of tickets, rummaged around for a few seconds, then withdrew a solitary piece of paper. There was a number on the front, which I read out, but there was also a name on the back, just to avoid any chance of confusion.

'Brenda!' I called out.

Brenda was actually standing just off to my left, and as I glanced around the room looking for her, I saw that she had tears rolling down her cheeks. I had the $500 cash rolled up into a thick bundle, and I pressed it into Brenda's hands, congratulating her.

And then an astonishing thing happened.

I watched as Brenda peeled off $20. I believed that she

wanted to make an additional contribution, celebrating her win with the chance to make an individual donation of $20. But she said, 'This is the $20 I bought the tickets with. I'll take that back, and I want you to give the other $480 to Acorns.'

I was speechless. $480 at any time of year would be a considerable amount from one individual. To pledge such a sum just days before Christmas was stunning. As keen as I was to reach my target, I could not accept what Brenda was offering. I argued with her, pleading that she keep the larger sum and donate $20. But Brenda was adamant. She'd never before had the opportunity to do something like this, and now she had this chance within her power. Moments ago she had nothing. Now at least she had her $20 back, and she could walk away knowing she had made a real contribution. I still maintain that this was one of the biggest acts of charity that I have ever personally witnessed. With regards to my fundraising activities, my year ended on a real high due to Brenda and Dovetail.

Christmas was upon me before I knew it, and I took the family to the Canary Islands where I would begin my first real taste of long distance sea swimming. Once I was back from holiday though, I suddenly found myself firmly into 'The Year of the Swim'. It was no longer a case of undertaking a challenge the following year, but instead I had to wake up to the reality that summer was approaching somewhat faster than I would ordinarily have liked. A change in perspective was needed. There was still a way to go in finding the remaining funds to pay Kevin for the boat, but I had to focus on the fact I *was* going to swim the Channel this year, not that I *hoped* to.

Yet there was only so far I could take this Positive Mental Attitude. Most importantly, I did not want to become flippant and blithely talk about the fact that I would undoubtedly get to the other side. I had faith in my abilities, but there were also plenty of unknowns. If the likes of Julie had once had to pull out, it was completely conceivable that something similar could happen to me. As Julie had encouraged, I was beginning to visualise myself staggering up the beach in France upon successful completion of swimming the Channel. But in no way could I bring myself to use the word 'when'. To the consternation of several people, I still said 'if'. And to me that was not being negative or doubtful - it was simply my way of showing respect for the scale of the challenge and for the Channel itself.

'I believe there's a rite of passage,' I explained to the film crew during one interview. 'The Channel will either let you cross, or it won't. You have to earn the right.' In the early part of 2014, I felt I was a long way from having done everything that was necessary.

I had to regularly reflect on the fact that swimming the Channel was simply a means to an end. The ultimate success or failure of the whole venture would be raising £10,000. In January, the pledged total was still less than £2,000, and I further required around an extra £1,000 to pay Kevin. Networking again helped me out on the latter point, with one of the parents at rugby training informing me that the hospital trust he worked for may be interested in providing sponsorship. He gave me the details of the person to contact at Spire South Bank Hospital Trust, and we began to exchange emails. It was a longer process than I would have initially believed. I had to provide a detailed outline of why I was doing the challenge, what it would involve, and where the money was going to. All of this would be presented to the board for justification of funds, and the initial reply from them was a request for yet further details. I'm pleased to say that my efforts were fully rewarded though, and in March of 2014 with just six months to go until the swim, the Trust pledged several hundred pounds towards the logistical costs.

Other, non-cash forms of sponsorship were also gratefully received. Simon from FT Images had already provided his photography services free of charge, and Vita Coco had also sent a shipment of drinks through. An old army colleague got in touch with a friend of his who worked for Zoggs, the swimming equipment manufacturer. They sent through a free pair of anti-fog goggles, and I was genuinely impressed by how comfortable and efficient they were. My previous pair of goggles had been painful to remove after several hours of swimming and felt as if a vacuum had been created inside them, sucking my eyeballs from their sockets. This new Zoggs pair were softly cushioned, fitted the eyes perfectly, and they never, ever fogged up once they were on. Even when my free pair eventually perished, I immediately went out and replaced them with an identical set. Furthermore, Julie told me she had actually got through no less than three pairs of goggles during one of her Channel swims, as two of them had ended up smeared with lubricant.

Consequently, I needed to have an absolute minimum of one spare set for my own attempt.

I was further lucky to have not just one, but two contacts within Glaxo Smith Kline. Matt, who was in the same class at school as Esta, offered to obtain some drinks and energy gels. I was getting through the gels at an astonishing rate, and at between £1 - £2 per sachet, the cost was mounting up. Matt arrived at my house one day armed with no fewer than four boxes full of Lucozade energy gel, along with several crates of the non-carbonated Lucozade sport drinks. Such a supply gave me the opportunity to begin to freely experiment with my feeding plan. Julie had advised that I needed to keep all feed stops as short as possible.

'Think of them as just that: feed stops, not rest breaks, ' she told me. 'You want to keep the duration down to less than a minute. In that time, you need to take on board enough fuel and liquid to see you through the next hour.' Julie went on to confirm and reiterate lots of the advice given on the CSA website. 'Don't forget you're going to be cold. You'll want something warm to drink, but not so hot that it burns you. And you don't want to be fiddling with energy sachets whilst you're in the water wither.'

As a result of Julie's advice, I tried mixing the Lucozade energy gels with the Vita Coco. The result was a rather thick and very sweet glutinous mixture. But it was full of quick release energy, and it quenched my thirst. As a side benefit, the mixture would also help overcome the taste of sea salt, albeit briefly. The combined help from Vita Coco and GSK had given me the solution to one part of my feeding plan.

In the year that a swimmer plans to undertake their Channel crossing, the CSA request the completion of a medical certificate by a doctor. Esta and I began to make enquiries at the medical practice we were registered with, and to our disbelief we were initially informed that there would be a fee of £200. However, the medical practice wanted details on exactly what was required of them as, perhaps understandably, certification of fitness to swim the Channel was not the sort of request that they usually received. In the end I managed to arrange to fax the forms over, adding a cover note requesting that Dr. Blaine be the one to be consulted. Clearly recalling our experiences with Harry, and being so closely involved from the outset, Dr. Blaine confirmed he was happy to perform the medical, adding that he would kindly waive any charge as part of his own sponsorship. Generous offers such as this all combined to make the swim at all possible. There seemed to be a hundred or more chargeable extras that went completely unknown until the last minute. Having a unexpected fee such as this one waived was a huge relief.

During the medical examination itself, Dr. Blaine was keen to understand what sort of training regime I was partaking in, and how long I anticipated the crossing to take. He was impressed at my level of commitment, though it was clear that he was relieved at not having to certify me 100% sane. He could certainly understand my motivation, and I obviously indicated I was sufficiently compos mentis, but wanting to swim 26 miles across cold and treacherous water hardly sounded sensible. The situation was reminiscent of Catch-22, wherein only an insane person could be excused from the war, but wanting to be removed from the war was a sure sign of complete sanity.

When Dr. Blaine had to put a final signature to the question 'do you consider this person sufficiently fit to undertake a crossing of the English Channel?' he laughed. 'I have no idea what it takes to swim across the Channel, so I'm not entirely sure how I answer this question.' He paused and looked at me, turning the question around. 'Do *you* think you are fit enough?'

'Absolutely.'

The answer was good enough for him, and with a flourish he signed the document. I was another important step closer to entering the waters of the English Channel.

Other smaller, but no less significant donation offerings came along. I had to be clear with all sponsors from the very outset in determining exactly how they wanted their money to be used. Some, such as Hallmark Hulme and Spire South Bank, were committed to ensuring the swim could proceed, and consequently pledged their funds towards the not-inconsiderable logistical costs of conducting the Channel swim. Others preferred their donations to be pledged directly to Acorns, increasing my total ever closer towards the goal of £10,000.

Examples of the latter came from events such as bake sales held internally within Dovetail, where £150 was raised by employees brining in cakes and pastries to sell to other members of staff;

Connagh, my second eldest, had his chest waxed in public on the Isle of Wight, drawing a small crowd who were eager to see if he was capable of enduring the pain. As a result of his efforts £150 was raised for charities, half of which he pledged to Acorns; our regular pub in Worcester, Charlestons, ran a raffle on my behalf, donating a three course meal for two as one of the prizes. I had a signed Worcester Warriors shirt which I also gave as a prize offering, and in total a further £250 was added to the pot.

I hit a stroke of luck when the Metro newspaper began to run a one-month campaign offering free advertising to ordinary people such as myself who were undertaking events for charity. The fundraising department at Acorns put me on to the idea, and though there must have been thousands of people who applied, my column was run in May. The article appeared in the paper the day after Stephen Sutton tragically lost his long battle against cancer. In all honesty, with the tremendous work that man had done, I fully expected any spare money the public may have to be pledged directly towards cancer research. Yet somehow over 30 donations were pledged by complete strangers, all of whom wished me the very best of luck. A further £150 duly materialised. My total was creeping up, but I was still a long way off the final target.

Listing all of the sponsorship in this fashion gives the impression that companies and individuals were tripping over themselves to offer help. In reality though, gaining access to all of that funding was seriously hard work. When I was not swimming or working, the remainder of my time seemed to be spent emailing or calling contacts, or pondering on how else I could expand my network of potential sponsors. It was hard work which seemed to occupy every spare minute and thought. It was a drain on any spare energy I had, but I was motivated by the nagging thought that failure to secure the funding would mean that everything else I'd been doing was utterly futile. Family life was all-but put on hold, and the longest conversations Esta and I seemed to have revolved around areas where she and the boys could possibly help out with anything to do with the swim. It was in this way that we managed to arrange for me to present my Channel swim plan to Perrywood Primary and Nursery School, where Esta worked.

The children were just due to finish what the school had termed 'Aspirations Week'. The pupils had all been invited to consider their role models, and to think about what motivated those individuals to achieve their goals. Likewise, they had to give thought to the aspirations of great leaders of state, or famous explorers, trying to understand what led these people on in their determination to succeed. In this way, of course, they were then led to inwardly reflect on any of their own desires or aspirations, and to use the motivation and determination of others to encourage themselves.

My challenge, with its year-long requirement to rise early each morning, for cold swims, and for a doggedly single-mindedness with regards to focus, fit in nicely with the theme. I was a local parent of one of the children at the school (Will), husband to one of the staff there, and consequently I was someone tangible whom the children could associate with.

I spent some time putting together a presentation I thought would be suitable for my target audience, bearing in mind the very young age of some of the children. Will was in the nursery side of the school at the time, and he and his classmates would also be attending the assembly. This meant that the age range of my audience would be from three to 11 years old, though obviously the teaching staff would be in attendance too.

My time spent coaching the boys and girls at rugby meant that I had a current CRB safety certificate, making it that little bit easier for the head mistress to agree to the idea of me taking an assembly. Unbeknown to me at the time, as I loaded the presentation onto the school computer in the assembly hall in preparation for a final last-minute check, Miss Kelly-Freer, the headmistress, had stopped Esta in the hallway. It had suddenly occurred to her that some of my subject-matter material would revolve around a poignant, delicate topic.

'Will your husband be talking about the hospice?' She asked Esta.

'I should imagine so. That's what the whole swim is in aid of, after all.'

'How will he deal with the subject?' Miss Kelly-Freer was naturally mindful of her youngest pupils.

'I've not seen the presentation at all,' admitted Esta. 'But he's a training manager. He knows how to prepare for his audience.'

I waited at the front of the hall as all 400 or so children filed in and sat down cross legged on the floor, chattering quietly and looking at me in expectation. The teaching staff gathered around the outside of the children, settling them down, hushing the noisier ones with a stern frown or a finger.

Miss Kelly-Freer took control by saying good morning, and the children had gave their sing-song reply: 'Good morning miss Kelly-Freer, good morning everyone.' A deep and expectant silence followed, the children's eyes torn between their headmistress and me, the stranger standing off to one side.

The scene was set, with the pupils all being reminded of the subject of study for the past five days, 'Aspirations Week.' They were told that I had something relevant to contribute by way of a challenge I was planning to undertake.

I opened the presentation by showing a picture of Esta and I posing together for the camera. It was a photo taken by Mike Henley at one of the Worcester Warrior end of season dinners. Every person in the room already knew who Esta was, so the slide was an excellent way of capturing their attention and giving me a point of reference from their perspective. I told the children that I was Esta's husband, and then showed them a photo of Esta and Harry.

'We had a baby, before Will, and after Lewis.' Half of the young audience knew Lewis, who had recently moved to high school, and the other half knew Will, who currently sat towards the front, watching me with a smile.

'But Harry was very poorly. Does anyone know where you go if you're not well?'

Many hands shot up in the air, with murmurs of 'The doctor,' or, 'The hospital,' clearly audible. I chose one little girl towards the front who gave me the answer of the latter.

'Yes. Harry went to the hospital, as he had a very poorly heart. But sometimes, sometimes, the hospital cannot make you better.' There was an audible intake of breath from the adults in the room, and a heightened sense of expectation. I put up a picture of a yellow, sad face, and pulled down the corners of my own mouth in exaggerated sympathy. 'That's sad, isn't it?' Many young heads nodded.

'But,' I continued, in a suddenly up-beat tone, 'Harry went somewhere called a "hospice". Now, the hospice cannot make you better, but it can look after you whilst you are unwell. So all the nurses and other people at the hospice all helped us look after Harry, and made sure he had lots of fun.'

At the back of the room I could see one of the other female members of staff hold Esta's hand as my wife wiped her face with her free hand.

'But it costs a lot of money to look after poorly people. It costs thousands of pounds.' There were gasps at the mention of such a large sum. 'So I want to try and raise lots of money for the hospice, so that they can help to look after other poorly children, like our Harry.'

The sensitive hurdle successfully cleared, the path was now free to talk about the swim itself. I showed a map of England and France, pointing out where we lived in Worcester, and then directing their attention by means of a laser pointer down towards Dover.

'Does anyone know what this place is called,' I asked, indicating the European mainland adjacent to our own island. A few hands tentatively rose, and the successful answer of 'France' was given. I asked if anyone had been to France, ignoring the comic grins of the teaching staff as they raised their hands in answer to this question. Involving the children as much as possible, I asked them how they'd travelled there. After my third or fourth try, someone said by boat, allowing me to proceed onto an image of the Channel. I described how I planned to swim to France across miles of sea (cue an image of the water under choppy, windy conditions) explaining that it would take many hours - longer indeed than a full school day! I proceeded to detail my early mornings spent practising in very cold water, and explained that raising money for Acorns was my 'aspiration'.

'Would you like to help me raise some money?' I asked, in a buoyant, positive and leading tone.

There were many eager nods and murmurs of ascent. *If only it was always this easy to get a pledge of sponsorship*, I thought!

'Well I'd like you to help me raise £400. Now, if I asked one person for £400, that would be a lot of money. But, if you could all raise £1, then we'd get there easily. So if I ask miss Kelly-Freer if you can come in to school one day in bright, non-uniform clothes, and you all bring in £1 each, that would be great.' Naturally I was not putting the head teacher on the spot, and the idea had already been pre-approved. Every school likes some positive press coverage, and fundraising for a local hospice benefits everyone all round. The assembly concluded with some awards for hard work, generosity and helpful behaviour, and many of the teaching staff came up to me after the children had left to pass on their best wishes. The PE teacher and the caretaker, Bill, both made a point of shaking my hand and wishing me good luck. Miss Kelly-Freer, now greatly relieved to see that her concerns had been alleviated, thanked me for my input. The non-uniform day was held in March, and an extra £248 was clocked up on my JustGiving website as a result. The local press were contacted shortly after, and some photos of me with a selection of brightly clothed children accompanied a short piece about Perrywood Primary and Nursery supporting a local father on his quest to swim the Channel for Acorns.

Due to the ever increasing number of contacts available from my expanding network, a huge boost in the total funds pledged directly to Acorns was unexpectedly taken during the second quarter of the year. In April I was contacted by Ross Prince, chairman of the Worcester Group of Chartered Accountants. As a contact of both Becky and Julian from Hallmark Hulme, Ross had seen the write-ups I'd been posting to LinkedIn. The annual dinner of the Chartered Accountants Group was due to take place in May, and Ross invited me to come and speak as a guest, with Acorns being the nominated charity for the evening. It was an invitation I took no hesitation in accepting.

The evening came round quickly, and it was another opportunity to dress up smartly, complete with campaign medals, and to spend an evening with Esta whilst fundraising. We arrived with the pop-up banner bearing the Dovetail and Hallmark Hulme logos, and brought a pile of the flyers which contained website addresses for further donations. Ross, whom I'd never met before, greeted us warmly, saying how impressed he was with what he'd read of the challenge so far. He offered us a drink from the bar, and whilst Esta could indulge in a gin and tonic, I was off the alcohol by this stage.

At our table we were introduced to our fellow diners, including the second guest speaker of the evening, the comedian Dr. Phil Hammond. The presence of Dr. Phil had given me a big boost when preparing my speech for the evening, as I knew that I could hit slightly harder with the cruel truth about poor Harry, safe in the knowledge that my words would not utterly ruin the evening. My speech even opened with that fact:

'Lady Macbeth once admonished her husband for displacing the mirth during their dinner,' I began. 'I will confess immediately that I will be guilty of a similar crime, but we do have a professional on-hand to subsequently re-generate your humour.'

There is a question I like to pose at the beginning of my talks, one that I like to think sets the listener on the right mental path. I posed this question next.

'I'd like you to ask yourselves something serious. Most of you have sons, daughters or other young loved ones. Please take a moment to pause and consider this simple question, as it's one I will return to at the end of my speech: Can you think of anything worse than being told that your child is terminally ill? Think on that silently. They're going to die, and there is absolutely nothing that you or anyone else can do about it. It may sound morbid, perhaps even highly dramatic. But I can assure you it is not dramatic, and that Esta and I were told exactly that about our son Harry. What could possibly be worse?'

All eyes were on me. The room was silent. Many of the women bore an expression of worry bordering on panic. Everyone was waiting to hear my story, and obligingly, I told them of our journey with Harry. It's always hard to know how much detail to include within a verbal retelling. The balance has to be right if you are to achieve and maintain empathy, without obscuring it with boredom. And though we were extremely fortunate to have the Acorns facilities and support available to us, it is vital during these speeches that the listeners do not perceive that support as the 'happy ending' to our story. Acorns made life bearable for us, and for Harry. But the outcome was always inevitable, and Harry's terminal prognosis was never altered. Though we could never have realistically asked for any more than we got, we still ultimately lost our son.

'So let me return to my initial question', I began to conclude. 'Can you imagine anything worse than being told your child is terminal?' Heads were bowed, and most people shook them slowly, determined after my retelling of Harry's ordeal that surely nothing could actually make such an experience any worse.

'I can think of something worse,' I said. Heads came up, expressions of puzzlement and worry etched onto faces. 'Our lives would have been made far worse, had we been told that there were no facilities or nurses to help us. Had we been informed that we had to face our journey unaided, without and means of help or respite... well I just don't know how well we would have coped.

'Acorns relies on charitable donations in order to continue the work that they do. So that is the reason I'm swimming the Channel in the summer - in order to help ensure that the hospice is still there when other parents receive the horrific news we were once given!'

Admittedly, it was a tough warm-up act for a comedian to have to follow, and only a professional could hope to turn tears of sadness into ones of laughter within a few minutes. But after shaking hands with me as he took my place, Dr. Phil duly managed to return the mirth to the room. The gloom was dispelled, even though I later found out that my story had hit home to more than a few of the audience.

Envelopes had been placed on each table, with the diners invited to place donations into. Ross arranged for the contributions to be collected, and we were all delighted to discover that on this one evening alone a total of £1,315 had been donated. Ross handed me the cash as though he'd known me for years, and it was a wonderful demonstration of faith to be trusted with such a bundle of notes from a relative stranger.

Even better, as the evening drew to a close and Esta and I began to make our way to our car, was the fact that Becky from Hallmark Hulme came running up to us, full of excitement and bursting to tell us some news.

'I think I've managed to secure the remainder of your sponsorship!'

Esta and I looked at each other in amazement.

'Hallmark Hulme are partnered with Kendall Wadley accountants. Jeremy from Kendall Wadley was really impressed with your talk. I'll confirm with you tomorrow, but between our business and theirs, we want to ensure you have the remaining funds you need!'

It was fantastic news, and meant that we headed home with a pocket full of notes to boost my increasing total, together with the peace of mind that comes from knowing that our sponsorship worries were over. We still had to raise several thousand if we were to achieve the £10,000 mark, but at least one problem was now out of the way.

There was little to stand in the way of my swimming to France now - except of course the weather, injury, and the large and foreboding expanse of water separating both land masses.

The game was truly on, and it was time now to switch all energies solely to the training front.

Training and Acclimatisation - Part 2

In early spring, the horrors of cold water acclimatization continued, mostly in the Parliament Hill lido at Hampstead. Though I could see the digital display of the water temperature beginning to rise day by day, I was despairing that my endurance was not escalating quickly enough. It was invariably the cold, as opposed to fatigue, that was driving me out of the pool each morning, as my face, toes and fingers were simply unable to bear any further exposure to such low temperatures.

And yet a massive but unexpected boost to my confidence was received one morning at the lido. A lady approached me as I was about to jump into the cold pool. There was a smile on her face as she walked over, and for a moment I assumed she had mistaken me for someone else.

'Have you swum the Channel, or are you training for it?' she asked.

I was momentarily confused as to how or why she would leap to such an assumption, especially considering I was just one of many swimmers at the lido. Sensing my dismay, the lady indicated the CSA swim cap clinging tightly to my scalp. All became suddenly clear.

'I've got a slot in August,' I explained. 'I've been training for it for around seven months.'

'I've swum it,' the lady said, casually. 'Are you registered with the CSA or the CSPF?' Any doubt I may have held over the veracity of her first statement was dismissed with this question, and I told her I was registered with the former organisation, and that Julie Bradshaw was mentoring me.

'Hey, I know Julie! Tell her Nuala says hello. I'll train with you sometime, if you like?'

I found the offer slightly disconcerting, not simply because I'd never met this lady before, but mostly because I was convinced I would not be able to keep up with another Channel swimmer. Furthermore, aside from occasional swims with Lewis, I was only used to training alone. I made an excuse about currently not being able to stay in the cold water for longer than an hour.

Nuala's eyes opened wide. 'You can stay in this water for an hour?' There was a distinct air of surprise and awe to her question. 'That's incredible. If you're already up to that level of endurance, you'll have absolutely no problem with the Channel, I can promise you.'

Hearing these words was absolute music to my ears. I would happily have paid someone to repeat such a statement to me, and I felt my confidence unbelievably boosted by this news, especially as the comment had been delivered from someone who had successfully completed the crossing themselves.

'But the Channel will only be a few degrees warmer, surely?' I asked, wondering if there had somehow been a mistake.

Nuala smiled and shook her head.

'We're not yet up to twelve degrees here. That's the magic breaking point, and as soon as it reaches that temperature you'll notice a big difference. But also, and I don't know how to explain this, but sixteen degrees in fresh water seems vastly colder than sixteen degrees in the sea somehow. It's weird. The metal lining of the pool here always makes it seem colder, too. Trust me, if anything, you'll feel warm when you get in the Channel.'

Having both wasted enough time chatting, we promptly got in and got on with our individual swims. The water failed to feel any warmer that day, but when I exceeded an hour of swimming, I was buoyed by the encouraging words I'd been given.

Later in the year, when my London accommodation plans had relocated me to the Union Jack Club in Waterloo, this new location meant that it was more convenient for me to continue my outdoor training at Tooting Bec Lido, as opposed to Parliament Hill. I joined Tooting Bec as a full member (another personal expense to add to the list), allowing me to swim in the out-of-season months before the facilities were opened to the general public. The pool is an incredible 90 meters long, and it's a favourite venue for many would-be Channel swimmers. As with Hampstead, Tooting has its own regulars, many of whom have been involved in Channel swimming to one degree or another, be that participating in an attempt or actively supporting another swimmer. I invariably got into conversations with many of the patrons, though naturally my main focus was on the swimming itself. After all, I already had a world-record holding mentor for advice and questions.

As spring progressed, my overall swimming distances began

to increase. Indoors, I was already capable of churning out length after length for five hours. The six hour mark was next on my radar, but this sort of commitment had to be carefully built into my working schedule too. I was rapidly burning through my annual leave entitlement, taking half-days regularly so that I could swim without the worry that other members of staff were wondering where I was. David Chance, my direct report within Dovetail, suggested that I begin to work US hours, thereby giving me the morning to swim, and the afternoon and evening to work. In this way, I would not use all of my leave on preparation for the challenge. It was another example of the fantastic level of support I was being offered from every angle.

The next step in my training was to begin to increase the open water swimming distances. The outdoor water temperature was gradually creeping up, and the first three hour swim in Windermere with Julie was rapidly approaching.

'You need to plan to build up to an eight hour swim one day, followed by a six hour swim the next day,' Julie advised me. 'The eight hour one will be over half of the time you should need for the Channel, and the six hour one will be a real test of endurance the next day. But if you can do this, you can complete the Channel.'

The real crunch in all of my scheduled training was the planned six hour qualifying swim, due to take place in the first week of June. To me, this date seemed too close to the actual swim, and I'd initially asked Julie if we could plan for the qualifier to be earlier.

'The water will be too cold.' Julie stated. 'We can book in a shorter swim - let's say three hours - as a trial or build-up swim. But I don't think you'll last six hours in the water before June. It won't have had time to warm up.'

As with most of Julie's advice, I paid heed. After all, it seemed madness to hire an expert and then ignore what they said. We booked a three hour Windermere swim for mid-May, with the full six hour Channel qualifier being just three weeks later. Julie assured me that there would be a significant and noticeable difference in water temperature between these dates.

To ensure I had milestones which would progressively move me towards being able to endure a six hour open water qualifying swim, I booked myself onto a challenge at Eton Dorney, the venue for the London 2012 Olympic rowing events two years previously.

Distances varied according to ability, but I booked myself onto the 10km (non-wetsuit) swim, calculating that it should take me around four hours to complete. This would mean that I would have a three, four and six hour swim, all within a three week period, still leaving me almost two months to really top-off my training regime.

By this point in my training I was regularly swimming for four hours in the pool at David Lloyd's. I'd completed a few six hour swims, and I was now closing in on the magic 40km/week mark that Julie had advised me to aim towards. One problem I began to suffer from was aches and pains. Being such a low-impact sport, it's easy to assume you cannot injure yourself by swimming. Trust me when I say that hours and hours in the water, week after week, month after month will almost certainly result in some form of suffering. For me, there were two areas of injury. The first one was due to the fact that my technique was still very poor, and as a result I was obviously not lying flat enough in the water. With fresh water being so much less buoyant that salt water, this meant that after a few hours my back began to ache from continually arching upwards. I've suffered from back ache for years, and it's a horrible pain that gnaws away at your patience, your concentration and your determination. During these swims I would have to curl into a ball every now and then and stretch my back the other way. Such relief was always only extremely temporary though.

The second effect was essentially wear and tear on the shoulders. The continuous rotation and pulling meant that I had developed an ache deep inside my shoulder muscles. During a swim this would initially build to an excruciating level of pain whilst the muscles warmed up. After half an hour or so, the pain would gradually fade (or at least plateau), but after a few hours it would once more begin to build. Swimming for hours was becoming not only boring, but also very painful. At the completion of each session I would have the satisfaction of knowing what I had just achieved. But this was offset with the knowledge of knowing I'd have to endure it all again, sometimes in as little as 18 hours.

In the end, the only way I could get through the pain was by regularly taking paracetamol and ibuprofen. The house became littered with packets of the tablets, and I would religiously have to take them every four hours to stop the pain from driving me to distraction. I'd take tablets with me to my swim, and at the appointed time I swallowed them along with the dark chocolate, glucose and Vita Coco I treated myself to during breaks.

In fact, I was spending so much time in the chlorinated water that the effects were beginning to manifest themselves in several ways. As well as my body shape being toned up, my skin and hair were actually turning grey, bleached by the prolonged exposure to chlorine. On top of this, Esta commented that I constantly smelled of the chemical. The odour had penetrated my very skin, and whenever I broke into a sweat it was as if pure chlorine were coming through my pores.

As far as my physicality and well-being was concerned, I was feeling good. I'd given up drinking several months previously upon return from a trip to the US office with Dovetail. The weather had been horrendous in the States, with deep snow drifts and freezing temperatures which made the roads lethal. I'd been over to New Jersey again, this time to interview for a new US-based trainer to work with me. However, the Dovetail office was forced to close for a day due to health and safety issues caused by the snow, so my interviews had to be pushed back 24 hours. Several other Dovetail staff from the UK were visiting the US for their own reasons, and as we were effectively trapped in the hotel we all met up one evening and started chatting and drinking. It was a long, expensive, heavy session. Though the interviews the next day passed without incident, it was actually during my flight back that I realised just how huge a session we had all indulged in. When I arrived home, looking even greyer than the effects of the chlorine could produce, I announced to Esta that I would stop drinking for a while and put some real effort into not just my fitness, but my health. The two subjects had always been very disparate for me. My days in the army had seen me extremely fit, but I cannot claim to have ever been very healthy. Alcohol is a poison, but it was my one vice, and one that I tended to indulge in more than I should. Even occasional stints of abstinence lasted no longer than a few weeks.

'You can't give up drinking just yet,' was Esta's surprising response.

I was bemused and shocked. 'Why not?'

'The Six Nations rugby starts tomorrow. There's no way you'll be able to watch the matches without a beer. You'll fail straight away, and that will discourage you.'

Harry's Favourite Thing

It was a logical argument. But I countered it with one of my own. 'The rugby will go on for several weeks. Giving up always happens tomorrow. I'll be fine watching the matches without a beer. I'm going to stop. Today.'

I was treated with a sympathetic, appeasing smile. It was not hard to guess what Esta was thinking.

I won't deny that it was difficult. To begin with, I was not truly expecting to go from February to August without a single alcoholic drink. The habit of relaxing and enjoying a pint, or a glass of wine, is a hard one to break. I found that sleep initially evaded me for the first few nights. But watching the rugby without an alcoholic drink actually turned out to be easier that I'd expected, and I think I genuinely shocked Esta with my initial abstinence. Temptation was often thrown in my way over the following months however, such as being offered complimentary glasses of champagne during subsequent flights to the US. Turning them down and asking for an orange juice seemed so alien to me that I could barely comprehend having uttered the words myself.

Along with my improved physicality and general well-being, mentally I was feeling strong and positive. My training plan, updated with my progress on a daily basis, showed me graphically how just well I was progressing. So though I was tired a lot of the time, and though my shoulders ached, this evident progress had an extremely positive effect. To alleviate the rubbing and chaffing that continuous hours of swimming inevitably caused, Julie had recommended making a 50/50 mixture of lanolin and Vaseline. Though I had never heard of lanolin, any mothers will know exactly what it is. Extracted from the wool of sheep, the product is a purified wax-like substance which penetrates the human skin well without turning rancid. Breastfeeding mothers use lanolin to treat chapped, cracked nipples, and Channel swimmers had also caught onto the idea of using it to prevent chaffing. The trouble was, it is an extremely gelatinous and thickly viscous substance. The tubs I had bought were neither liquid nor solid, but managed to hover somewhere in-between, a sticky solution akin to tar. Applying it was actually quite painful unless I did it gently and slowly, as it would simply drag my skin along with it. Julie had suggested mixing the raw lanolin with Vaseline to ease the application proce͏͏ In the end, I chose to use it straight out of the tub, awkward a͏ was, as in its pure form it did not wash away at all, even on the longer swims. At this point, of course, I had yet to perfect the technique of applying the lanolin. Once on the fingers, the stuff was almost impossible to remove. I quickly realised that touching my goggles with any of the lanolin residue on my fingers made them smudged and impossible to see through. This was another bizarre area of Channel swimming that needed thought and practice, and was one reason why swimmers often went through so many pairs of goggles during a Channel crossing.

The mental benefits of knowing I would not suffer the discomfort of chaffing were quite significant, as this was one less niggle to worry about. The pain in my back and shoulders could be held at a manageable level due to the painkillers, so the only thing that really remained to stand in the way of a 100% positive mental attitude was boredom.

For me, every swimming session was rapidly becoming a battle with sensory deprivation. With nothing to hear but the sound of my own breathing, nothing to see but the side of the pool, and nothing to taste but chlorine, all for hours at a time, I was beginning to dread the boredom of a swimming session more than the pain that came with it. Having time to one's own thoughts is a luxury many people would love. But when you have anywhere between four and six hours within which to mentally occupy yourself each day, you rapidly run out of things to think about. I have to admit that sometimes the boredom won. On more than one occasion I stopped swimming simply because I could not face the monotony of even one more lap. It was a dangerous habit, but I'd be lying if I pretended it never happened, and each time I did this I would convinced myself that the actual Channel swim itself would be different. During the actual challenge I'd simply keep going, I told myself.

'You absolutely have to get the mileage in!' Julie admonished me. 'Above everything else, your body must be capable of achieving the distance, and your mind must realise this. Do whatever it takes, even if you have to get an MP4 player for during your training.'

So that's what I did. It seemed strange suddenly swimming accompanied to music, and it did offer some respite. But the habitual length-counting still continued at a subconscious level from sheer habit, and a further appreciation of the duration of each training session was paradoxically delivered due to realising just how many albums I'd listened to during each swim.

I'm not sure exactly when or how I made the decision, but once the spring arrived and the weather began to make sea swimming a realistic possibility for me, I realised I was not going to go and practice in Dover harbour after all. With the exception of a few training sessions with Julie, my swimming had all been solitary. Whilst this had a price tag of boredom attached to it, I suddenly knew without doubt that I did not want to begin swimming training with anyone - especially not with a group. I was painfully aware that I was a slow swimmer, poor in technique if strong in stamina. My perception was that my confidence would take a hammering if I were to meet up with fellow swimmers down in Dover, and regardless of whether that may have been a fair assessment, I determined that the first time I would arrive in the vicinity would be just prior to my own Channel attempt.

Sea swimming practice is vital, of course, so I was lucky that I had further business trips enforcing visits to Bournemouth. With the long, safe sea-front and easy access to the beaches, Bournemouth could offer me everything in terms of facilities that Dover could. Whenever there was call for me to take a trip down to the coast, I made the most of the opportunity to get as much sea swimming under my belt as was possible. This would often mean an early morning in the water at sunrise, swimming as far as possible before having to get back to the hotel and ready for work, followed by another session in the evening.

The weather in the late spring of 2014 was looking good, and I soon became fixated on the weather forecast and the temperature of the Channel. Prior to being reconstructed, the CSA website was crammed with useful tips and suggestions, but lacked some of the more immediate data I needed, such as the conditions in the Channel and the temperature of the water. The 'rival' governing body, the Channel Swimming and Pilot Federation (CSPF) site had this information readily to hand, and I found myself checking on an almost daily basis, watching with fear as the water at first stubbornly refused to rise above 13 degrees. Such a temperature was manageable in April and May for an hour or two, mainly thanks to enduring those winter temperatures down to five degrees at Parliament Hill, but my mind was continuously thinking of a swim in excess of 12 or even 14 hours. For a swim of that duration, I needed the water to be 16 degrees at the least.

Consequently, I prayed for the sun.

Before I knew it, mid-May had arrived, and it was time for my first major milestone: a three hour open water swim in Windermere under the watchful eye of Dr. Julie Bradshaw. It was a big event, and though I knew I could swim for six hours in a pool, I'd achieved nowhere near this time in the open water thus far.

I'd booked the day off work, and Ali and I had arranged to drive up to the Lake District. This swim posed the first opportunity for us to work as a team, with Ali being in charge of feeding me and ensuring I was generally ok. We had little idea of the geography of the lake, or where or how the feeding would be done, but we planned to sort out the final details once we arrived.

The weather was forecast to produce the hottest day of the year so far, and during the three hour drive from Worcester it certainly looked to deliver on that promise. But as we neared the town of Windermere itself the skies began to cloud over and a nasty wind picked up. The radio kept telling us what a gorgeous day the rest of the country was enjoying, but for my part it looked like I would be swimming in the same wintery conditions I'd experienced for the past eight months.

Ali called up the film crew, who had already arrived ahead of us, to get final directions from them. We parked up next to the docks and met up with Emma and Steph, both of whom seemed far more enthusiastic about this swim than I did. The drive itself had been long enough - I was now due to be in the water for that same amount of time, and then drive back home.

Whilst the film crew got their gear ready, I set off with Ali to locate Julie. In true military fashion we'd arrived in plenty of time, so my aim was simply to confirm where we would be meeting up at the allotted time. As luck would have it, no sooner did we turn the corner into the private dock than we ran directly into Ms. Bradshaw. Seeing us there so early shocked her. She was only just on her way back from the gym, and had not expected us for some time yet. She pointed out her boat, 'Butterfly on the Lake', told us where we would meet later, and headed off to get changed.

The wait allowed the film crew the opportunity of catching some footage of Ali and I. It all seemed very unreal to us, as we've known each other many years, and we generally sit in comfortable silence enjoying the quiet company of the other. For the film, we were required to be far more vocal, of course, and it seemed very forced for both of us, regardless of us understanding the need for it. All the while though, my trepidation at what I was about to endure was increasing. The weather conditions were actually deteriorating, and there was no sign whatsoever of the sun, nor of any heat produced by it. Instead, threatening clouds and a wintery wind battered us. I was feeling the cold with my clothes on. I had yet to strip off and get into the water.

When the cameras stopped rolling, I told Ali that his primary role today had changed. His aim was no longer just to feed me. More than that, he was now responsible for ensuring I did not get out of the water in anything less than three hours - no matter what I said.

'How am I supposed to do that?' He complained.

'Don't worry. It may never happen,' I replied, with far more confidence than I felt.

When Julie arrived there were introductions to do. She had spoken to the film crew, of course, having been the one to initially pass my details on to them. This was the first time they had actually met, and obviously the crew were eager to capture some footage of Julie, Ali and I in conversation. For her part, as I've mentioned, Julie is a no-nonsense lady. There was no big plan to discuss, and all she wanted to do was get me in the water and get me swimming.

'I'll tell you everything you need to know on the short walk to the start point. Let's get going.' Without further ado, she trudged off, leaving us to fall in behind her.

Despite Windermere being a vast lake, to keep costs down we were not going to be using the support boat for this swim, hence saving on the expense of fuel. As a consequence, I would be reduced to swimming in a bay within sight of the 'beach' where the others would wait. The bay was far from sheltered, and I could see just how choppy the water was as we approached. The beach was small and narrow, and consisted mostly of pebbles. There was a large grassed slope that ran towards the water though, giving a lovely panoramic view of the lake and which would have provided a perfect picnic spot, had the weather been nicer.

'The entry to the water is quite rocky,' Julie told us. 'You'll have to watch your step going in, and be particularly careful when coming out. When your feet are cold and numb you can easily cut yourself without realising, so don't be in any rush to get out of the water. It's actually good practice for the Channel, as you may well have the same issue when you arrive in France.'

The bay was full of boats. They were moored up and were all facing away from the shore due to the wind blowing directly towards us. It was quite picturesque for those not about to strip off and go for a swim, I guess.

'We will wait around here. You see that boat with the red flag on it?' Julie pointed down to her left. A few hundred meters away there was a wooden boat, beautifully varnished and looking ready for a pirate captain. 'Swim down to that, come around and back up to the buoy here. That will be your circuit.'

I was actually bitterly disappointed. I had envisaged a much larger route requiring me to swim maybe two or three laps in total. The small circuit I was restricted to would not take me very long to complete, even at my slow pace, so I quickly calculated that I would have to endure many more laps of this small route than I'd anticipated.

'Get changed and get ready,' Julie ordered. If this had been an American film, I would have felt the need to salute her.

It's hard in retrospect to appreciate the incredible sense of trepidation and reluctance that was mounting inside me at the very thought of commencing this particular open water swim. I kept praying for some form of reprieve, some event that would cause us to call it all off for a few days. I have no idea what I was worried about, or why I was scared. All I know is that I really, really did not want to get into the cold water at all, let alone in front of Julie and the camera crew.

Ali helped me apply the lanolin to my arms and between my legs. It was a job that he was clearly less than impressed with, and the result was somewhat brutal. The substance was cold and hence more viscous than normal. It clung to my skin as though it were barbed, dragging my poor flesh with the harsh, rapid strokes with which Ali was applying it. I stood it for as long as I could before telling him he'd applied a sufficient amount, and the first direct result of this open water swim was an acknowledgement that I had to find a better way of applying the lanolin.

'When you're ready to feed, after your first hour, swim to the shore.' Julie told me. 'Be careful of the rocks, as I've said. You won't be able to come all the way in, so Ali will have to throw you food and drink, as when you're on the boat.'

Due to the absence of an escort boat for this swim, and to enable the shore party to safely keep an eye on me, Julie had requested that I bring along the high visibility float I'd been practising with in the Canaries. I secured the straps around my waist, holding the float which would trail behind me, and posed for a photo. In the shot I admit that I look calm and focussed. In reality, I was unaccountably terrified.

With no other reason to delay, and with Julie understandably becoming more impatient to get the swim underway, I ventured into the water. I'd psyched myself up to such a pitch by this point that I'd genuinely expected the water to be bone-numbingly freezing. It was certainly cold, but no more so than the lidos. By the time I was in up to my waist, having slipped and clambered over the algae-covered rocks and boulders, I determined that I just needed to clear my mind and start swimming. I shallow-dived into the murky water, careful not to smash my head into any submerged obstacles, and struck out for the buoy on my right. The water was choppy, and I soon realised that the entire swim was going to be a battle. I would never have credited the water being so rough so close to the shore, especially given that the wind, though blowing, was far from storm strength.

Around 1991, whilst in the army, I'd been lucky enough to partake in an expedition to Canada, canoing 750 miles along Peace River in Alberta. At one stage we'd had to cross a vast lake, so wide that we could not see landfall on the other side. In cinematically dramatic fashion, the weather suddenly changed when we were halfway across, and our group of two-man canoes were forced to break formation and just individually head for the safety of shore. The waves were crashing over the gunnel of the boats, and I remember that I was the one who put my head down and dug deep with the paddle whilst my companion busied himself with bailing the canoe out to keep us afloat. We all arrived safely on the other side, but it was an example of how even a freshwater lake could be severely disturbed by the weather conditions.

Windermere was currently nowhere near as bad as that Canadian lake. But in the Canadian example I had been above the water. Now I was in it. The waves made it hard to see where I was going, and compared with the luxury of only having to glance sideways in a swimming pool, I now had to check my forward course regularly as I rounded the buoy and headed towards the boat with the red flag.

It transpired that a single lap of my small circuit took me eight minutes. With 180 minutes of swimming to endure, this meant I was destined to complete over 20 laps. I began to tick them off, doing my best to ignore the cold. If anything, paradoxically, the rough water conditions actually helped keep me warm. I seemed to be fighting the waves continually, consequently expending far more energy than usual. I was frustrated and annoyed though, as this swim was not turning out to be anything like the pleasant and picturesque lake swim I had envisaged. All I wanted to do was get it finished, tick off milestone number one, and head home.

As I swam, I recalled something I'd read on the CSA website. When the wind is blowing it's the flesh that is exposed above the water that endures the cold. The temperature outside the water is genuinely colder than in it. Each time I plunged my arm into the lake, reaching forward to take a stroke, I could feel the relative warmth of the water compared to the brief exposure to the wind. With this in mind, I changed my feeding plan 'on-the-fly'. I calculated that clambering across the treacherous rocks towards Ali, all the while exposing my whole body to the cold wind, would not be a pleasant experience. If I were to feed every hour, it meant I'd have to do this not once, but twice. Conversely, if I decided to delay my feed by half an hour, it meant I could get away with a single stop, and hence have to endure the exposure only once.

The main problem was that I had no way to communicate this change of plan to Ali. I decided I would have to endure his bemused wrath and apologise to him later.

At the one hour point I could see the poor guy frantically jumping up and down, waving to me to indicate that it was time for a feed. I tried to somehow mime that I would do another three laps first, but clearly my signals were only causing more confusion. In the end I simply swam on, knowing that if they did not work it out for themselves within 30 minutes, then I'd be able to tell them in person soon enough.

When I did stop, Julie was severely unimpressed. She listened to my explanation, and as I crammed some chocolate into my mouth, washing it down with some warm soup, she admonished me.

'You simply cannot change your plan without communicating it to your support crew. Communication is vital at all times.'

She was completely, utterly correct, of course. And yet I could not feel any regret over the action I'd taken. I was unhappy with the swim, I was not enjoying it in the slightest, and at least now I could get back into the water knowing that I merely had to repeat my earlier number of laps once more. It was a huge mental milestone for me, and I believe that ultimately that change in plan helped me complete that first lake swim.

I cramped up slightly towards the end, when the cold finally began to bite. Three hours of being submerged in water at 12 degrees was beginning to take its toll, but to have survived that long without throwing the towel in was all purely down to the acclimatisation work I'd endured over the winter period. I emerged from the lake to cheers from the film crew, a big relieved smile from Ali, and a congratulatory nod from Julie.

Milestone one was securely under my belt.

Until this point in the challenge the days had generally passed slowly and almost torturously. My constant attention to the weather, the temperature of the water, and the conditions of the Channel all ensured that I was crossing the days off the calendar at a rather slow rate. As a direct consequence of me planning these milestones so close together, that situation soon changed. After all, if there is one sure way of making time pass faster, it is to arrange to do something you're really not looking forward to doing.

The 10km swim at Eton Dorney came round far too quickly for my liking. It was a warm and sunny day when I collected Ali and we headed down the M40 towards the venue, and it was for this reason I neglected to take a coat, or indeed any form of warm clothing, with me. As we drove, the temperature soon dropped and the rain began to set in. It was what we call in Britain a drizzle, often referred to as 'that slow steady rain that gets you wet'. The sky was a slate grey, and the world seemed to lack any colour whatsoever. Ali must've seriously wondered what he was getting himself into. Primarily he was there in order to practice our feeding techniques, but as we paid closer attention to the detailed instructions provided about the event, we noticed that there were (of course) already dedicated feeding stations along the route. Consequently Ali's role morphed into one of pure moral support.

We had to park some distance away from the actual start line, and without a coat my clothes were soon soaking wet. I checked myself in at the registration area and headed towards the changing tent in order to get ready for the event.

The swim was primarily a series of three differing distant events, all of which were designed to be races. There was a choice of 750 metre, a 5km, and a 10km distances. For my part, this was purely an endurance distance event, and I had calculated on four hours open water swimming. Most of the competitors were triathletes clad in wetsuits. Only a few individuals were swimming without wetsuits, and all of these appeared to be doing the same 10km event I was doing. Despite this being a regular open water series event, the lady starting the race expressed her incredulity that anyone should choose to do this without the benefit of a wetsuit.

It was a truly miserable day. What could have turned out to be a very pleasant open water swim in the sunshine in late spring was instead a somewhat drab and dreary event. For my part all I wanted to do was start the event, get out, get dry, and head home. After a similar experience at Windermere, I had a sinking feeling that this outcome or expectation was all I could hope for each time.

The venue was the site of the London 2012 Olympic rowing events. As I looked at the site layout, I could see a wide, long, straight expanse of water stretching out before me like liquid runway. To the left-hand side of the main expanse was a narrower auxiliary channel, presumably used by the rowers for warming up, or practising, whilst the main channel was in use. Our swim would take us 1.25km up the main channel, across a short distance of around 30 meters, and then back down the auxiliary channel. We would complete this loop four times, comprising the overall 10km.

For health and safety reasons the swimmers were allowed to enter the water early prior to the start of the race via the gentle slope down towards the water's edge, as opposed to a mass sprint into the lake. I heard the race controller say that the temperature of the water was 16.5 degrees. These were heavenly words, especially as the temperature outside of the water, standing still, semi-naked in the drizzle, had now dropped to just 9 degrees.

I felt a strange, smug, almost childish sense of pride and

satisfaction when I saw some of the other swimmers shiver at the water temperature and heard them complain of the cold. To me the water was bordering on being warm. I floated around quite happy and content, looking forward to the start of the race.

I was no open water swimming connoisseur. I had little other experience other than Lake Windermere to compare Eton Dorney with. But when the whistle went to commence the start of the race, I put my face down and began to swim. The water was far from unpleasant. It had no particularly foul taste, and though it was far from clear, neither was it murky or thick with algae. The route we were to take around the lake was in an anticlockwise direction. I knew from swimming in the men's ponds at Hampstead Heath that this would result in me being unable to clearly ascertain whereabouts I was, or even to swim in a straight line. The result was, as at Windermere, I had to regularly look up ahead to avoid veering wildly off course.

To keep the numbers controllable and manageable, the non-wetsuit swimmers were set off a few minutes ahead of those wearing wetsuits. To my utter disbelief, and to provide further proof of just how slowly I did swim, I was overtaken by a triathlete in the first 10 minutes of commencing my swim. Tempting as this may have been to speed up, I resolved to keep plugging away at my regular rhythm and pace.

With nothing to judge distance or time against, the first 1.25km length of the lake seem to take forever. Even practising in a 90 metre pool provided little experience or preparation for such a long, straight line swim. This was of course, ideal Channel swim practice.

Eventually the first left turn arrived. A few strokes brought me to the reserve channel lying parallel to the main rowing strip, and I began the return leg of the first lap. Again, due to breathing to the right my visibility was reduced, and as a result I failed to notice the feeding station positioned on my left towards the beginning of the return leg. This was no major problem so early on in the swim, and when I realised my mistake, I made a mental note to stop when I passed the feeding point on the next lap.

The swim proceeded with little memorable event. I completed the first lap in 59 minutes, the second lap two minutes slower, and the subsequent laps slightly slower again. Though I was probably the last swimmer out of the water, I was nevertheless very happy completing the distance in four hours 12 minutes. Moreover, I was neither tired nor cold. I had not seen Ali during the entire event. There had been no need of his services, given the professionally organised feeding stations, and he had sensibly taken refuge out of the rain in the on-site cafe.

I can't honestly say I enjoyed nor disliked the Eton Dorney swim. It had purely been a matter of business: A 10km swim, successfully completed in open water in May. It was an important physical and mental accomplishment.

It would be logical to assume, and lovely to pretend, that every successive swim could successfully build on the back of the last, progressively moving forward and increasing the distance and the time I was in the water.

Unfortunately that was far from the case, and it would be untruthful to say that this actually happened. In reality, a successful and enjoyable swim one day was no guarantee of completing a target on the subsequent day. Shortly after the Eton Dorney swim I decided to attempt a three hour open water swim at the Tooting Bec Lido. In theory this should have been fully achievable, presenting no real difficulties. However, one hour into the swim I remembered the words repeated to me by Nuala Muir-Cochrane at Parliament Hill, namely that by some strange and unaccountable reason, the water temperature in the lido is nothing akin to the water temperature in the sea or in the lakes. On this occasion the cold seemed to seep into my body, steadily and gradually wearing away at my nerves and my concentration. Once I realised that my target of three hours was not achievable my resolve quickly crumbled and I found myself exiting the pool long before my assigned target. This was a bitterly disappointing psychological blow. I berated myself continually for the remains of the day, blogging a self-derogatory posting online, and determining that I would return to the pool later to complete a subsequent swim. When you are warm and comfortable, it is so much easier to convince yourself you will be able to stay in the water longer next time. But it is amazing how each failure can psychologically far outweigh those of any success, and in many ways I felt that my two successful milestones been very much negated by this recent setback.

Sometimes the cause of these failures only became apparent

a while later.

As May progressed, the passing of time seemed to be gathering pace, accelerating steadily. Before I knew it, and certainly before I felt comfortable about it, the time had almost arrived for my six hour qualifying swim at Windermere. In anticipation of not wishing to do the return drive back to Worcester immediately after the swim, Ali and I were preparing to spend the night at a campsite, sleeping in a tent. I had not used our large, family four-man tent for several years, so on the final day of May we decided it was prudent for Ali and I to practice erecting the tent in order to ensure it was still in a serviceable condition. Putting up a tent is hardly an arduous physical activity, but once we had finished I suddenly found myself collapsing to the floor, sitting plump on my backside and staring in disbelief at the fact that my legs had given way beneath me. As soon as I was able I drove Ali home and returned to go straight to bed, despite the fact that the sun was shining and it was a beautiful day outside. I had simply been over-training. Trying to achieve 40km swimming per week on top of a standard full working day was severely taking its toll on my body. I awoke the next morning aching down to the core. I had no strength and little mental resolve. The only realistic thing to do at this point was to reassess my training plan and begin to factor in more suitable and practical rest periods. This began with the immediate cessation of any physical activity prior to going to Windermere. Whilst on the one hand this would help my body recover, it was hard to reconcile that decision with the mental anguish of believing that I was wasting valuable training time. Besides which, my qualifying swim was only three days away. I actually had very little time in which to recuperate.

Less than one week after my physical collapse, and the day arrived to pitch myself against the official six hour open water swim time required of any solo Channel challenger. At 06:15 on 6th June, Ali and I once more jumped into my car and made the three hour journey north towards the lakes. Ali and I rarely have deep meaningful conversations when we're together, and the journey towards Windermere was no exception on this occasion. However, it quickly became apparent that Ali was worried about my physical condition. He had witnessed the last three hour swim in the lake, and was aware that I had been physically ill for the previous seven days. I was now required to double my previous achievement, and neither of us knew whether I was currently physically capable of doing such a thing.

Almost a full week laid up sick had resulted in well-rested muscles, but appreciating that my health was still not 100%, my plan was simply to take the swim as gently as the water temperature would allow. But this plan also relied on one crucial factor that up until this point had been against me for the entire training campaign: the weather!

As it turned out, my break had finally come. As we crested the rise overlooking Windermere on the A591, we were rewarded with a gorgeous view of the lake basking in the early morning sun. It was clear even from such a distance that there was barely a breath of wind to disturb the surface of the water, and I knew that for once I'd have the luxury of the sun warming my back as I swam.

We soon met up with Steph and Emma from the film crew, and then with Julie, the latter of whom would be ratifying my qualification swim. In all honesty, having the secretary of the CSA confirm I was qualified to undertake a Channel swim felt like some high prestige indeed. After all, no one was going to doubt the veracity of my claim with such an esteemed witness to the event.

It was necessary to make some minor alterations to our original plans for the day, courtesy of the film crew's willingness to allow us to use their hire boat (something Julie was thankful for, having sliced her finger open the previous night, and not really wanting to pilot her own boat single handed). I was in the water by 11:30.

The first hour was spent cruising round the small harbour bay as with the three hour swim, warming up my muscles and getting used to the water temperature. Despite Julie having assured me previously that the water would have warmed up appreciatively in a matter of weeks, I was still surprised just how comfortable the temperature felt within the bay area. The surface of the lake was calm, the sun was out, and everything was altogether very pleasant at this stage.

At the first feed stop I looked up to find Ali passing me some energy gel from the hire boat close by. Julie, experienced on the lake and qualified to pilot her own boat, was in charge of the vessel. James the cameraman was filming me closely whilst being overseen by Emma and Steph. The mechanics of the feed-stop itself was somewhat clunky (as most of them turned out to be), but Ali and I knew this trip would very much form a 'lesson's learned' exercise ready for other long practice swims. In all honesty, I'd been eating and drinking Lucozade for the entire three hour journey up, and felt as if I could have swum for six hours without any sustenance at all.

The real idea was to get used to feeding (and being passed food and drink) whilst actually in the water, all in preparation for the anticipated 16 hour Channel crossing.

Once fed, Julie drove the boat down the lake some three or so kilometres, with me following alongside.

Though this journey down the lake made for an easier swim than dodging in an out of moored boats and avoiding raised propeller blades, it did bring its own, entirely new experience: temperature variances! Whilst the sheltered bay had been fairly consistent in temperature, now I found myself swimming through huge swathes of bitterly cold water, before finally emerging again into a warmer area.

The cold patches were truly bone-numbing, and brought on an almost instant and deep-set shivering. Even with the acclimatisation training I'd done, I would not have been able to survive the total duration of this swim had the water had been so uniformly cold.

The strangest sensations though, came from the water which was warm for the top few centimetres, but was then bitterly cold underneath. Here, my arms would be warm whilst reaching forward, and then I'd have to plunge them into the unpleasant, numbing darkness for a few seconds, rotating constantly, warm/cold, warm/cold. I soon lost all track of time, and the second hour seemed to last an eternity. I honestly thought that everyone on board had become preoccupied in something else and had forgotten to feed me.

One thing that had never fully dawned on me during my preparations for this qualifier was the actual date of event. It was only on the journey up, whilst listening to celebrations in France via the radio, that I realised the irony of an ex-soldier qualifying to swim the Channel on the 70th anniversary of the D-Day landings. We were given regular reminders of the on-going celebrations courtesy of various military fly-bys, including a Lancaster Bomber and a Euro Fighter Typhoon which went roaring overhead. My own landing on a French beach still seemed like a long way off at the time - as did the end of my qualifier.

With 2.5 hours left to go, Julie dropped me off back at the

harbour. This was my most dreaded part - the final hours of swimming round and round the bay, again dodging the boats, and continually having to look up and check my position. I found this put strain on my back, unaccustomed as I really was to wild swimming. In a pool, of course, there's no requirement to keep checking ahead and confirming the direction you are swimming. Consequently, I found I could not 'switch off', and this made every remaining minute seriously drag. In the end, though I knew Julie would not be happy, I realised that the only way I could cope with the remaining time (mentally, not physically) would be to swim further along the harbour than I really should - and to do so a little further out from the shore.

Before doing this I came into the shore for what should have been my penultimate feed. Clambering across the rocks to get close enough to the beach to be passed the food was a real pain. But what was worse still was then swimming back out through the warm shallow water and into the cold depths once again. I shouted to the film crew, asking them to tell Ali I would skip my last feed. The next time I crossed those rocks would be to get out of the lake, not to feed.

Somewhat surprisingly I found that the last hour of the swim was in fact the easiest. A slight wind had picked up, and even at the outer reaches of the harbour the water temperature was consistent and comfortable, with no patches of cold, dark water to wear away at me. For the last 30 minutes I closely analysed my condition, asking myself how much longer I could swim for, if I really had to.
Bizarrely, my mind came up with two answers, even though only one was relevant:
1. I was fairly sure I could do the entire six hours again if I really needed to (and I would soon need to, and more - but feeling this way at this juncture was fantastic)
2. Steak and kidney pie.

Quite where the second answer came from I've no idea, but the thought of a warm, filling, pub meal did help, and in the end I did enjoy this treat when Ali and I joined Julie post-swim at the lakeside pub.

I emerged from the water after six hours feeling fresh, comfortable, and not too cold. Most importantly, however, I was pleased that even when not 100% fit, I had been able to endure a lengthy swim in the cold water, and to ultimately qualify for my actual attempt on the English Channel in August.

Ten Week Countdown

Before I felt I was actually ready for it, I found there was only ten weeks to go until the Channel swim itself. I remember blogging that it was happening the month after next, and like a student who suddenly realises they've left it too late to revise for their exams, I suddenly felt as if I'd not made the best use of every available day.

What was worse in many ways, however, was that I'd so far only raised £5,500 of the target £10,000, so more fundraising and awareness effort was also needed. Though I had by now secured the complete amount of required corporate sponsorship due to generous donations by Dovetail, Hallmark Hulme and other local sponsors, I took it upon myself to increase my blogs and communications pleading for financial support. To further raise the profile of the swim locally within Worcester, we began to arrange for additional press interviews, and Esta even arranged for some polo shirts to be printed bearing the title 'Swimming for Harry' on the front, and the URL to my web site on the back. We had them made for various members of the family, and everyone seemed to take great pride in wearing them.

It would be nice to say that after so much effort during the previous 11 month build-up, and being so close now to the swim date itself, that everything went according to plan from this point onwards and that I had no further failures. Unfortunately, that was far from the case. Though the water temperature had now increased to the point that swimming outdoors was no longer painful and unpleasant, this one misery was being swiftly replaced by another more troublesome problem.

On 16th June I made a record of another disappointing training session. Whilst on my way to New Jersey for work, I had planned to stop and complete a four hour (10km) swim at Tooting Bec. In the end, however, I stopped after just an hour and a half (3.75km). Though I could have tried an avenue of denial, attempting to attribute this failure to a host of reasons, in reality, each was to be unhesitatingly dismissed:
1. The cold - except I was not cold. I can hardly claim to have been warm, but neither was I driven out of the water by the temperature, as in the past

2. The weather was not good - no, it wasn't. It was cloudy, cold and windy, and it looked like it was going to rain heavily. But then I'd only been fortunate enough have had one sunny swim up until this point (Windermere), so I could not blame the weather
3. I was tired - nope, not in the slightest
4. I didn't have time - well I did. In fact, by finishing early it meant I had to hang around in the departure lounge at Heathrow for hours.
 If anything, getting out of the pool when I did caused me more of a problem.

So what was it? There is only one answer I could give, in all honesty:

I was bored.

Having successfully completed three, four and six hour swims, another four hour swim should have been be easy. But that is simply looking at it from a subjective point of view, trying to apply a form of mathematical logic that simply does not stick.

For me, these pool training sessions seemed to be getting harder as they increase in duration. Swimming is not like going for a run or cycle and being able to admire the scenery. It was also not as if I was swimming from one location to another either. The training consisted of endless laps of a pool, and was akin to training for a marathon on a treadmill. Facing a wall. With no music or TV.
 Also, I had already conquered the challenge of swimming in a pool for six hours at a time, so now it seemed like nothing more than mental endurance. And sometimes (like one this particular day) I just do not feel able to take the mental torture.

During this particular swim, I found I had nothing to think about from 10 minutes in. From that point onwards I could not take my mind off putting one arm in front of the other. It was soul destroying. I kept thinking, 'I'm not cold, I'm not tired, I have plenty of time.... but I SO want to stop and get out!' So in the end, one hour and 20 minutes later, I did just that.

Worryingly, of course, I knew I still needed to keep on training, and I had to be able to get over this boredom blockage somehow. I'd already decided that not only was I not a lover of long distance swimming, I'd was prepared to go as far as to say I actually disliked it. It was not a good discovery for someone who had yet to face the Channel in nine weeks' time! It was clear that of all things, more open water and wild swimming experience was required.

Somewhere amongst all of this, however, I also needed to fit in some actual work, and this included overseas trips to Clients across Europe, and to the Dovetail US office in New Jersey.

Fortunately for me my US employee at the time, Neil (who is actually South African), knew of a family who lived immediately alongside a freshwater lake. He asked them if his crazy English boss would be able to swim up and down the lake for a few hours, and as much out of curiosity as out of their deep Christian good will, they readily agreed.

The lake was situated around a half hour drive from the Dovetail office. It was around five or six hundred meters long, unspoiled, surrounded by trees... and I had the entire thing to myself.

It was not without a sense of bemusement that the family watched me enter the water semi-naked, wearing nothing but skimpy swimmers, a hat, and a pair of goggles. They had clearly expected me to be clad in a wetsuit, and I was secretly happy to surprise them.

This lake was a world away from Windermere. A few small boats were moored alongside docks at the water's edge, but the entire main body of the lake was available to me, without the necessity of having to dodge vessels and to watch out for raised propeller blades. I quickly learnt that I was able to calculate my bearing from glancing right at the edge of the lake when I breathed, and this meant I only had to look up and ahead very occasionally to see how far from the end I still was.

It was picturesque, serene, relaxing, and as close to enjoyable as I could expect. Under different circumstances, I genuinely think I would have loved it. By this point in my training, however, all I wanted to do was finish the Channel attempt one way or another, and hang my goggles up in a gesture of swimming retirement.

Around mid-June, in the desperate battle to overcome the sheer monotony of swimming, I bought myself a bicycle. I was fully aware that cycling would bear little muscular relevance to swimming, but at least it would be an additional, alternate form of physical activity, and it would offer me some scenery whilst I cycled.

My first bike ride was just over 16 miles. My legs and backside ached, but physically I felt good. The ride had taken me just over an hour, so I quickly decided that my next venture out should be around double the distance, and that I should do it the following week, mixing the occasional cycle ride in with my normal swimming regime.

The 25- miler took me two hours. I was sweating and puffing when I arrived at the top of the big hill leading from Worcester city centre up to our neck of the woods, but all in all I was pleased that I had achieved such a distance on just my second outing, having done no serious cycling in my life prior to that point. And it was with that mentality foremost in my mind that I noticed the poster on display in David Lloyd's when I next went there to swim: 'Worcester Classic Bike Ride. Join us for a 50, 85 or 100 mile cycle in aid of Acorns.'

It was too tempting to refuse.

My calculations were thus: As I could comfortably swim for four hours whilst training for a potential 16 hour swim, then it stood to reason that having successfully complete 25 miles that I could therefore achieve a 100 mile bike ride. Before I had time to change my mind, I signed up. The event was within a matter of weeks, so it transpired that I would not have time for another trial ride before the 100-miler. The escalation in distance had been staggering. I'd had my bike less than a month, and I was due to compete in a very serious distance event. The fact that I could even consider such an undertaking was testament to my level of physical and mental fitness at that stage in my swim training.

With the event due to start early in the morning on a Saturday, I bizarrely had no choice but to cycle to the start. To take the car and deprive Esta of it for the entire day whilst out on my bike was simply not on. I left the house whilst everyone was still asleep, and slowly, gently, cycled the three miles to David Lloyd's.

The place was abuzz with excitement. The local radio were covering the event, an Acorns tent had been set up to promote their cause and offer any advice on their services, and a waggon was busily selling bacon rolls to cyclists and spectators alike. I knew no-one in the crowd, so my new bike and I, accompanied by a Garmin Sat-Nav device which I'd only used twice, waited quietly to one side. As I mentally prepared myself for a long, hard day, a man approached me.

'Are you the guy swimming the Channel?' He asked.

I confirmed that I was indeed the idiot he must have heard about, and we began chatting. The man's name was Tom, and he had seen me in the final stages of my 1000 press-up challenge some months previously when I was trying to raise the profile of my swim. He too was ex-army, and he had entered the cycle ride as a personal challenge, dragging along his business colleague, Darren. Like me, both were also competing in the longest of the three challenges, namely the 100 mile event.

Naively thinking we'd each now have some company during the upcoming eight or so hours, we lined up together at the back of the pack, awaiting the horn which would announce the beginning of the race. For my part, my only real aim was to complete the distance in one piece. I had no interest in any particular finish time, as no matter how long it took me it would still be a personal best. 100 miles was, after all, four times further than I'd ever cycled in my life.

No sooner had we set off than Tom disappeared into the distance. I had no intention of even attempting to keep up, so I happily chatted to Darren for a few minutes. Darren, however, had clearly been expecting me to be much faster on my bike than I actually was, so after a short time he told me he wanted to catch up with Tom. Within the first few miles I was already on my own at the back of the pack.

It was actually a beautiful day to be outside, so I stuck to a pace that I anticipated I could endure, ensuring I was not too out of breath as the miles slowly disappeared beneath my wheels. Though the route was fairly clearly marked as we rode, I'd downloaded the entire route map onto my Garmin as an extra precaution. This had the huge drawback of enabling the tiny device to calculate my anticipate completion time, and after more than an hour of cycling, mostly alone, the Sat-Nav was telling me I still had over six hours of peddling to reach the finish line.

Despite the added benefit of some beautiful countryside scenery, as with the swimming, time dragged.

At around the 25 mile point, we hit the first rest stop. Coincidentally, I caught up with Tom at this point, and we chatted for a few minutes as we both took on board some much needed liquid and fuel. The event organisers had done a fantastic job of ensuring that the riders would not go wanting for anything, and bananas, pasta, energy gels and sweets were all in plentiful supply. Tom told me that his business partner had already sped far ahead, so

I held out little hope of seeing Darren again that day. Before I had recovered enough to continue, Tom was ready to set off. Once again, I was alone.

The film crew had equipped me with a Go-Pro camera, wanting me to record a regular diary as the actual swim approached. I'd fitted the tiny camera, enclosed in its waterproof case, to the crossbar of the bike, facing me. Though I saw little point in capturing eight or so hours of me grimacing in pain and exhaustion, I did switch the recording on at various times. I also detached the device occasionally to record a snippet of my thoughts. One such time was around the 30 mile point.

The location for my video shoot was utterly unassuming. The only thing that made me chose such a point was that it was now undoubtedly the furthest I'd ever cycled, and that it represented almost one third of the distance I'd be cycling that day.

On reflection, however, I would have been better off waiting just a few more miles before I chose to stop.

As I completed my video, a local resident approached me. He'd been happily cutting his grass in the sun, and was interested to know what I was doing. I explained the cycle event, and the bemused gentleman asked me why I'd then chosen to stop at the bottom of the upcoming large hill, and not at the top.

In all honesty, I'd had no idea there was even a hill ahead. 'Is it very big then?' I asked, not truly wanting to know the answer.

'I believe they call it a grade three?' He ventured, somewhat unsurely. For my part, that meant little either, but the fact that it had been given any grade and any number surely meant that it must be far from insignificant. I smiled at him nervously and set off again.

The hill began subtly, rapidly increased in incline, and went on forever. With its arrival went any hope of completing the cycle without ever having to gasp for breath.

It was around this point too that my back began to ache. Unused to leaning forward for hours on end, despite supporting my body weight on my handlebars, the muscles in my lower back began to scream at me. From this point on I had to regularly stop and straighten up. Each time I had to do so, it felt as though I could feel tendons snapping. I was on my own in the middle of nowhere, 70 miles from home, in pain, and the fun had long-since stopped.

After what seemed like hours of head-down peddling, and

just when I thought it would never end, I eventually reached the top of the hill. There were two route-signs at the top, one indicating the road to take for the 85 mile route, and one for the 100 miler. The strength of will required not to suddenly cut out 15 miles cannot be adequately expressed in words. It would have been the easiest thing in the world to turn right. There were no witnesses, no tracking system, and no-one would have ever known. Without giving myself time to consider it for more than a second, I turned left, continuing along the longer route. Moving on immediately meant I missed out on the luxury of any rest at the summit of the hill, but I simply did not trust myself with enduring the temptation of taking the short cut.

The track down from that huge grade three hill was no more than a path used for horses. I tucked my body into a small shape and enjoyed the feel of the wind in my face as my legs had a rest. The gradient increased, and so did my speed. The track was filled with lethal potholes, and risking a rapid glance at my Garmin I saw that I was moving at a pace of 42 miles per hour. If my wheels hit a hole at this speed, not only would by bike be wrecked, but I'd be lucky to escape without considerable injuries.

The hill ended abruptly in a T junction. I leaned the bike over as far as I dared, and took a right-hand turn at around 25 miles an hour. Though the path had levelled out now, I began to pump my legs again to ensure that I maintained my rapid pace for as long as possible. It was not until two miles later that I regretted this decision.

Along the ride thus far, there had been two incidents where the tac signs marking the route had been at odds with the map I'd downloaded onto my Garmin. Invariably, within a short distance, the two once again tallied, but until that time I'd had to accept that there was indeed a discrepancy between the downloaded route on my Garmin and the one being indicated by the signs.

At the T junction, where I'd sped right, my Garmin had again complained that I was off-course. On that occasion, I should have listened. After two miles of assuming I was actually heading in the right direction, I eventually conceded that I must have imagined a tac sign telling me to head right, and with no other choice I had to perform a U-turn and retrace my steps for two miles. In effect, I'd now unwittingly added an additional four miles onto the 100 mile course. And that was not taking into account the three miles I'd cycled to the start.

Depressed as I was with this unforced error, it actually resulted in a hidden benefit, for shortly after regaining the correct route I somehow managed to catch up with Tom. Neither of us could quite work out how this happened, given that I'd been off course for four miles, but from that point on, and for the remaining 60 or so miles, we kept each other company. Tom was faster on the level ground than I was, and I tended to overtake him on the hills, but this variance in speed, together with regular breaks to enable the other to catch up, meant that we were able to encourage each other over the remaining hours. By this stage, we were both despondent, tired, and wondering why we'd ever thought that this would be a fun way to spend a day.

When we reached the half-way point of the race we were both convinced we could now complete the distance. Neither of us were any longer in any doubt as to the scale of the challenge we'd taken. Tom was almost as new to cycling as I was, and for him too the fun-factor had long since stopped. Events that broke up the tedium and monotony were few and far between, and when they did occur we would retrospectively decide we would have been better off without them. The first of these was a rear-wheel puncture for Tom. Being as naive in long-distance cycling as we were inexperienced, neither of us had a repair kit. We looked at each other stupidly, wondering how two ex-soldiers could possibly have found themselves in a situation whereby they were utterly helpless in the face of such an obviously expected occurrence. And yet before we could even begin to make any decisions as to our plight, a group of fellow cyclists drew up. I don't think they were on our actual event, as there is no way these guys could have been behind Tom and I otherwise. Regardless of this, they saw our situation and within seconds they were stripping Tom's back wheel off and replacing the inner-tube with one of the many spares they were carrying. In this instance, the Samaritans rode bikes. Without their assistance we would have had to ride one bike and carry the other to the next checkpoint somehow.

The second noteworthy point was when we somehow managed to catch up with another group of riders. One of their members had a puncture, so I pulled over to see if they were ok. Not appreciating that Tom had cycle shoes with cleats in them, I stopped in front of him without allowing him time to unclip his feet. The result was that he sprawled into the road in front of car. The vehicle narrowly missed his head as it sped past him. Having survived tours of the Gulf, Tom was nearly killed instead by a freak accident (through my stupidity) on a country road in England.

From our euphoria at half-way, my energy, enthusiasm and mental attitude took a nose-dive at around 70 miles. Whilst this distance represented a huge percentage of the overall mileage, I could not help but focus on the fact that I still had another 30 miles to go. And 30 miles was still a significant amount when considering my very limited cycling experience.

Tom and I had stopped talking through an unspoken mutual agreement, simply to preserve energy. We also had little to say that was at all positive, and we knew from past training that there is nothing more dangerous or depressing than to tell your fellow travellers that you are in pain. Everyone is in pain at times like this - the trick is to suffer in silence, thus mutely encouraging everyone else to keep quiet and to keep going.

With my back screaming at me in defiance, I pulled over to a small petrol station to buy some Red Bull and some paracetamol. How I'd ever managed to neglect bringing any of the many, many packets of paracetamol I had at home I would never know. The cycle was turning out to be an eye-opener in many ways. I could not afford to be this stupid or full of neglect on the swim.

The remaining miles ticked away slowly. All Tom and I could do was put our heads down and keep peddling, comforted only by the knowledge that the road, and hence the remaining distance, was slowly and surely passing beneath our wheels.

With 10 miles to go, we were back on familiar soil within the county of Worcestershire again. But now, when we really did not want or need it, a wind had picked up. And that wind was blowing directly into our faces.

My Garmin was telling me that I'd been cycling for almost seven hours. It was now also displaying the remaining miles in single figures, which was undoubtedly a blessing. Not that those miles were being ticked off any faster. If anything, with the strong wind, our speed had dropped.

Knowing that there was now no way we would fail to finish, we stopped waiting for each other, simply wanting our own individual efforts to be over. I finally arrived back at the Sixways stadium a few minutes ahead of Tom, having been riding for a total of seven hours, 42 minutes and 16 seconds (not including breaks). I was exhausted, I hated my bike passionately, but I was utterly elated at what I'd somehow achieved. When Tom arrived he gave me the same 'never again' look I must likewise have been wearing, but we thanked each other for the mutual support. It would be impossible to say whether we would have been able to complete the entire route without a companion - but that was academic at this point. We had finished, albeit right at the back of the pack, and that was all that mattered to us.

I had the choice of either cycling home another three miles, or of calling Esta and begging for a lift. It was no real choice, of course, so I waited with Tom and his family before gratefully piling my bike into our car and heading home for a rest. To this day, I've never been out on that bike again.

What was really called for, of course, was more open water swimming.

I could appreciate now the benefit felt by those who headed down to Dover week in, week out. In my army days, the best way to ensure you would actually get your lazy bones out of bed early in the morning to go for a long run, was to arrange with a colleague or two to run together. Tempting as it often was to switch off a noisy alarm and enjoy another hour or so of sleep, this was almost always overcome by the dread of letting a colleague down through being unreliable. So I could well imagine a similar camaraderie and sense of responsibility being felt by those individuals in Dover who had said goodbye one week, with promises that they'd be back the following weekend.

Instead, I arranged to take occasional days off work, scheduling trips down to Bournemouth with Ali. Two of these outings were noteworthy failures.

On one occasion, having planned a six hour sea swim, I notified the film crew of my intent. Emma and Steph wanted to record my various swimming experiences in order to compare and contrast such footage with that which they were capturing of other swimmers in Dover.

The drive from Worcester down the M5 is pleasant one, taking considerably less time than a journey up to Windermere. The weather was lovely on this particular occasion, though it was soon to become clear that trying to second-guess sea conditions by looking at the sky can often lead to disappointment.

I'd learnt from Julie's swims at Windermere not to waste any time procrastinating, but to get straight down to business. Once we'd parked up, I quickly got changed and got into the sea. Once more, I was grateful of my acclimatization training over the winter, as the temperature of the sea was no longer bothering me. At around the same point the previous year, when I'd come to this very beach during my eldest son's stag weekend, my body had rebelled at getting into the water, and my head had actually hurt when I'd submerged it. Not only was I now fitter, stronger, and healthier, but I was totally impervious to the effects of sea water at 14 or so degrees.

My jubilation did not last long.

Pool swimming is a luxury, by many comparisons, to sea swimming. Though occasionally annoying when you pass another swimmer and swallow a mouthful of water courtesy of their wake, by and large a pool is flat calm. One of the many reasons actual sea swimming practice is called for is that you need to gain experience in swimming with waves. Many swimmers find they suffer from sea sickness if the waves are coming from a particular angle, such as behind them. Turning your head to breathe, only to find a wall of salt water where air would normally be, takes hours of practice to get used to. The swimmer needs to be sufficiently fit that they can last until the next breath without having to stop swimming and lift their head up to gulp in water.

But what happens when this unpleasant phenomenon, that of effectively breathing in salt water, happens every other breath? That was the lesson I was going to learn on this particular trip. For whilst the day was warm, with only a fairly gentle breeze, if that wind has been blowing long enough and far enough across the sea, it results in a sizeable swell. From in the water, literally up to my neck in it, the waves were hiding me from Ali on the beach until I was lifted up onto a crest. I was wearing my safety buoy, but despite its high visibility orange, Ali was regularly losing sight of me.

For my part, I was getting more and more frustrated. The lack of forward progress due to the swell was inconsequential, as I was here for the sea swimming duration, not the distance (the two are often at odds with each other when you find yourself swimming against the tide). What was annoying me was the vast quantity of seawater I was inhaling and ingesting. Eventually, with a belly full of salt water, and angry at my constant lack of good fortune during my planned outdoor swimming sessions, I determined I was going to end my swim early. I had completed several laps of the Bournemouth to Boscombe pier swim, and I was due to meet Ali for another feed when I next reached Boscombe again. I also knew the film crew would be there, and that my words and actions would be captured by the cameras, but I simply I didn't care. All I wanted to do was stop, and to enjoy breathing without inhaling water.

That particular episode, of me leaving the sea early and complaining about the waves, was one that made it into the final production of the televised film.

Had I been at all superstitious about my many misfortunes with the weather, attributing such bad luck to portents from the Channel Gods, I would never have got as far as entering the water in Dover.

When next travelling down to Bournemouth, I determined that I would not, under any circumstances, be driven out of the sea by the weather on this occasion. I had endured far worse in the Atlantic when swimming off the coast of the Canaries, so this time I would man-up and stay in there, whatever the elements had to throw at me.

I was only partly right: It was not the weather that thwarted me this time.

It was a stunningly beautiful day. There was not a breath of wind to be felt, and though Ali and I kept our reservations to ourselves prior to seeing the sea itself, we were left speechless to notice that not a ripple was to be seen on the water. The sea looked as calm as a bath. There were no waves whatsoever, and locals and tourists alike were gazing at the glass-like surface of the water with incredulity. I had seen conditions like these once in the Red Sea, but never, ever in the UK. I grinned at Ali like a child. This was going to be like swimming in the Tooting Bec lido, except with the buoyancy of sea water.

Some people argue that our primeval fear of the sea stems not from a dread of drowning, but from a terror of what lurks within the water. I had no fear of sharks around the waters of the UK, and indeed I have been diving with sharks on a few occasions in various seas and oceans around the world. What made my blood run cold that particular day, and drove me out of the water very quickly indeed, was something altogether different.

Being so still, the water clarity had also increased, as sand and other sediment had slowly sunk to the sea bed beneath me. At first, when I glimpsed the undulating white object, my annoyance rose at the thought of some idiot throwing a plastic carrier bag into the ocean. The object vanished for a breath or two, but when it reappeared, so close that my hand almost brushed it, I must confess that I panicked slightly.

Right before me, as large as child's space hopper toy, was a live jellyfish. I watched in horrified fascination as it pulsed, swimming in its own fashion, a creature very much alive and thriving in its own element. It was at the same time beautiful and terrifying. I knew from many foreign trips that not all jellyfish can sting, but I had absolutely no idea how dangerous this monstrous thing in front of me might be. It was vast. And it was directly in my way.

I determined that on my return swim back to Boscombe pier, in an hour or so, I'd have to remember to watch out for this thing. I made my way carefully around it, and carried on swimming.

The next jellyfish surprised me about 10 meters further on. Then the next. And each one was larger than the previous one. I found myself surrounded by the things, and I was suddenly worried that I would not be able to get out of the sea. I really did not want to find out the hard way if they were harmful, but as I could only see them when I was almost on top of them, it was inevitable that I was soon going to reach forward and thrust my hand right into one. Or worse still, ram one with my face.

Fear drove me out of the water. I'd been in less than 20 minutes. Ali was incredulous when he saw me walking across the sand, until I managed to spot a jellyfish that had been washed up on the beach. Pointing it out to him, he swore.

'Do they sting?' He asked.
'No idea. And I don't intend to find out.'
'How many are there?'
'Lots. I was surrounded.'
Looking up the beach, we could see several jellyfish bodies

littering the sand. A man was cleaning the beach, picking them up with a shovel and placing them into plastic bags. We asked him if the animals were dangerous, but as it turned out he spoke no English. As the sun beat down, we made our way along to the lifesaving station. Two lifeguards seemed to be at odds with each other as to the harmlessness of the creatures when we enquired.

'One guy says he just swims over them,' we were told.

'Well I'm not swimming over them!' I said.

Ali and I walked up Bournemouth pier to look down into the water. It was a scene like something out of a horror movie. The sea was crowded with alien-looking lifeforms, most of which were an unbelievable size - over a metre across. The jellyfish were a variety of colours, from light blue to various shades of purple. They looked tranquil and strangely beautiful from the safety of the pier, but there was no way on earth I was venturing back into the sea whilst they were floating around in such huge numbers.

Despite the perfect weather, it was another day wasted.

Interspersed amongst these failures, as disappointing and disastrous as they seemed to me at the time, were many daily and weekly successes. My object in listing the less successful ventures is to highlight the brutal reality of a gruelling year-long regime. This regime, remember, was intended to take me from an occasional recreational swimmer to one of the limited number of individuals ever to successfully swim the English Channel. It would be tempting to expect a continuous upward trend, a progression week by week. My experience, graphically indicated on my spreadsheet, was more like a roller coaster. Some weeks my accumulated distance would rocket upwards, and other weeks it would plummet. In such cases, it was important to keep my spirit up. An overseas trip for work would play havoc with my training schedule. Exhaustion would not only stop all physical activity, but could actually knock me backwards. My primary concern at such times was to be able to identify an overall upward trend, not dictated week by week, but over a longer term. And, of course, I had to bear in mind that the real goal was the financial input to Acorns.

As long as that amount continued to increase, everything else was secondary.

Final Preparations

In the army there are various voluntary courses that can be undertaken, such as Special Forces training. These courses invariably involve a phase generically known as 'beat up', where week by week the candidate is put through ever-progressive physical tasks. In my final weeks of training for the Channel, I too devised my own beat up. Bear in mind, that though I had hired Dr. Julie Bradshaw to act in an advisory capacity, offering expertise guidance and experience, my personal background was very different to that of Julie's usual clients. And whilst I was relatively new to swimming, I had years of experience of putting my mind and body through rigorous regimes. I was acting in the only way I really knew how.

Unfortunately, as became more apparent when I began to go running with civilians once I'd left the army, one very important factor that the military never really instill into their staff is the vital importance of giving your body sufficient time to rest and recover. For military staff, it's all about training your body to recover during whatever brief down-time if available, be that hours or minutes. But ultimately, this is not sustainable over long periods, and the body suffers. It's not without thought that the army generally retires staff after just 22 years' service. A typical soldier, having done a 'full' career in the army, will be receiving their first pension at the age of 40.

I was 46. I may not have done 22 years' service, but my 14 years had nevertheless taken its toll on my body. I'd had a seriously prolapsed disc that had resulted in me being unable to walk properly for six months, and every part of my body seemed to have taken its similar share of wear and tear.

Swimming an average of four hours a day most weeks, burning the amount of calories necessary to exercise and generally work normally, the weight had been dropping off me. I'd been around 86 kilograms when I started training (13.5 stone, or 190 pounds), but now I had lost over 4kg (8lb). This was despite me eating and drinking everything I seemed to be able to lay my hands on. I'd start the day with a pint of full fat milk and a mars bar, consumed whilst on my way to whatever swimming venue I was heading to that particular day. During the swim, it would be dark chocolate, Lucozade gel provided by GSK, and coconut water provided by Vita Coco. After the swim I'd be quaffing down protein powder mixed with another pint of full fat milk. And all of this was before I'd even started work.

I was not on an intentional weight-loss diet. And in reality, I could not actually afford to lose so much weight. Julie was telling me that I'd need some fat reserves for the swim, both to keep me warm and to help with buoyancy. And yet, week by week, my clothes were feeling looser, no matter what I consumed. I actually had very little body fat by this time, and this factor meant I generally had to work harder at staying afloat. And muscle sinks.

Though I could feel the physical change my body was going through, I could not see the difference in the same way others could. I contacted Simon Fall-Taylor from FT Images, the photographer who had done the first promotional shots, and asked if he would be interested in doing another set for comparison. He gladly agreed, and when I posted the images side by side there was a striking difference. Not only had I now grown my hair and a beard, but my shoulders looked noticeably more powerful, and overall I appeared far trimmer. A rigorous 10-month fitness program of early mornings and cold swims is not a regime I'd personally recommend to anyone wanting to lose weight, but it certainly worked for me at the time.

In the meantime, my beat up continued. I was not enjoying it, and even three days in I was making notes of how tired, weary and mentally drained I was. Even after a good night's sleep, I'd wake up to an early alarm and lay there for a moment contemplating the pending long, cold swim. My body would rebel at the first movement as I began to get out of bed. I blogged that I just wanted it all to end, for the entire thing to be over and done with. And yet that particular week, the first of six progressively harder physical weeks, was nothing compared to what I'd need to be coping with during the actual swim.

Secretly, without even telling Esta, I really just wanted to somehow run and hide from it all. One tiny part of me, hidden away, wondered if there was any way to call it all off legitimately. But I knew there was no cancelling it. You cannot run and hide from yourself. This self-arranged physical hell was one of my own choosing. I was not as young as when I was in the army, and at 46 I was feeling it more, deep inside, at the nervous-system level. I was tired, weary to the bone, and mentally exhausted.

Yet there were just eight weeks until the big swim.

And then the small question of 26 miles separating England from France. A task that was due to take me at around 16 hours to swim.

But paradoxically, somehow, the challenge still thrilled me. Whilst some days I felt far from prepared, this was not the norm. Usually, when I got out of the pool I just wanted to get on with it, to pit myself against this ultimate swimming challenge, and take my chances. It was a rare opportunity that I'd been given. I knew of no-one (aside from Julie and Nuala of course) who had ever even attempted this. From what I could tell, no-one in the Worcester area had taken on the challenge of the Channel before, and this factor, small as it was, buoyed me during my times of despondency. Family support, and the encouragement from friends and work colleagues was always there of course, but I think that they too had become desensitised due to the prolonged build up. It was this level of commitment required by a Channel swimmer that the film crew aimed to capture. Standing on the beach and setting off for the opposite shore is the tip of a very big iceberg.

Finally, there was just one more week to go. I had been ticking the days off regularly, and with the event being so close now, interest began to pick up again. One work colleague stated that I would no doubt be as equally elated and triumphant as relieved when it was all over. He hit the nail precisely on the head.

Throughout the duration of my training, but more so now that it was so imminent, I'd been asked a set of what I referred to as 'frequently asked questions'. Probably top of the list was, 'What do you think about whilst you're swimming?' This is one of the huge challenges. Any Channel pilot, along with any swimmer who has attempted it, will tell you that 50% or more of the swim is mental. The swimmer has to be in the right mental space. This comes from the hours and hours of practice they must have put in in order to succeed. The practice not only accustoms their body to the rigours of swimming, but also their mind to the hours of lonely monotony. If you can't swim in a pool for four hours without getting so bored you stop, don't waste £3,000 thinking you will survive 12 hours plus. That sort of achievement won't simply happen on its own.

Harry's Favourite Thing

For my part, I thought about everything. I'd planned speeches, I'd run through work scenarios, I'd recited poetry and I'd even thought about sex, because the truth is that you absolutely have to keep your brain from focussing on how long you have been swimming for, or how long you have left to go. Sure, in the back of my mind I still counted the lengths, and at times I'd catch myself thinking, 'Oh no, another 400 laps to go!' But then I'd begin to break things down into manageable chunks. I'd say, 'Yeah, but I'm almost at lap 30. So that's almost halfway to the hundred. And at 100, I stop for a brief rest and some chocolate.' Because 600 lengths is just too much to try and hold in your head with any positivity.

And at times I had meditated. With a constant rhythm of breathing and the soothing sounds of the bubbles and the water, this was often a great way to switch off. Sometimes it was somehow elusive, which could be frustrating, but when it could be achieved the time, and the laps, would melt away.

Some colleagues seemed to miss the point of why I was doing all of this. I'd often find myself being asked if I was yet preparing for my next challenge. What was next on the cards, once I'd achieved the swim? I had to admit that not having to train for several hours per day would at first leave a big gap in my routine, but I was seriously looking forward to just lazing around and enjoying some spare time with Esta and the kids. And when I did go to the gym, it would be at a much reduced level of effort. I was doing this purely for Harry and Acorns.

And then suddenly, one morning I found myself leaving Tooting Bec lido with the surreal realisation that my very last training session was now behind me. There would only be one more long swim, and that would be the big one. As I walked away from the pool I reflected on 14 months of hard work, planning and organising that was now behind me. 750 kilometres had been notched up during the 307 hours of swimming I'd recorded on my spreadsheet. Interspersed with this had been multiple circuit sessions, long runs where I'd burned off 1,100 calories in an hour, and a 100 mile bike ride. And abruptly there was nothing more I could do. I was either ready, or I was not, and only the final test would reveal the truth. Nevertheless, it felt strange leaving the lido, knowing that in all probability I would never be back. I had no excuse now for late starts at work, and getting to and from either

Parliament Hills or Tooting Bec was a real pain. I was not going to miss those early morning journeys.

On Wednesday 13th August I phoned Kevin Sherman, pilot of Connemara, to confirm everything was still on, and to see if he had any last minute advice. I'd not spoken to him prior to this point, as communication had been via email. Luckily, he was not out supporting a swimmer when I called, so he had plenty of time to go over a few things with me.

Most of the approved Channel swim pilots arrange their swimmers in 'slots', allocating them position one on the actual day of their swim. Should they not be able to swim that day, due to conditions or any other reasons, they can be allocated a lower slot on another day. These pilots often find themselves returning from one swim support and immediately setting out on the next in order to satisfy the demand of their customers. At most they can expect a few hours' sleep on the boat per night during the Channel swimming season.

Kevin explained that he did not work like this. Being semi-retired, he can happily manage by taking on just eight to 10 swimmers per season. Not only does this reduce his own workload and leave him time for a life, but it means that his swimmers are not allocated slots. Nor is a swimmer keeping his fingers crossed for the weather to be agreeable on a single allocated day, as Kevin allows a window of three or four days per swimmer. This was all fantastic news to hear, as arguably my biggest fear after all this time was that the weather would be unsuitable on my allocated day, and I would not be able to even begin a Channel attempt. Kevin could sympathise with this when I told him, and he reassured me that even if my window passed, assuming I was still in the vicinity, I could always go after the next swimmer, if they completed their crossing within their own window. In short, every opportunity to make an attempt would be made available to me. He even asked when I would be down in Folkestone, on the off-chance that we could go early.

Kevin next enquired about my swimming background and experience, so I told him why I was doing the swim, and of course mentioned Julie to him. Knowing the tides as well as he does, Kevin explained that we'd be going as close to the neap tide as the weather would allow. This of course meant that the difference between high

Harry's Favourite Thing

and low tides would be at the lowest point, due to the moon being either half-waned or half-waxed. He told me how only the most experienced Channel swimmers would ever ask to swim a spring tide. Such tides resulted in a far greater volume of water pouring into and out of the Channel. And with greater volume came greater speed.

Next came some personal advice gained through successfully guiding many swimmers across to France. 'Swim hard for the first four hours. We need to get to a certain point within that time to prevent you being pushed back when the tide turns. After that, you can relax a bit. But I need you to be ready to have another two hours of hard swimming towards the end when we round a certain buoy. These two efforts could be the difference between an early landing and a potential extra four hours in the water. Understand?'

I did, but it worried me. I only swim at one speed. I can put in extra effort, but my speed barely increases by any noticeable amount. All I could do was see what happened.

'Now I also want you to keep feeding time RIGHT DOWN,' Kevin continued. 'Every second you stop, you are drifting back over water you have just swum through. The tide pushes you towards England and away from France, so it's really not doing you any favours when you hang around. And don't bother with idle chit chat, procrastinating. Eat, and swim.' He seemed to have a similar no-nonsense attitude to Julie.

The pilot next asked how long I anticipated the crossing to take me. I told him between 14 and 16 hours. He grunted, probably unimpressed with my slow swimming.

'From the boat, and from my experience, I'll know how well you are doing, and roughly how long it'll take you to land. On a first swim, you'll have no idea. Looking back is pointless, as you can see the cliffs from over halfway across the Channel. The best indication for you is how often I have to engage the motor on the boat. If you hear it kicking in regularly, that's good.' He left the second part of that statement unspoken.

'I'd probably get into trouble telling you all of this. I know the governing bodies certainly don't like the pilots giving you advice during the swim,' he said. This seemed ridiculous to me. I was paying a pilot for his experience after all, and that knowledge could be vital in keeping me alive. Why would he not be able to offer pearls of wisdom?

'Shall we meet when I get down to Folkestone in a couple of days then? If you go over some of this with my support guy, Ali, he might remember it better than me, and can relay it to me when I'm in the water.'

That arranged, Kevin asked me if I had any questions.

'I have a film crew coming along to produce a documentary. You mind if they come on the boat?'

'You're not just hiring me, you're hiring the boat. There are five spaces. As long as they're legal, they have passports, and they don't get in my way, you can bring who you like.'

Folkestone

I kept a diary for the days immediately prior to the swim, as I knew my memory would muddle the actual sequence of events later on otherwise. My mind was in turmoil and my nerves were on edge. The culmination of a serious amount of effort was imminent, yet I knew there could still be delays and setbacks. Like every other swimmer, I was now at the mercy of the micro-climate surrounding the Dover area. At this point in the proceedings, with no more training to be done, it was important to try and relax, and to be as methodical and focussed as possible.

It may be tempting to imagine that a swimmer simply turns up in the Folkestone or Dover area and gets straight into the water and on with their swim. My personal experience was anything but that.

Saturday 16th August 2014:

I woke up early, my heart leaping at the first thought of heading down to Folkestone and to actually lay eyes on the challenge that I was about to undertake. I rose to finish packing the swim equipment, along with the supplies and other articles that Esta and the boys would need for a week down at the coast in the apartment we had rented. I was also anticipating the arrival of the film crew, who were coming along to capture the moments immediately prior to our departure.

Ali and I had spent the previous evening going through every conceivable item we would need for the swim itself. It was like planning for an expedition, trying to second-guess what eventualities we might have to cater for, when in fact neither of us had any practical experience on which to base our logic. Julie had told me that the feeding part of the swim was very personal, so though she'd told me of her own preferences, this was purely to be used as a starting point - she did not expect me to emulate her. As such, we decided to pretty much stick to the regime I'd been using thus far, drinking the Vita Coco and Lucozade gel, and snacking on dark chocolate and jelly babies. The only addition to this was the provision of some spicy soup, courtesy of the chef at the Bird In Hand next to where Ali lived. This soup would not only warm me whilst I was in the water, but would also assist with taking away the taste of the ever-present sea water.

There were still everyday practical matters to attend to, of course. I'd bought some chickens several months back, wonderful animals which made great family pets - not to mention the fresh eggs they provided. But what with it now being late summer, the chickens did not go home to roost until dusk, which was around 10 O'clock. This was too late to expect my mum to come and secure them away for the night, so instead I'd arranged for them to be boarded at Newland Poultry, the farm from which I had originally purchased them. Lewis and I rounded the chickens up, and the camera guy for the swim itself, Keith, jumped in the car with us as Emma and Steph followed in their car.

Sean, the owner of the poultry farm, was slightly perturbed to see us arrive with cameras, but when I told him about the documentary and the challenge I was undertaking for Acorns, he promptly waived the boarding fee as his part of the contribution. It was a kind gesture, as that fee would otherwise have come out of my increasingly-empty pocket.

When we arrived back home, Esta and Will were ready to go. It was 11:00, and we had to collect Ali before we could begin the four to five hour journey down to Folkestone.

Ali's family were waiting outside his house when we pulled up. Iona, the eldest, was smiling. Next to her stood Fraser, her younger brother. Fraser was born shortly after Harry died, and I've known both kids all of their lives. Fraser is generally a very quiet and serious young boy. The only words he spoke that morning were just as we were about to pull away.

'Don't drown,' he advised. I had to admit, drowning had never been in the plan.

Getting to Folkestone from Worcester is a huge pain, to put it mildly. We stopped twice on the journey so that everyone could get some air and stretch their legs. The M25, as is often the case, was effectively a car park for some time, and Esta took over driving (or sitting in the driving seat and waiting for the traffic to move) whilst I took a nap. Sleep is something you can't stock up on, but it is certainly too easy to get a lack of it. I needed to be as fresh as possible for whenever Kevin gave the green light to get into the water. We had already been informed by him that the following day,

Sunday, was out of the question for commencing the swim, as the forecast was predicting force four to five winds. Nevertheless, I'd been advised by both Kevin and Julie that such things could change very quickly.

We arrived at the apartment just after 16:00. Whilst the boys began exploring the new accommodation and Esta unpacked, Ali & I went to collect Connagh, the second eldest of my sons. On the way to the train station we drove past the small harbour, and I joked to Ali that we may see our boat. Lo and behold, there was Connemara, floating safely at the end of a line of boats in the calm, sheltered waters. It was strange to think that this vessel would be spending hours alongside me as I swam, and that it would be occupied by Ali, Connagh and the film crew during my crossing. On the way back, there would be an additional, tired and cold occupant. Hopefully, that additional passenger would be smiling.

Folkestone is a small but pleasant harbour town. The beach at the bottom of the hill from the apartment was large and sandy, though we hadn't appreciated at first that come high tide there would be no sand left to be seen. After hours in the car, Lewis and Will needed some exercise, so with Connagh now in tow, we set off exploring the sea front on foot. From the shore itself we got our first real indication of what the weather was like out to sea. The wind was on-shore, blowing directly at us, and the waves had large, white crests. Aside from some adventurous sailing, or generally playing in the waves, it was evident that no real distance swimming could be achieved in such conditions.

Being somewhat naive at the time, I was surprised that I could see the French coast so clearly from Folkestone. I had imagined no more that the suggestive smudge of land, but I could see cliffs, a beach and even vehicles moving. I pointed out the distant land to Will, telling him that our trip here was all because daddy would be swimming over there, to France.

'Doesn't look far,' he said with an uninterested shrug. I wondered how many people had said that exact same thing.

Sunday 17th:
Much to my annoyance, I slept badly that first night. It was a combination of a new bed and of being so close to the sea, yet so far from the commencement of the crossing. My habit of regularly

checking the weather had naturally increased now that my situation was so directly affected by it. The forecast was grim. Force four to five winds were being predicted for the entire week. It seemed so unfair. I'd always somehow thought this was meant to happen and that I would at least get a shot at giving the Channel my best. But suddenly, events seemed to be conspiring against me. The weather had been my constant enemy these past 14 months, and it appeared that things were not about to change now.

I called Emma from the film crew. From their interaction with the Channel swim communities over the months, the crew had made many useful contacts. Emma informed me that one pilot predicted Tuesday was looking favourable for a crossing. I promptly sent an SMS to Kevin, asking him what time we could meet up that day. I was hoping that there would be an opportunity to get together sometime in the morning, but Kevin's reply said 16:00. This was all proving to be a lesson in patience.

My main problem was that I'm generally used to being highly proactive. I wouldn't say I'm a complete control freak, but I do like to have influence over events that affect me. Suddenly, I was powerless. Worse, there was no garden that needed tending and no work to do. Going for a run was unadvisable, and anything more than a recreational swim was madness. Granted, I had been gifted a day with the kids and family, yet my mind was distracted by the possibility of an imminent swim to France. We played on the beach in the huge sandy bay, occupied only by us, a few other families, and swooping, crying gulls. The calls from the birds reminded me of my teenage years in Gurnard on the Isle of Wight. Combined with the smell of the sea, it was a powerful reminder of my time there as a child, over 30 years previously.

There was a Thunder Cat boat race on that day, with speedboats racing rapidly and noisily around a buoy-marked circuit. Despite the strong, cold wind, I played at the sea edge with the boys, me dipping into the water regularly to keep cold and acclimatised. I soon got chatting to a safety guy who turned out to be ex-army, telling him about my pending Channel swim. Looking out to sea, with France no longer visible due to squalls just off the coast, the entire venture still seemed surreal.

Ali and Connagh had left us alone for the morning whilst they went exploring the neighbourhood. With me not drinking, and

Harry's Favourite Thing

them being on holiday, it also meant they could go to the pub without having to watch me drink Coke. I'd not been particularly missing the alcohol until then, but it was tempting to think of sitting outside a pub enjoying a pint in the sun. I promised them I'd join them for a drink the minute we got back from the swim.

Later that day when we'd all met up again we wandered around somewhat aimlessly, killing time whilst waiting to meet Kevin. At a café by the harbour, whilst the kids ate ice creams and Esta chatted to Connagh about what he'd been up to that day, I sat there studying the boats that bobbed gently in the shelter, safe from the unpredicted force seven gale that had just passed. The wind was now dropping slightly, and the sun was coming out. As I looked, I saw a man walking along the promenade with his wife. I watched him for a while, and I somehow knew instinctively that it was Kevin. I pointed him out to Connagh, but by the time he looked the couple had disappeared around a corner.

Time dragged and my patience was wearing thin. There was a pebble beach near the harbour, and we went there to let Will throw stones at the waves. One look at the water was enough to show that the weather was worse than the previous day. The tide had now pushed the sea right in, covering all the sand we'd been playing on round the corner earlier in the day. With the tide currently running against the wind, the water was choppy, rough and angry. Worse, there was no reason to believe it would change any time soon.

At 17:30 we met up with Ali, all of us now hanging round to meet Kevin Sherman, the man who would be responsible for guiding me safely across to France. The film crew were on their way, planning to arrive in time to witness us rendezvous with our pilot, but suddenly I saw the man and his wife I'd seen earlier. My conviction that this was Kevin was stronger than before, so when I told Ali of my thoughts he called across to the passing couple. The man stopped and turned round, clearly surprised to be addressed by people he'd never met.

Kevin was with his wife, Paula, and though we weren't scheduled to meet for another 20 minutes or so, they took a seat with us anyway, and we all started chatting. By the time Emma, Stephen and Keith arrived, we'd all-but finished covering everything of importance. We were miked up, and went over some of the most vital points again. Most importantly, Kevin thought we were looking good to attempt a crossing on Tuesday or Wednesday. We agreed I'd call him the following day, Monday, at 18:00 for an update.

In the meantime, the waiting continued.

Monday 18th:
Possibly the frustration and anticipation was wearing me down, but whatever the reason, I finally got a good night's sleep. Monday started off with a forecast for force five winds most of the day. The following day was predicted to be the same, at least for the morning. I was guessing that when I called Kevin at 18:00 he would say that late Tuesday was possible, but that Wednesday was more realistic. Now, more than ever, I had to be patient. I wanted to ensure that I made my attempt not just at the *first* opportunity, but at the *best* opportunity.

The film crew wanted to capture some of our routine during this waiting period, and were due to arrive at 09:00. Unusually Will, who is normally awake by 06:00, was still asleep at 08:10. Esta wanted to be ready to face the cameras, but she similarly hated to waste the chance of a lie in. She was supposed to be on holiday, after all.

With the swim so close now, the local radio had been keeping listeners updated with events. BBC Hereford and Worcester called me for an update that morning. Their offer to cover the story and highlight my fundraising for Acorns was certainly appreciated, so it was frustrating not to have any positive news of a commencement date that I could provide them. I was also contacted by Free Radio, asking if I could give an interview. When I stressed that I needed to mention my JustGiving link in order for listeners to pledge funds they refused, saying there would not be time within the snippet. I subsequently declined the interview. If it could not be used to increase donations to Acorns, it was of no interest to me at this late stage.

Despite the continual uncertainty, we actually had a fun morning playing with the boys in the sand whilst the film crew recorded us. On the shore, the weather was nice, and the sea was noticeably calmer... but that in itself was actually deceiving, as it was still possible to see white horses out to sea. I'd been warned of many swimmers becoming angry that their pilots would not let them commence a crossing, ignorant of the fact that just a mile or two off the coast, the sea was utterly unswimmable.

Time seemed to slow down as 18:00 approached. I found myself continually checking my watch, anxious to phone Kevin and hear his recommendation. When the film crew arrived to capture the call, we'd been sheltering in a pub from a sudden shower. Connagh and I stepped outside into the quiet of the street in order to make the call. I'd been looking at the forecast closely all day, and had been hoping Kevin would concur with my own thoughts.

He did.

Tuesday was predicted to still be blustery, with a force four wind. This was due to die towards the end of the day, dropping to a force three on Wednesday... which was also forecast to be a sunny day. If I was to have any window of opportunity at all, it was to be on then!

We agreed to rendezvous at 05:15 at the harbour on Wednesday.

This news was a slight disappointment to Emma. She was due to fly to Spain to take care of her kids, so this extra one day delay meant that having followed my progress closely for months, she would not be able to join us on the boat for the attempt itself. Connagh also had a deadline of setting off for home on Thursday, but though this would be cutting it fine, he was hopeful he would still be able to make it.

From my own perspective, it naturally felt fantastic to finally have a firm date and time. The pressure of uncertainty had been lifted from me. The tide would actually be more favourable for a crossing on Wednesday too, as it would be further into the neap tide frame. All that remained for me was to update my blog, and to let everyone know of the appointed schedule.

One lighthearted point during all this waiting was when Connagh suddenly asked me how I would go about relieving myself if I had to go during the swim. Of course, not being able to touch the boat at all means that swimmers must do this in the water, should nature call. I instinctively hit on an opportunity to wind him up, so told him straight-faced that we could not be seen to pollute the sea with untreated sewerage. If I had to go, he would have to fish the result out with a net. Ali and I did actually have a net. It was for passing me food without the need to throw it. Julie had recounted situations where the swimmer had be smashed in the face or on the head by well-meaning support staff throwing them supplies. It made far more sense to gently pass food and drink in a net.

But Connagh now thought the net had a much different practical purpose. He was horrified at my suggestion, of course.

'I'm not doing it. I didn't realise I'd have to.... do THAT!'

'Well I can't exactly just throw it onto the boat, can I?' I responded. 'And Ali is responsible for sorting out the food. You don't have to keep the net afterwards. We'll throw it away when we get back.'

He was absolutely fuming. How we all kept straight faces, I'll never know.

We never did tell him it was a wind up.

Tuesday 19th:

I spent a large portion of the day glued to the local weather on TV. It looked as if there would be a narrow window within which swims could take place, starting on Wednesday morning and stretching into Thursday. After that, the wind was due to pick up again. Friday was forecast for heavy rain. It was hardly glorious weather, but at least the predicted opportunity had not completely vanished. For a while, I had wondered if the entire venture would ultimately come to nothing, with me getting no closer to France than the coast of Folkestone. Now, as least it appeared that I would get a slim chance to make an attempt at the crossing.

I had a final pre-swim interview with BBC Hereford and Worcester, promising them I'd be in touch again with news of the swim as soon as possible.

And with nothing else to do, and whilst hoping with all our hearts that the weather predictions were right, we sat down to await the coming day.

The Swim

The pounding and booming of the base gradually broke through my sleep. I came awake groggily, unsure at first where I was, or why it was so dark. Esta was awake next to me, and I could see she was worried.

'How long has that been going on?' I asked.

'Since straight after you went to sleep. I'm surprised you managed to sleep at all.'

The people in the flat upstairs were having a party. It was well past midnight, I had to be up and getting ready in less than four hours, and all I wanted to do was get to sleep. The thumping of the music was shaking the walls, and the beat was making sleep impossible. I bore it for another five minutes before leaping out of bed and putting on a pair of shorts. This was what Esta had been worried about.

'Please ask them nicely. Don't hit anyone. I'll be here alone with the kids when you're swimming don't forget.'

I ran up the stairs and knocked on the door. Loudly.

There was no answer.

After the third unsuccessful attempt, I ran to the front door, three floors down, and kept ringing the bell until I got a reply. The man who answered came down to our floor, stoned out of his brains. Esta arrived on the scene just as I got there. Her presence possibly prevented a nasty altercation and the music was quickly turned down, but by now I was wide awake and angry. This was not the restful pre-swim night I'd had in mind.

The remaining few hours of the night crawled by. I slept, if at all, fitfully. When my alarm finally went off at 04:00, the very last thing I wanted to do was swim the Channel. My mindset could not have been worse, and I had just over an hour to change from a tired and irritable human being into a calm and focussed athlete about to take on the biggest challenge of his life.

I'd planned on a big breakfast, but I simply could not face anything heavy. I had that gritty, grimy feeling that comes with a poor night's sleep, not to mention the huge anticipation of what was to come. I knew I needed as much fuel as I could take on board, but yet I didn't feel like eating a thing. I grazed on breakfast biscuits and almonds, constantly sipping Lucozade. Ali and Connagh quietly and calmly went about re-checking their own kit. They left me to my own ruminations. Neither had slept particularly well either, and they were already worried what effect the interrupted night might have on my performance. They could tell I was grumpy and unsociable.

At some point during my preparations and research, I'd read an article by Lewis Pugh. Lewis is famous for his swimming exploits, and his advice on a Channel attempt was to ensure you left all doubts on the beach in England. Taking him at his very word, I had a stone engraved with the word 'doubts', in much the same way as we'd engraved Harry's stone. This item was in fact one of the 'spare' ones I'd brought back from Egypt when I went there with Lewis, as we'd been told that some of them shattered when they were being carved. I intended to take this particular stone with me and place it amongst the many other stones on the beach before I set off on my swim. Before I left the apartment, along with my goggles, swimmers, hat and lanolin, I ensured I had this stone with me. Ali and Connagh were in charge of food, passports, and the balance of the cash for Kevin.

Lewis crept out of bed just before 05:00 to wish me luck. I kissed Esta goodbye, and we all sneaked out of the flat silently.

It was cold, dark and quiet outside in the street. A few gulls cried as the sun began to peak above the horizon to our left, and a chilly breeze blew gently. We made our way silently to the harbour, not seeing another soul along the way. The water was slowly creeping across the mud of the dock as the tide came in, and Connemara was on the verge of floating. I felt a nervous anticipation as I watched the tide rise, and I had to consciously avoid the temptation to pace up and down. It was going to be a long day, and nervous pacing would not help me.

Fully aware that there was still a chilly bite to the early morning wind, I removed my sweatshirt so that I stood in just jog bottoms and a tee shirt. It was cold without the extra layer, but I wanted to ensure that when I first entered the water there was no shock of the cold hitting my system. If the swim started in that way, it could only get worse. I just hoped my plan worked, and that I wasn't needlessly wasting energy trying to keep warm.

Kevin and Paula arrived, and with a curt nod and a brief 'good morning', they quietly and efficiently slipped into work mode, taking a dingy across the rising water from the dock steps to Connemara. We watched as Kevin climbed aboard and went through his obviously familiar routine of ensuring the boat was ready for its cross-Channel voyage. The starting of the engine broke the silence of the morning as a puff of diesel fumes erupted from the exhaust. Connemara was underway.

Emma, Steph and Keith arrived and quickly set about miking us up. There was little chat to record. I remained silent, concentrating on what was to come, beginning to focus on a hard day's work. I asked Connagh if he could be responsible for making notes, such as the timings of various events.

At 05:35 we climbed down the stone steps towards the boat which was now waiting for us. Kevin proudly helped us all aboard his vessel. A third crew member had now arrived, and Kevin introduced us to Malcom. The CSA would normally have sent an additional independent observer, but in this instance they had decreed that Kevin's wife, Paula could perform that task. It saved a place on Connemara, which was already fairly full. As Malcom took control of the boat, easing us gently out of the dock and into the main harbour, Kevin briefed us all. Safety was paramount, as can be expected, and the swim would proceed only as long as every other safety consideration was met. This did not just extend to me as the swimmer, but also to the safety of everyone else aboard the vessel. We totalled nine souls in all, as Emma had managed to rearrange her plans such that she could be present to witness my actual attempt. She was due to head to Spain and her kids early the next day. Kevin was adamant that whatever else may happen, he would return to England with the same nine souls that he left her shores with.

'We have a journey of around 45 minutes to your start point,' Kevin continued. 'I'll let you know when we're around 10 minutes away, and at that point I need you to start getting ready: goggles, hat, grease etc. When we're there, I'll turn the boat broadside onto the shore. I want you to get into the water as quickly and safely as you can. Make your way to the shore, climb out and wait for the signal from Paula to start. Then you're on your way. Any questions?'

Wait until I say so; get in the water; swim to France. Seemed simple enough. I had no questions.

I'd planned, campaigned, trained and waited 14 months for this opportunity, and now it was here. It was real, despite feeling anything other than real. France was visible in the brightening morning sunlight, and the weather looked set for a gorgeous day. The Channel Gods were smiling on me. All I had to do was play my part: Just keep swimming. And swimming.

I can honestly say I have never been so focussed in my life. All thoughts of the previous night vanished into historic memory as the seriousness of my situation began to take a firm grip. I was about to do it. I was about to jump into the Channel and attempt to join the exulted ranks of the thousand or so individuals who had successfully made it to the other side. I was about to test myself against that same challenge that Captain Webb had undertaken so many years before.

Those 45 minutes to our start point flashed past. Before I knew it, Kevin gave us the 10 minute warning. Ali helped steady me as I stripped my tee shirt and jog bottoms off. One thing Ali and I had learned since Windermere was that applying lanolin was best done using a pair of disposable surgical gloves. If I did this myself, being careful not to coat my fingers at all when I removed the gloves, it saved me a lot of pain, and Ali a lot of embarrassment. I put on my gloves and plastered the viscous lanolin liberally under my arms, between my legs and across my right shoulder to allow for several thousand neck rotations as I turned to breath. I'd never had any chaffing in either of the latter two areas, but now was not the time to start. I put loads of the stuff on. It matted my beard and clogged up my armpits, but if all went according to plan, I'd never need the lanolin again anyway. I stripped the gloves off, turning them inside out, and handed them to Ali before putting in my ear plugs and slipping my CSA hat on.

Abruptly, Kevin cut the engine.

As Connemara began to drift into a broadside position to the shore, I focussed my sight on the English coast. I was utterly unaware of anything other than the task at hand. Connagh captured me in a photo which shows me in an almost stoic state of pure concentration. The film crew had ceased to exist to me. I checked I had my stone, slipping it into my swimmers so that I would not drop it, and I leapt over the side of the boat and into the green waters of the English Channel.

My immediate reaction was an overwhelming sense of relief: The water felt warm! My plan had worked! During the short trip to the start point I had gradually acclimatised to the cool breeze, and rather than being initiated to the water with any cold shock, I felt very pleasantly warm. All of this was also no doubt helped by the many hours of excruciating cold water acclimatisation I'd endured over the winter. Nuala had been right.

Now all that remained was for me to swim a marathon.

The English coast lay around 100 - 150 metres from the boat. It didn't take long to get there, and I climbed up the pebble beach to well beyond the high water mark before I retrieved my stone from my Speedos and gently set it down amongst millions of other stones. At this point I was both physically and mentally leaving my doubts on the English shore. What I was about to embark on, was in memory of Harry.

It was time to get on with the actual swim.

At 06:16, without further ado, I plunged into the sea again and began to make my way back towards Connemara. From this point on it was all about patience. I couldn't afford to dawdle, but neither could I rush things. I had a long and boring day ahead of me. All of my training had to come into play now, with my mental strength also being given a true test of character. I had never swum for longer than six hours, and had not swum further than 15 kilometres. I was now expecting to surpass both of those milestones by a several magnitudes, but I felt confident that I could achieve that.

I had deliberately left my watch at the flat and had instructed both Connagh and Ali not to mention how long I'd been in the water. All that was important to me was whether I was on the French beach or not - and I wouldn't need them to confirm that fact for me. Everything else, such as my speed, stroke rate, and duration of my swim were incidentals which I wasn't overly concerned with. I knew I swam at a fairly consistent speed when in tide-free waters, but how the tides and current would now affect me remained to be seen. Being told I was not making much headway, for instance, would only be counterproductive. I'd rather simply not know. I just had to keep swimming.

And so I put my thoughts to the task at hand, mechanically reaching one hand in front of my head at a time, methodically pulling myself forward, stroke by stroke. As in the majority of my training, there was no music, little scenery (just Connemara to look at every time I turned to breathe), and little to occupy my thoughts.

The latter aspect is one that makes the Channel so difficult: The sheer boredom and monotony of it all. And though you know you are swimming in the Channel, in reality you are only aware of your immediate surroundings. There is no concept of being miles from shore, of swimming across one of the busiest shipping lanes in the world. You actually see and notice very little.

I was aware of the sun continuing to rise, though at no time did I really feel the heat or strength of it on my skin. Nuala had told me she'd actually had to move so that she was swimming in the shadow of the boat in order to avoid being sunburned. I admit to being envious of that image. I saw Connagh strip off his top as the morning wore on, and I knew it must easily be warm enough to sunbathe in, but these were fleeting thoughts. My world was centred around the taste of salt, the sound of my bubbles and the throbbing of Connemara's engines. The waves were gentle, and though I'd taken a sea-sickness tablet just in case I may need it, I don't think the gentle swell would actually have caused me problems anyway.

I was surprised how quickly the first hour went by. Before I knew it, Ali was holding up the large green card to catch my attention. I was surprised when he then held up five fingers, letting me know I could feed in five minutes. If every hour went by that quickly, I would feel lucky indeed. After a short stop to take on board half a Mars Bar washed down with my usual Vita Coco / Lucozade energy gel mix, I got straight back to business. With nothing else to look forward to in the immediate future but the next quick feed, I began to break down each hour into an estimated three parts. I had no way of judging exactly how much time had passed, other than the hours and hours of experience of swimming training, so somehow I simply knew when I'd swum for around twenty minutes. Certainly I found that no sooner did I begin to think that my final third of an hour must be close to ending, than I saw Ali with our large green card. I'd stop, I'd feed, and the monotonous cycle would begin all over again.

According to the log that Connagh diligently kept, I spotted the first jellyfish shortly after the first feed stop. It was a gorgeous shade of purple, with long trailing tentacles. It was a marvellous specimen which drifted along serenely with its slow and rhythmic pulsing movement. The animal was slightly below the surface, and I had to ensure I did not brush it with my next arm stroke. As with the large box jellyfish I'd seen in Bournemouth, I had only noticed this one when I was almost on top of it. My real worry was of charging into one face first, and this is something many swimmers have done. Avoiding jellyfish stings to the face was the main reason I'd grown a huge, shaggy beard, in emulation of Sean Connway who'd done the same when he swam from Land's End to John O'Groats. I hoped my beard worked for me as well his did for him. I called out to the boat during my next breath, telling them I'd spotted a jellyfish, and I watched them exchange quick looks of concern.

It was almost a full hour later, three and a half hours into my swim, that I received my first jellyfish sting. I saw the creature too late to avoid it, and it brushed against my right thigh as I swam past. In truth, I think I must have avoided the worst of its tentacles, for though the sensation was of a serious nettle sting, I'd been expecting much worse. I called out to the boat that I'd been stung, more for the log than any other reason, and immediately carried on swimming. The pain was certainly not worth abandoning the attempt for, and even had I not been in the midst of a Channel challenge, I knew that the best place for my stung leg at this point was actually in the salt water. With my concern of further stings now fully justified, I tried to heighten my concentration of keeping an eye out for further jellyfish. The positive side effect of this was that it took my mind off the pain in my leg, and within a short space of time I had forgotten about the sting completely. Forgetting about jellyfish was another matter. The sea was becoming thick with them.

During my fourth feed I experienced my first bout of leg cramp. I don't use my legs a great deal when I swim. I kick somewhat lazily, and not very consistently. Besides this amateur style, the main leg muscles used in swimming are the front ones, the quadriceps femoris. From having been face-down in the water for so long, effectively trailing my legs straight behind me, the sudden use of them to tread water was a shock to the other muscles. They complained in no uncertain terms. All of the major muscle groups at the back of my right leg, the biceps femoris, vastus externus, semitendinosus and the adductor magnus went into an involuntary spasm, contracting violently. The pain was unbelievable, and I clearly remember crying out in agony. That shout of pain was captured by the film crew, and was used in the final production. The only thing I could do to alleviate the condition was to straighten my legs again, which meant that from that point onwards I would have to eat lying flat on my back, as opposed to treading water upright. This was hardly disastrous - it simply made eating, and especially drinking, that much more difficult.

    These various incidents, the jellyfish sting and the leg cramp, were very transitory. For the vast majority of the time it was simply business as usual: keep swimming, and endure the monotony. Though I may have been bored, I could take comfort from what was absent: namely cold and fatigue. My harsh winter of acclimatization was continuing to prove to have been worth the effort, and though the gloriously warm summer had heated up all of the outdoor swimming venues, my body did seem to have remembered how to deal with the cold. At no time do I recall feeling even chilly, let alone cold. My fitness too seemed to be paying off, despite not focussing exclusively on swimming training. I felt strong, fit and very, very focussed.

    Before I was expecting my next feed, I was surprised to see that Ali and Connagh were signalling me with the card. Had the fifth hour passed even faster than the previous four?

    'We'll have to feed you early.' Connagh shouted, ensuring I could hear him through my ear plugs.

    'Why?' I asked, not unreasonably.

    'So you don't get run over by that boat, of course!' Connagh pointed behind me.

    Never having been able to master the art of bilateral breathing, I'd just spent over four hours constantly looking to my right. As Connemara was tracking me on that side, the only visual sighting of anything other than jellyfish had been my constant view of our boat and its occupants. Turning now to look to my left I was greeted with a truly awesome sight. Not more than one hundred metres away was a container ship of unbelievable proportions. Though I didn't know it at the time, we had been on a perfect collision course with this beast, and hence Kevin, who had been in regular contact with both the coast guard and the ship's captain, had been ordered that we must give way. When I later searched the Internet for more information on this particular ship, I was quite staggered at its dimensions, even after Steph had told me they had effectively watched something the size of a city float past their small vessel. The ship was a Maersk container vessel name Cornelia.

Measuring almost 350 metres in length, it was over three football/rugby pitches long. The ship was 43 metres wide, and had a draft of 14 metres. With an equivalent load capacity of 173 million bottles of wine, the vessel had a dead weight of an incredible 110,000 tons - equal to roughly the weight of 398 airbus 380 aircraft. Powered by engines which output 63,000 horsepower (on a par with 64 formula one cars), a ship of this weight and mass will take around two miles to bring to a stop once it is moving. It takes around a mile just to begin to alter course. And considering this particular ship weighed almost 1.3 million times more than I did, I was happy to concede that giving way to it was the correct decision.

With nothing to do but wait, I lay on my back, kicking my legs out straight in order to avoid cramp, and munched on some jelly babies whilst swigging some Vita Coco. The ship passed with surprising speed, given its incredible size, and after bobbing through the wake for a few minutes, we were soon underway once more.

One consequence of only breathing unilaterally, aside from being unable to spot 110,000 ton container ships, is the wind. After over five hours of swimming in the lee of the boat, I gradually began to feel sick. For a while I worried that it was sea sickness beginning to take a grip, and I asked Ali for a tablet, just to be sure. It was not until a short while later, with the sense of nausea increasing, that I worked out what the problem was: diesel fumes. In an effort to increase my pace, which had been at a steady speed since the start of the swim, Malcom had edged the boat slightly ahead of me. Due to this, the stern of the vessel was now roughly level with my head, and the wind was gently blowing the exhaust fumes directly in to my face. It was a distinctly unpleasant experience, and I had to yell to Connagh and ask them to ease back on the throttle. I was extremely reluctant to swim any faster than the steady pace which I had practised at for hundreds of hours. Burning out through exhaustion was simply not an option.

The message got passed to Malcom. The boat eased back into position alongside me, diesel fumes were replaced with fresh sea air, and the monotony of swimming returned.

As their name implies, cross-Channel ferries ply their trade in taking passengers and cargo from one side of the Channel to the other. One of the main responsibilities of a pilot boat captain during a Channel swim, after the obvious paramount inclusion of safety, is to ensure that the swimmer does not drift outside set boundaries. Swimming the Channel is not simply a case of getting into the water anywhere in England and landing anywhere in France. If the swimmer is taken too far north, and into the path reserved for the cross-Channel ferries or towards the French docks, the coastguard will insist that the attempt is abandoned. Likewise on the French coast, if the tide takes the swimmer too far south outside of acceptable limits, the challenge will be terminated. The pilot would have no option at this point but to comply with the coastguard, and the swimmer would be ordered out of the water. For the first few hours of my swim Kevin had to keep guiding me slightly south, away from the cross-Channel shipping route. Connagh took a fantastic photo of me during this phase of the swim, alone within a vast area of sea with only a MyFerryLink ship as a backdrop.

But the vast majority of shipping traffic within these waters move up and down the Channel, rather than across it. On a typical day over 500 ships pass through the Strait of Dover. Being such a choke point, to ensure the safest possible passage for all sea-going vessels the Channel was split into shipping lanes after several instances in 1971. The left hand lane on the English side is for southbound ships, and the right hand lane on the French side is reserved for traffic heading north. After just over six hours of continuous swimming, the furthest and longest I had ever done, I was slightly over halfway across the Channel, and was now beginning to enter the southbound shipping lane.

I was greeted by a smack of jellyfish. And yes, 'smack' really is the collective noun for these creatures.

It is a common occurrence to find the predominance of Jellyfish concentrated around the middle of the Channel, and this was certainly proving true for me. I was spotting them regularly now, and though I was being warned by Connagh and Ali on the boat to be careful, there was absolutely nothing I could do apart from keep swimming and hope I didn't bump into any. It was like negotiating my way through a thick jellyfish soup. It certainly kept me focussed.

The next three hours continued in this fashion. Whenever I stopped to feed I had to be conscious of my immediate surroundings, and at one point Connagh called out that there was a jellyfish drifting directly towards me as I ate. Instinctively (and stupidly) I swatted the animal away with my hand, simultaneously stinging myself and spilling my drink. Connagh scooped the creature up with the net and flung it far away, but by that point the damage had been done. With a sore hand and angry at the interruption to my brief swimming respite, I swum on.

The French coast was now tantalizingly close. I had long since lost count of the amount of feed stops I'd had, so I was at a complete loss as to how long I'd been in the water for. Connagh passed on Kevin's advice that I'd narrowly missed being able to get passed the inshore marker buoy before the tide turned. This meant that I was now facing around another four or five hours' worth of swimming. I assessed my condition, looked at the French coast, and knew I was going to do it. I felt fit, I was strong, and my determination and focus were at a peak. I put my face in the water, and swam on.

And at that point, after 10 hours in the English Channel, just when I became absolutely certain that I was going to succeed, it all suddenly started to go wrong.

At 16:25 I realised that the sun had disappeared behind thick clouds, and that the wave height was gradually increasing. Every now and then when I turned my head to breathe, the space that had previously been the domain of fresh air was suddenly replaced by sea water. The waves were beginning to break over my head. My experiences off the coast of Gran Canaria in the Atlantic suddenly became hugely relevant. Whilst at that time I had been alone with nothing other than my high visibility float, now I had a safety vessel right alongside me, with observers continually keeping an eye on me. I was strong, I'd swum is seas far worse, and I felt no fear.

Yet the situation deteriorated rapidly.

Suddenly, I realised that the French coast, once so clearly visible, had disappeared. Looking behind me, I saw that the famous white cliffs were also absent from view. I optimistically put this down to the distance I'd covered, when I abruptly realised that Connemara was now also invisible. My safety boat had vanished.

No sooner had I comprehended this, than she came rising up on the top of the next huge swell. The wave height had increased from gentle rolling swells to two-metre waves within a matter of 20 minutes.

'We're in a squall,' Connagh yelled. 'Kevin says it'll pass.

Are you ok?'

I told him I was fine (which was true), but the fact remained that I didn't know which way I was supposed to be going. Was the boat still facing France? There was no time to begin a conversation, and Connemara was once more disappearing into a wave trough on the opposite side to the one I was sinking into. There was little else I could do. I set off in the direction I assumed would bring me on to the French shores.

At 16:45 things had begun to get serious. I was being buffeted around by the waves, and I was sure I was no longer making any headway. I became gradually aware of a rasping in my breathing, and though I felt fine, I was very conscious of this new and worrying sound in my chest. I no longer felt that I could get sufficient oxygen into my lungs. This wasn't through lack of trying. It was just that the air seemed to have thinned somehow. For the first time in the swim, the minutes had begun to drag.

Confusingly, I looked up to see that Connemara was now facing directly 180 degrees in the opposite direction to me. I assumed I had become completely disoriented, so I swung myself around and set off the way the boat was facing. I was beginning to get washed under by the occasional wave, and the rasp in my breathing was increasing steadily. With the boat now only visible when we were both on the crest of a wave, I had to be patient and wait to catch sight of her. When she had been absent for some time, I stopped and once more looked about me, only to discover Connemara behind me. How had she managed to get from my right side and onto my left so quickly? My sense of bewilderment was growing with the waves.

At 17:15 I again caught sight of the boat and saw Kevin peering at me closely.

'The storm is lasting longer than I thought. I'm going to give it another half an hour.' It was an ominous, non-negotiable warning. Before I'd had time to reply, I was swept under the water by a huge wave. When I surfaced, Connemara had vanished into a trough. I did the only thing I knew how to do at this point, and carried on swimming.

Unbeknown to me, the passengers on the boat were becoming increasingly worried. Discussions were taking place with Kevin about terminating the swim. I was not to discover the nature of this argument until later the following day, but the result at this point was that they agreed to wait a few more minutes.

For his part, Connagh had seen me disappear under the water once too often, and all aboard Connemara were more aware than I was that I had in fact been pushed farther away from the French coast in the last half an hour. At one point I had been just 2.8 miles from land. Within only 10 minutes that distance had increased to well over three and a half miles. Kevin finally decided he'd seen enough at 17:25. Ali relayed the message, shouting that the swim needed to be abandoned due to safety reasons, and I could see the worry on his face as to how I'd bear the news.

I bobbed in the water for a few seconds, my breath harsh in my throat, and glanced around me in dismay. How did this all go wrong so quickly? Where was the glorious sunshine? How was it possible that I could no longer spy the coast that had just recently been so unbelievable close? Was this really going to end here?

It took only seconds to acknowledge that the decision was the right one to make. The sea was now clearly as rough as when I'd swum in the Atlantic, and I was now regularly being submerged by the waves. Though I did not physically feel the need to quit, I had to admit that 11 hours of swimming meant that I was not at the peak of my energy levels. I'd done the best I could, the decision was beyond my control, and my Channel swim attempt would end here and now, three miles shy of the French shores. I put my face in the water, swore viciously, then made my way towards Connemara.

It took longer to reach the boat than I'd have credited. The boat was still occasionally vanishing from sight behind a huge wave, and for a while it felt as though the distance between us was not being decreased. This fact gave me my first real appreciation of how little progress I'd been making in the last hour. I was fighting the waves, the tide, and a very strong current.

Once alongside the boat I had to wait for a swell to lift me higher before I could reach over the side. Hands reached to grab my wrists and hauled me in, but it was far from an elegant boarding of the vessel. My legs had not bourne my weight for hours and they were not keen to do so now, at only a moment's notice. I squirmed over the side before staggering and collapsing into waiting arms. Kevin quickly guided me into the warm comfort of the wheelhouse, and Ali draped a warm seafarers jacket about my shoulders before helping me into my jog bottoms. With control of the steering being passed to Malcom, Kevin set about attentively ensuring I was well. He quickly fetched some hot chocolate to drink, and constantly checked on my condition by talking to me, asking me questions in order to look for any signs of hypothermia. I assured him I was fine, if understandably disappointed with the result. And all the while the cameras were rolling. The film crew were capturing everything.

After a short time I began to feel seasick. I don't travel well on boats, and it didn't take me long to wish that I was actually back in the water. I left the wheelhouse and sought the cold fresh air outside.

I was being violently sick over the side of the boat minutes later, in full view of the rolling camera. Vomiting is never a pleasant experience, but until that point I had not appreciated how much sea water I had ingested. My belly seemed full of the stuff, and I heaved again and again, my body simply wanting to void itself of this vast quantity of unwanted fluid. Even when I'd retched myself dry, I felt extraordinarily unwell. All I wanted to do was to step onto dry land and get off of the boat. But I'd swum a long way, and in the rough sea conditions it was going to take Connemara a long time to safely negotiate her way home.

In an attempt to distract myself from the violent sea sickness, I reached for my phone. I saw I had four SMS messages, and no fewer than 54 emails, all of which were well wishing and full of encouragement. Neil in the US had sent an SMS telling me that during my ordeal I'd finally broken the £10,000 barrier. It transpired that this was helped in no small part by Lewis's rugby squad. The head coach, Gareth Llywelyn, had been drumming up interest and support amongst the other parents, and the closer I got to France, the deeper they seemed to dig. On top of everything else I'd already raised, another £1,500 was pledged whilst I was actually in the water. This news cheered me up tremendously, even if it did nothing to alleviate the nausea.

It was over three torturous hours later that I finally stepped back onto the dockside in Folkestone. I felt debilitated by my seasickness, and this feeling obliterated any other emotion, desire or thought. I was shaky on my legs, I had no strength, and my world was still rocking violently from side to side due to the after-effects of the boat journey. I'd left Ali and Connagh to gather all of our stuff together, and they joined me as I said goodbye and thank you to Kevin and Paula. The three of us then trudged silently towards one of the coastal pubs as the film crew captured the final footage for the day.

In all honesty, despite having abstained for eight months, the very last thing I wanted to consume at that point was alcohol. But I'd promised Connagh and Ali I would celebrate the conclusion of the swim with them, so I slumped on a wooden bench outside the pub whilst Ali went inside to get us all a beer. Connagh took a photo of me nursing my first drink in eons, and someone later commented that it looked as if I'd entered the Channel when I was 40 years old, and had been pulled out when I was 70. The combination of seasickness and fatigue had aged me around 30 years in a single day. My skin was grey, my face was etched with exhaustion, and I was feeling sick. I looked terrible.

The drink took a long time to consume, but eventually I forced the last of it down and we trudged up the steep steps back to Esta and the boys. The Channel challenge was finally over for me. I'd given it everything, and in the end I'd been thwarted by the bad weather that had dogged me at every step. At least now that it was all behind me I could return to my family and resume a normal life, without the need for four to six hours of swimming training per day. That thought alone was a massive relief, and despite still feeling like death, I walked back into our rented flat to smiles of relief and congratulatory hugs.

It was a relief to everyone that I was back safe and well, and that the training and fundraising effort was now all behind us.

Having just completed the toughest challenge I'd ever faced, and having reached my target of £10,000 for Acorns, it was an easy decision that night to agree on Harry's favourite thing.

Aftermath

I had fully expected to sleep well, given the fact that I had undergone 11 hours of exercise in cold water, not to mention the lack of sleep from the previous night. But the unwell feeling remained, and I slept fitfully. At 03:00 in the morning I woke up feeling nauseous again. My stomach was empty, and I desperately wanted to avoid dry retching into the pan next to me. I switched the light on and sat up.

Esta was awake in an instant and asking if I was ok, all concerns directed at my wellbeing, though she too must have been exhausted from the weeks of relentless build up to the swim. I decided to have some of the dry breakfast biscuits I'd been using as part of my training diet. I ate them slowly and carefully, though my tongue felt thick and awkward in my mouth. I didn't fully appreciate at this stage what that sensation meant. In months gone by, Esta and I would have sat up and had a drink, maybe a glass or two of wine, and chatted before trying once more to get back to sleep. But I could not have stomached a drink if I was paid, and Esta could take it or leave it after so many months of supporting me through my own abstinence. Eventually my nausea subsided, the biscuits stayed down, and we both lay down to sleep.

When the house started to rouse in the morning normality had already begun to reassert its grip once more. Ali and Connagh needed to catch an early train to London - Ali to return to Kate and the kids in Worcester, and Connagh to get back to work on the Isle of Wight. There was little talk of the swim. Despondency, which would previously have been considered as inevitable, was not even conspicuous in its absence. In abandoning the attempt, the correct and sensible decision had been made, and I'd had no choice but to concede. I would not have been in a position to argue, and everyone, including myself, was fully aware of that. The swim was history, and now I had to focus on the aftermath, and the final push for fund raising. But whilst despondency may have been lacking, an undeniable sense of disappointment was growing. To have been so close, within clear sight of France and yet to have failed anyway, was hard to believe. The one huge consolation which I had to return to again and again was the fact that the Channel had always been a means to an end. The primary goal, that of raising £10,000 for

Acorns, had been achieved.

Fate had no consideration for my prior exploits, nor for my sense of underlying disappointment. On the way to taking Ali and Connagh to the train station, I ran over a socket that had been left, presumably deliberately, in the middle of the road. My car tyre was ruined. The morning after almost swimming to France saw me sitting on a roadside kerb and hand-cranking my car up on its jack to change the wheel.

One of the items that I had handed to Kevin upon boarding Connemara the previous day was a copy of Admiralty Chart 2675, purchased from a specialist provider of nautical charts and shipping books. Kevin called me the following day, telling me he had annotated my personal chart on my behalf, clearly showing my location within the Channel each hour of the swim. I'd seen one of these charts on Julie's wall, of course, and now my own was ready for collection. We arranged to meet at 11:30, confirming with Steph that we'd then meet her directly afterwards. Esta and I walked the boys down to the harbour, treating them to an ice cream on the way. I was a lovely sunny day, but that belied the fact that a force five was blowing steadily out at sea. The Irishman due to swim after me was clearly going to miss the first day of his window, and in fact the forecast did not look good for him to get away at all. I could feel a tremendous amount of empathy for him, regardless of the fact that my own chance was already history.

Kevin arrived precisely on time. He took us all into a small cabin within the port, and talked us through the chart. Apparently, the rocking of the boat on the sea swell had been so violent that the satellites had actually lost sight of us, resulting in the fact that the tracker had been unable to update our actual position for the last hour or so of my swim. It was only on the way back that we were again detected, and accordingly it showed that we were heading back after the last confirmed location - around 10 hours into the swim. Kevin showed us what had actually happened. Between hours 10 and 11, I had stopped making forward progress due to both the current and waves pushing me away from the French coast. This much had been evident to me in the water, but I had not appreciated how far south I'd been drifting. The swells had now reached a height that had begun to concern Connagh. He had not come on this voyage to witness his dad drown, and he had suggested the swim be abandoned. But Kevin is a sailor. He knew the sea, and he'd seen people swim in these conditions before. Whist far from flippant, he also knew this attempt could be my one and only chance. He could see I was strong, and wanted to give me every opportunity to prove myself. Ali was caught in the middle. He knew what this swim meant to me, and how hard I had trained, but as with Connagh, he too was worried about my safety. It was at this point Kevin had suggested they would give it another half an hour. Nine minutes later, with the weather deteriorating further, Ali and Connagh were becoming increasingly anxious. Kevin could also see I had lost a significant amount of ground. At this point I had already gone under the boat once, partly due to the waves hurling the craft around like a cork, and there was every likelihood that it would happen again if the boat was too close to me, so Kevin had had to increase the gap between me and Connemara. I was rapidly going backwards though, and with the storm increasing, and sensing the futility of my battle, Kevin conceded that enough was enough. The swim was officially abandoned after 11 hours and nine minutes.

'Could you, honestly, have stayed in there another four hours?' he asked me. 'Because that's how long it would have taken you in those conditions. The tide needed to turn, and then you would have had to swim back across ground you'd been pushed back across.'

Swimming for another four hours in calmer waters would not have been a problem. Swimming in those conditions was another matter entirely. Even whilst standing on dry land the next day, there was no fooling myself or anyone else that I would have been able to reach land whilst battling those waves.

Kevin was glad to hear my answer. It must have been heartbreaking for him to have had to make the call, and clearly he'd had people question such a decision in the past. I took possession of my chart, shook his hand, and left.

Having said goodbye to Kevin, we walked back to the pub to meet with Steph. Emma had already departed for Spain to reunite with her kids, and Steph and Keith were ready to head back to London themselves. There was no camera, and no sound recording. They came along purely to find out how I was.

Steph was unsurprised to hear how ill I had been feeling. Her experiences with following the other swimmers for the documentary, and her research into the physical effects a Channel swim can have on the body, were quite eye-opening. Apparently, in conditions such as those I'd been enduring for the last hour, the swimmer slowly drowns without realising it. With the spray of the waves, and the unpredictability of knowing whether there will be air or water in the space to which you turn your head to breathe, the swimmer gradually begins to fill their lungs with water. This was undoubtedly the reason for my rasping breath towards the end of my swim. And what is worse is that the swimmer has no idea that they are drowning. Steph explained how this phenomenon was akin to high altitude pulmonary edema, where the lungs of climbers slowly fill with fluid once they pass a certain altitude. Even once out of the water, a swimmer can suffer dry land drowning if enough water has penetrated the lungs. Things had not progressed anywhere near as far as this with me, but Steph was convinced that my episode of vomiting on the journey home had been more down to the amount of sea water I had undoubtedly ingested than anything else.

  To rub salt into my wounds, it transpired that the world record for the oldest man to swim the Channel had been broken on the same day as my abandoned attempt. Cyril Baldock, a 70 year old man from Australia, had set off at around 02:00 and had consequently missed the storm that had disrupted my swim. Cyril's boat had been docked in Dover. Not having to wait for high water to float the vessel, they had consequently been able to depart that much earlier than us. Connemara, docked in Folkestone, was stranded on dry land until high tide. Though this nugget of information could potentially have led to the inevitable 'what ifs', there was no mileage down that road. There had been absolutely no reason for us to set off any earlier than we had. The weather had been forecast to be clear until much later on the Thursday, and if those conditions had held true, we would have been back in Folkestone long before the wind had picked up. To have voluntarily set off at the previous high tide, and swum through the night for no apparent advantage, would have been seriously questionable at the time. At least the date of my attempt, being marked by a world record, now had some additional credence.

  Steph then mentioned the fact that a lady called Irene Keel, another Australian, was also waiting in Dover in an attempt to claim not one, but three records. If Irene could swim the Channel, she would simultaneously be the world's oldest woman, the world's oldest person, and Australia's oldest person to have achieved the crossing. Unfortunately, Irene knew she needed in the region of 19 hours for her swim - and in the last five weeks, such a window of fine weather had simply not been available. Obviously by this point, Irene must have been on a standby list - she could not have expected to charter one pilot for the entire duration. It looked highly likely that Irene's opportunity was not going to present itself. My worst fears, that of returning home without ever having had the opportunity to prove myself, looked like a reality for poor Irene. My four days of waiting paled into nothingness next to the very idea of Irene's five weeks. Enduring such anxiety must have been Hell.

The film crew were scheduled for some down time. They had been working seven days a week for months, dedicating themselves to their self-imposed project of recording the journey of Channel swim preparation. They were exhausted, they missed their respective families, and the filming was now all-but complete. The next stage was to begin the daunting task of sifting through the hundreds of hours of footage in order to start the process of editing it all down to just 90 or so minutes of quality and entertaining footage. That process could wait a week or two, whilst everyone spent the final few days of the summer holiday with friends and relatives.

Esta and I were finally alone with Lewis and Will. The swim was over, Ali and Connagh had departed, and even the cameras and microphones were gone. With most of my annual leave used up on ad hoc days off swimming in lakes and the sea, my final few days, like the film crew, could now be spent with my family.

I expected a huge weight to be lifted from my shoulders. The massively daunting prospect of swimming further than most people have ever run was now behind me. There was nothing to train for, no reason not to have a drink, no requirement to get up early, and no obligation to watch my diet. Moreover, there was no imposing mental and physical challenge to occupy my every waking, and indeed sleeping, thought.

But the absence of these factors did not bring the instant relief I was expecting. There was a surreal edge to normality, like I'd missed a train that was due to take me somewhere important, and no-one was bothered about it. I had no responsibilities, and it felt somehow purposeless. Enjoying the relaxation of such freedom is what most people would call a holiday, especially considering I was at the seaside with my family. But I was left with the empty feeling of a missed opportunity. It had all seemed too easy and too quick. Eleven hours of swimming had gone past in a flash. I did not ache anywhere close to the degree I'd been expecting. I'd escaped with only two minor jellyfish stings, which was miraculous when I considered how many of the things I'd seen in the water, and at no point had I felt chilly, let alone cold. And even towards the end, when the waves began to make any headway impossible, I had felt strong, yet in no way did I disagree with the need to abandon the swim.

Yet I somehow expected to feel more.

There was no feeling of relief. Similarly, there was a complete absence of euphoria, and I put this down to not having fully completed the challenge. But there was also a total lack of accomplishment. I was already being told that I'd accomplished something incredible, and that I should focus on the positives and be proud of what I'd done. Esta was certainly brimming with pride. But I was void of that emotion.

Much later, having had time to reflect, I realised what was missing from everything I'd undergone: The challenge I'd been looking for.

That must sound partially ridiculous, given that I never completed the swim. But I had been expecting to have had to endure the cold, and to have battled extreme fatigue. I'd been expecting the possibility of having to overcome seasickness and the physical agony of painful jellyfish stings - not just the slight discomfort equivalent to brushing against a stinging nettle. Had I climbed into the boat with the last of my physical strength and collapsed on the floor of the boat, I would have known the experience of swimming as far as I could possibly push myself. And had I stepped onto the beach in France, whether exhausted or not, I could have claimed the jubilation of a completed Channel swim. But the waves came on so quickly that they were impossible to swim against before I'd even begun to tire. Staying in the water until I was exhausted (had the decision even been mine, which it was not) would have proved nothing when I was being pushed backwards by the tide and the waves. So in effect I was caught between the two: stopping short of the end, yet with plenty of energy and determination left. My intention during the training was that I should indeed find the challenge less strenuous than it might seem. I pushed myself hard, not just in the swimming, but in the cardio vascular training and even with the weights. This had all been intentional, and it certainly looked to have paid off. But I had not been able to put all that training to full effect. I would never know now just how far I could actually have gone. Though I was convinced that I could have swum for the remaining three or so hours it would have taken to reach France in calm conditions, I would forever be unable to prove it, or to know in what physical state I would have reached the shore.

It was a challenge unrealised.

As we walked the boys along the sea front, throwing stones into the sea, or playing on the giant wooden climbing frames in Lower Leas, Esta and I talked this over. We always came back to the same point: I had surpassed my goal of raising £10,000. The challenge had been a means of reaching this end. I should be happy with that, and just let the events of the swim go.

Spending those last few days in Folkestone made it impossible to stop thinking about the Channel, of course. On most days, France was still visible, so tantalizingly close. We'd occasionally see Kevin at his boat, cleaning and checking it, preparing it for the next crossing. I kept looking out to sea, wondering if anyone was currently making their own attempt, and wondering if Kevin's next swimmer would get his chance. Thursday and Friday looked completely impossible, leaving only Saturday as an available option. I could completely empathise.

Though neither my arms nor shoulders ached, other physical effects soon began to manifest themselves.

One unpleasantry to be endured was the consequence of having effectively used sea water as mouthwash for 11 hours. Gradually, over the course of three days, all of the skin inside my mouth and throat came away. My tongue, which had been feeling thick and awkward from the moment I came out of the water, was soon stripped bare of flesh. My taste buds were gone, and large, stringy pieces of skin hung off the inside of my cheeks. Food and drink tasted bland, and eating and drinking at all was understandably somewhat uncomfortable to endure.

Following on closely from this was a vague feeling of nausea. I can only imagine that through ingesting so much salt water, a similar unpleasant occurrence to the one in my mouth was also taking place in my stomach. My appetite dropped rapidly, and my energy dropped with it.

Finally came the fatigue. I'm convinced that this was brought on not by the swim alone, for which I'd been training anyway, but from the culmination of events. With the anticipation, anxiety, doubt and expectation now all absent, I think my body and subconscious mind simply slumped in relief. With that relief came a bone-numbing fatigue that sleep alone would not shift. I suddenly found that walking up the steep steps to the accommodation was a huge struggle. My feet were shuffling, rather than walking, and the prospect of walking uphill into town was wearying in thought, let alone deed. Needless to say, though we remained by the sea, I did not go for a swim.

We went home on the Saturday. It was a beautiful day, with clear skies and a gentle breeze blowing across the sea. I simply could not help but log on to see if Connemara was out to sea. She was. Irishman Keith Gary successfully crossed the Channel that day, and I confess to a certain amount of jealousy. The fine weather stayed with him all day.

We had to split the drive home between us. After two hours I was exhausted, the fatigue again coming over me in a wave. Esta took over at the wheel of the car, and within minutes I was fast asleep. In the end, it took my body a long time to shift this exhaustion. I spent weeks going through bouts of initial high energy, only to feel utterly drained moments later. It may well be that I had caught some kind of bug. All I do know is that it made returning to any form of regular training very difficult, as even walking Will to school was a struggle one day.

When we pulled up to the house on returning from Folkestone, Esta turned to me with a smile. I hadn't noticed at first, but when I looked at the house again I saw a large banner hanging from the bedroom window above the front door. It said, 'Well done Dad. We're really proud.' When I opened the front door there were balloons hanging from the walls, and another large banner in the front room also reading, 'Well Done Dad'. On the kitchen table was a bottle of sparkling wine, and no sooner was I through the door than my mum, Graham and mother-in-law all turned up to congratulate me and welcome me home. There were cards from the neighbours with donations and congratulatory messages too. It was quite a moving homecoming - more than I'd received in the past when returning from an operational tour of duty in the army. Mum insisted on treating us to a take away, and Graham was looking forward to being able to have a glass of wine with me again after all this time. It was like returning from a moon walk. My family were all effervescent and highly enthused, though all were also glad it was over with: They didn't have to worry about my safety any more.

Whether I had ingested something in the sea, or simply picked up a bug at Folkestone, it took some time for my body to recover. Training at the gym had to be resumed slowly and carefully. It's hard to maintain such a high degree of intensity even when there is a deadline. Without one, having a few days off here and there seemed perfectly acceptable. With my energy level continually varying from feeling perfectly fine all the way through to suddenly exhausted, it was an awkward time to plan much in the way of training. I made an impromptu arrangement to meet up with an old running buddy, Tom, and without really meaning to I ended up running seven miles with him around the parks in London. We pushed the last mile hard, as we always do. It took me a week to recover from that run.

As far as work was concerned, I found I had taken on a mild celebrity status. I had been aware that the hyperlink allowing staff to follow my progress on-line had been emailed around the organisation. But what I had not anticipated was how disruptive my swim had been to production at Dovetail. Working through my emails I discovered that the main client meeting room in the London office had been set aside for the entire day, with the overhead projector beaming the current position of Connemara onto the screen. In the US office in Parsippany, a screen in the dining area had similarly been set up. As I spoke to people on both sides of the Atlantic during my first days back, most confessed that they had been transfixed to the tiny dot depicting my pilot boat, with little work being done at all. They had watched with interest as Connemara came face to face with the Maersk container ship, and everyone had gasped in disbelief when the updates showed us returning to England slightly shy of the French coast. What they did not know at that stage was why we had turned around.

To add further interest to the updates, the US office had

created a huge panoramic scene of the Channel along one long wall in the communal kitchen area. In the sea were fish, sharks and seaweed, whilst on the surface of the water they had stuck a photo of me swimming. The photo was moved along the scene according to my current location. In London, the staff were all given large printed letters and arranged in a group so that the words 'Congratulations Alan' were spelt out. The level of support that had been shown was quite staggering.

Once I was back in the office, people immediately wanted to congratulate me and ask questions: What had happened? Why did I turn back? Was it correct that I did not make it all the way? How far had I actually gone? I could have spent the first two or three days going from desk to desk answering the same questions. Anticipating this I'd prepared a 30 minute presentation, and arranged to deliver it to both sides of the Atlantic (to the US by remote presentation, to save them having to wait for my next visit). Both presentations went down well. Most people voiced their opinion that not only had I swum further than they would be capable of even running, but also that as I'd covered just under 22 miles, I'd effectively swum the Channel as far as they were concerned. Very few people focussed on any disappointment, or spoke of a task unfinished. Not making it to the French coast was a mere technicality to my colleagues, despite being crucial to me and the Channel swimming fraternity. Instead, there was a general sense of awe and appreciation, with rounds of applause and handshaking. When I spoke to Ali, he was similarly adamant that to his mind I had completed the swim. Connagh posted on his Facebook status that I had achieved something he could never think of doing, and that he was a proud son. Having had such a long time to personally come to terms with the scale of the challenge, the reaction in others as to the distance I'd completed across the Channel seemed quite strange to me.

One of the first people I encountered back at work was Martin, the CEO. As we chatted, I recalled the initial email he had sent, offering the initial deposit for Connemara. I racked my brains, trying to remember the exact wording, as I half-expected Martin to request a refund. After all, the deposit had been conditional. It was the phrasing of that condition that I was thinking about as we discussed the events of the swim. Martin brought the subject up a few days later, joking that on this occasion he was happy for me to keep the deposit, despite not completing the challenge. Checking back, I saw that the email actually stated that a refund was due 'should you not go through with the attempt'. It would have been a hard taskmaster indeed who argued I had not met the conditions of the deposit.

Not everyone was as forgiving about my attempt as my work colleagues however. Two weeks after the swim I met one of the children who had been at the presentation I'd given to the local school. He came bounding up to me, full of enthusiasm.

'Did you swim the Channel?' he asked with a big smile. I must confess that at first I thought he was asking if I was the person he'd seen in the paper. I simply replied with a yes.

'What, you got to France?' he asked, wide eyed.

'Oh, no, not quite...' I began. But his face fell and he walked away with his shoulders slumped. He wasn't interested in any excuses. It was irrelevant how close I got, or what had stopped me. All he knew was that I'd said I would swim to France, but in fact I had not done so. As with my own attitude, and that of the Channel swimming community, close was not enough for him. I could imagine him going home and telling his parents that the man who said he would swim the Channel had not done it after all. He would probably regret the pound spent on the non-uniform day. Another adult had let him down. It was quite a tragic experience to watch his demeanour change in the blink of an eye. It was worse to know that I was the cause of it.

Strangely, I found the child's attitude completely acceptable. For the truth was that I was finding the adulation and congratulations hard to take. People I had never met were greeting me, having seen my picture in the paper, and offering donations. They shook my hand and told me what a magnificent feat I had achieved. Being unable to ascertain if anyone from the Worcestershire area had ever attempted a Channel swim before, I appeared to have undertaken a challenge that had stunned the community. But in my mind, I had not complete it. It was black and white to me. Yes, I'd swum a long distance. Yes, I was close to the end. But not many climbers will talk about almost making it to the top of Everest. There is a niche group of swimmers who have swum the Channel. There is a far larger group who have failed. I belonged to the latter collection, and membership of the elite listing had ultimately proven to be elusive, regardless of the reasons or the sea conditions.

Don't ge me wrong: I had an immense feeling of gratitude at the opportunity given to me. Reflecting on the photos of me in the middle of the Channel, a passenger ferry in the background, really brought home to me what I had been part of. Whilst swimming at the time, I had only been aware of my immediate surroundings. There had been no concept of ever being nine or more miles from shore. Aside from the Maersk ship, I could have been back in Windermere, or even in Tooting Bec (had it not been for the salt water, of course). From the moment I got on board Connemara, I had been utterly focussed on my task and had been determined to succeed. In some way this concentration had blotted out any excitement, enjoyment or even appreciation of the event I was actually undertaking at the time. It was purely business, with the single goal of making it to the other side. My memory of the events was vague too. We cannot store the details of hours of boredom, and there was a void in my memory as a result. I know I must have been bored, and I had isolated incidents and events to break up the monotony, but otherwise the experience had largely been ordinary, even mundane. It was only by delivering the presentations and reviewing the photos Connagh had taken that I was able to fully appreciate the rare opportunity I had been able to experience.

But ultimately I had to contend myself with talking about my Channel swim 'attempt'. That last word rankled. And whilst my audience, friends and family all dismissed it, I could not let it go. The army don't talk about 'abandonments' or 'aborted attempts'. There is a culture of do or don't do, of success and failure. You don't 'almost' capture a stronghold or 'almost' defeat an enemy. And whilst I would love to have been able to adopt the attitude of my civilian friends (we describe ourselves as ex-forces, not civilians), old attitudes die hard.

Inevitably, one or two people asked if I would make the attempt again. It was an issue my family were all dreading. But a Channel swim is a bit like a moon walk. It's not simply a case of making another attempt immediately. Slots are booked years in advance. And even if there were any availability, there was the question of funding the boat, paying for accommodation, taking more leave, checking that Ali would be available (and even willing) to act as support again. The list was long. Were I to consider doing it again the following year, it would mean another 12 months of continuing to train, and to maintain my acclimatisation to the cold water. Not only could I not put myself through all of that again, I could not put my family through it either.

I had failed to swim the Channel, and that was that. I had to accept it and move on.

Another thing I had to accept was a return to my old routines. For the first few days I found myself waking up early in the Union Jack Club and getting ready as normal. But without having to cross London and go for a swim, I was ridiculously early for work. I ended up going to the gym for a leisurely sauna and shower, but even then I found myself in the Dovetail building before 07:30. I had to re-learn how to make use of my spare time. I was once again free to return to my enjoyment of reading without worrying that I should be preparing for a massive physical challenge. It would take time to adjust. The same was true of my diet. My final few weeks of training had seen me drinking several pints of full fat milk, of eating Mars Bars and drinking regular Coke. All of these had to go, to be once more replaced by more healthy options. And unlike the gradual build-up to all of these activities, the resumption of a normal lifestyle and diet was sudden and brutal.

Even though the swim may have been behind me, I wanted to ensure that the publicity and fundraising continued as long as possible. With the original target of £10,000 now well and truly smashed, I wondered what limit was suddenly possible. The donations continued to stream in. Within the first week back at work I had smashed £11,000, helped in no small way by one individual and anonymous contribution of £550. I later accidentally discovered who the benefactor was, and I thanked him profusely. Embarrassed at being identified, he begged to remain anonymous.

Suddenly, we were closing in on £12,000. Without any prompting by me, the HR department of Dovetail again jumped to my aid, organising events in both of the major offices once more. Another £400 seemed to be raised with little trouble, belying the effort that really went into arranging these fundraisers. For their part, Acorns were ensuring I featured highly on their Facebook page, with the media quickly picking up on what the hospice described as 'an inspirational fundraising effort'. This helped sustain the

Harry's Favourite Thing

momentum too, as some hugely generous donations from people I'd never met continued to increase my overall total. Before we knew it, the previously unimaginable total of £12,000 had been surpassed.

Whilst the balloons were still inflated at the house, and before the local fame had subsided, I arrived home one week to find an envelope addressed to me bearing the logo of the House of Commons. Inside was a personally written letter from Robin Walker, our local Conservative MP. Esta explained that Robin had called to the house canvassing, and had spoken to her mum, Pat. Intrigued as to the reason for the banner saying 'We're really proud', Robin had been told by Pat of my recent undertaking. The letter was his written appreciation, with an explanation of where he fit into the scheme of things with regards to palliative care:

Dear Mr. Gale

I happened to be canvassing in your street the other day and came across the splendid poster which your family had put up to congratulate you on our epic Channel swim. I spoke to your mother who told me how proud they all are of you and I was sorry not to be able to congratulate you in person.

As well as being a member of the All Party Parliamentary Group for Hospices & Palliative Care, I have been a regular visitor to Acorns Children's Hospice in recent years and I have always been enormously impressed by the good work that they do. It is fantastic that you have done so much to support them and I know that they will be very grateful.

A friend of mine who is ex-army swam the Channel when we were working together a few years ago and from him I got an idea of the enormous amount of hard work and training involved. I am in awe of anyone who can do it and wanted to write to pass on my personal congratulations.

Best wishes,

Robin Walker MP

I admit I felt very proud of this official communication, and I inserted it into my portfolio of other official letters from Her Majesty's Ambassadors and High Commissioners - a collection I had accumulated whilst working for the Foreign and Commonwealth Office a few years previously.

At this stage I decided I needed to put and idea of Ali's into practice. I contacted Acorns to arrange for an official handover of the money, but also suggested to them that the funds should be put towards acquiring something tangible that we could put Harry's name to. I spoke to Jorj Jarvie, Director of Fundraising at Acorns. Jorj had an official hospice 'wish list' to hand, and she asked if I'd be happy for the money to be used to procure a specialist child's safety cot. This highly adapted piece of equipment enabled certain children to sleep securely without harming themselves in the night, whilst also offering the nursing staff easy sight and access to the child. Being a very specialised yet low demand item, the cot was almost prohibitively expensive. When I was told that the cost would be £9,000, I replied that there would be plenty of change remaining.

'How much have you raised then?' Asked Jorj.

'Over £12,000.'

There was a delighted gasp at the other end of the phone. 'In that case, you could also fund a new hoist for the hydro pool? The existing one is worn out.'

In effect then, my swim would mean that not only would a family now be able to fully enjoy the respite offered by the hospice, knowing that they finally had a suitable safety cot for their child to reside in overnight, but also that other families would be able to use the hydro-pool facilities, courtesy of a newly-replaced hoist. With the warmth and comfort of the pool being the such a favourite sensation for Harry when he had been a resident at the hospice, the link back to water via the swim was perfect.

I took charge of arranging the handover, firstly liaising with Wayne at David Lloyd's to ask permission to use the venue. With the club facilities forming the majority of my training, and with it being local, it was the obvious choice. I then contacted Becky from Hallmark Hulme, and Jeremy from Kendall Wadley, to confirm they could make it to my intended presentation. The date for the handover was set for 12th September. Jorj from Acorns, appreciating the enormous amount of money generated from a one-person event, ensured that a trustee of the hospice named David Watts would be there to receive the cheque. Like myself and Esta, David and his wife were 'Acorns parents' too.

In addition, I ensured that the local paper would be in attendance, and I asked Steph and Emma if they would like to be there with the cameras. I topped off the crowd with Ali, my mum and Graham.

Our only disappointment was that Esta had an Ofsted visit that day at Perrywood. She was scheduled to be taking a class, and there was absolutely no way that could be changed, so unfortunately she missed the event.

The day itself went perfectly. Mandie Fitzgerald from Acorns was there early to greet us, armed with a big cheque and some large orange Perspex numbers. With the media somewhat reluctant to use the clichéd 'big cheque', the numbers allowed us to offer something different for the photographs. Once we had all arrived, we gathered by the outside pool for the press photographer. Six of us crowded in a line holding one Perspex figure each to give the accumulated rounded total of £12,800, with big smiles all round. Hallmark Hulme and Kendall Wadley had sent along their own PR lady, Caroline, and Simon from FT Images had once more kindly offered his services so that we could indeed capture me presenting a cheque to David Watts. Until this point I had managed to get away with wearing a suit and tie, and avoiding once more donning my Speedos and goggles.

That ended when we started to look for a novel way of using the Perspex numbers.

Someone asked if they would float, and as the pound symbol was lowered into the water Ali immediately pointed out that Perspex would sink. The next logical step was for me to offer (before anyone else did) to place the numbers on the bottom of the pool and stand next to them in my swimming regalia. With the orange figures contrasting brilliantly with the pale blue bottom of the pool, the resulting images were the perfect visual finale to the challenge.

With all photographs completed, congratulations were said, hands were shaken, and the crowd quickly dispersed back to work. Steph and Emma had requested the use of a quiet room at the gym in which to film me, and Wayne had granted them sole use of one of the large studios. My final interview was promptly conducted and concluded, I waved goodbye to the film crew, and my last official Channel swim event drew to a close.

And yet a full sense of closure remained amazingly illusive.

Certainly, a void in purpose and a lack of a training goal now pervaded. Friends and colleagues immediately enquired as to which challenge I would take up next, and the temptation to immediately replace that training target was strong. But again it was important to focus on two things: Firstly that the aim of raising money had been the driving factor all along; and secondly that I had promised Esta and the boys that I would not undertake anything which would so severely impact upon our precious family time.

At least not for a couple of years.

And as to the Channel? Towards the end of my training I vividly remember stating on several occasions that I would never be an ambassador for the sport. I was sick to death of the training, and could hardly have imagined me ever having a positive word to say about the very notion of swimming the Channel, let alone the deed itself.

Julie Bradshaw contacted me with congratulations on the achievement of raising so much money. She knew from my previous comments that I would be highly unlikely to make another attempt at the Channel, and she was fully aware that the expenses of this venture had been financially crippling to me. On the off-chance that I may reconsider a second attempt, she ventured, she would be more than happy to mentor me again - this time as a friend. It was an extremely touching and generous offer. I thanked her for everything she'd done in helping me come such a long way, but said I really did not think a re-visit was on the cards.

But the Channel can get under your skin. To now look back and appreciate what I accomplished, physically, and to comprehend how far I finally swam, is incredible. I had the rare opportunity to partake in something that few would ever want to contemplate, yet something that others can only dream of. And I'm under no illusion that any of it came easy. Every step of the way, from the initial conception, through to the actual day of the swim was a continual effort, a constant fight. But I would not change that. The challenge of the Channel is not just a 26 mile / 42km swim. A swimmer does not simply arrive at a beach on the south-east coast of England and head off across to France, despite any publicity leading to this perception. Before that can happen, the swimmer has undergone a long, hard journey that culminates in that final swim. Taking on the challenge of the Channel is an experience that will consume your spare time, your waking thoughts and your life - for the duration of that journey. And at the end, long after the taste of salt is just a memory, when the spattering of fame subsides, and when you have forgotten the last time you felt cold, a Channel swimmer is left with an incredible sense of achievement. I certainly felt that way, despite the final 2.8 miles remaining elusive.

So without a doubt, despite any earlier comments to the contrary, I would encourage anyone contemplating an attempt on the Channel to give it a go. If you cannot afford the logistics personally, find the sponsorship somehow. Forget the excuses: find the time; rally the support; give it your best shot.

I did, and prior to doing so I'd hardly swum further than a mile in any one go.

If you really, genuinely want to do it, the only thing standing in your way, is you.

Film Release

It's amazing how quickly time passed. Routine has a way of establishing itself without invite and without conscious effort, as we'd discovered with Harry. The swim became a memory, the memory became a legend, and the legend became a myth, as the saying goes. And this happened over the course of a just few months. Occasionally I would bump into someone I'd not seen since the swim, and if they knew the outcome they would commiserate with me and ask for details, and if not they would ask how I got on. Each time, it took me longer to summon up the memories. That swim already appeared to have been the adventures of someone else.

In 2016 I was busy with work. I had been travelling to Canada and to India. If I thought at all about the Channel, it was to wonder how on earth I would ever have had time to train had work been this hectic two years previously.

I was in the city of Chennai in India when I received an email from Emma about the film. We'd been in sporadic contact, and I knew that a lot of work was being done on the final production. Delays were caused by the team's need to undertake paid work whenever it presented itself, and the task of cataloging the footage, selecting which parts to use, and editing the entire film all had to be done as a secondary task. In addition to this, negotiations were underway to sell the final production. But this email, over 18 months after my Channel attempt, was to tell me with elation that the film had now been purchased by the BBC, and that it would air on BBC4 in the summer of 2016.

A thrill passed through me at the receipt of this news. I would be on national television! I had half-envisaged a production that would be aired at a film festival and would then disappear into the archives of obscurity. But Emma and Steph had clearly produced something worthy of the BBC, and this was immediately intriguing.

On the backdraft of this was a nagging worry. The reason the military are ordered to say nothing more than their service number, rank and name is that it is very easy to edit and splice footage into something completely different from what was originally said or intended. Countless politicians and celebrities have found this to be true. And whilst I wasn't worried about any chance of being portrayed as a villain, I was wondering if I would come across as a niave and ignorant challenger who had never stood a chance in hell of completing the swim.

A while went by. I'd made mention of the film at work, and over the following weeks I was repeatedly asked for the actual date. I was far more eager to see the production than those asking, so I was also on tenterhooks awaiting confirmation for the date of airing.

The film was scheduled for Monday 17th July. Previews started to hit the papers the weekend before, with both the Independent magazine and the Telegraph running articles. The Independent ran a piece called 'Hell in High Water', and broadly outlined how far more people had climbed Everest than had successfully crossed the Channel. It went on to speak of 'a BBC4 documentary airing next week that follows three people as they attempt the swim.'

The film crew had actually followed more than three swimmers, and they had accumulated over 220 hours of footage during the filming stages. It was later decided to include only a young lady called Georgina Halford who suffered from diabetes, a previous four-time Channel swimmer Mike Cross, and me. The final documentary was edited down to just under an hour.

For their part, the Telegraph spoke of 'the agonies and extasies of the ultimate open water swim'. Individual reviews were also given, as with the one by Crispin Thorold who talked of 'a story that is told with a gentle touch and affectionate humour is never far away.'

Naturally, Acorns, the local paper in Worcester, and my sponsors Hallmark Hulme were all using social media to its upmost to increase the viewing audience, and I was ensuring nobody at work could possibly be unaware of the opportunity to see the documentary.

For my part, I watched the film on-line, alone in my single room in the Union Jack Club. Even as it aired, Tom Adams, the man I'd cycled the 100 mile bike ride with, began texting me. It was fantastic to know that so many people were now getting the opportunity to see the real conditions which had thwarted my efforts. And it was encouraging to know that friends and family up and down the country could begin to visually appreciate everything I had been through.

After the airing, the Daily Mail spoke of 'a finely crafted film about those who want to swim the Channel'. The brief article rated the film as four stars, and said 'Few are so deeply motivated,' when speaking of my attempt. It was a tribute to Harry, and I admit to feeling proud at the words.

Typically, throughout all of the articles, one of two photographs were predominantly used: one showed a group of swimmers in Dover making their way across the pebble beach and down into the water; the other showed me and Ali on Bournemouth beach, looking out to sea and in mid discussion. The photo was taken by the film crew at the point of my failed six hour sea swim, and I was explaining to Ali how big the waves actually were, despite how it might look from shore. It was strange to see this image of Ali and I so often, in newspapers and magazines, and in the end I too used the image in some of my own posts.

The social media machine was still running strong after the program had aired. Congratulations poured in from highly impressed viewers, many of them deciding to follow me on Twitter and saying how distraught they were at finding out I had failed to make it across the whole way. One man on Twitter was chatting to me for a while assuming I was a fellow viewer. When he realised I was the swimmer he had been watching, he told me, 'I was heartbroken. I had a proper tear in my eye.' He promptly pledged £30 to Acorns, and the hospice told me they had also been receiving other donations since the film had appeared on TV. To me, this was the best possible outcome, as the continued contributions took me over the £13,000 mark.

With regards to the production itself, my own view was that the real indication of its success was the incredible level of empathy it managed to create within the viewers for the swimmers that they were watching. I believe that this was predominantly achieved by cleverly contrasting my own story and preparation strategies with those of Mike Cross. Ironically, my failing to complete the swim also contributed towards this contrast. As a result of this empathy, family and friends watching the film found themselves wishing against logic that I would somehow reach France, despite the fact that they knew the actual outcome well in advance. And those who watched the documentary unaware of the ending seemed to experience a real sense of disappointment and disbelief when I was ordered out of the water for safety reasons. A final contrast, of course, was provided by the visually dramatic weather differences we each encountered. My son Connagh was of the opinion that the camera-work of the operator was actually so professional that he accidentally minimised the real severity of the storm.

As brilliant as the final production undoubtedly was, when editing 220 hours of footage, decisions have to be made as to what ideas will take priority, and which will be left on the cutting-room floor. Many individuals, such as Dr. Julie Bradshaw, did not make it into the final film. Snippits of conversation were also lost, of course, and both of these factors lead to questions being raised by family and friends. None of these questions in any way degrade the film, but they did prompt me to include the answers within this book, as two in particular are worthy of explanation:

Firstly, my mum had to query my initial claim that I had not been tired at any point, and that I feel confident I would have made landfall had the conditions held.

'But you hear your captain (Kevin) saying that you're getting disoriented, and that you keep swimming the wrong way,' she stated by way of question.

It's an excellent point, and one I allude to in the chapter about the swim itself.

One of the main briefing points from Kevin (after safety), recalled something my mentor, Julie, had said to me the first time I met her. I'd been studying her swim chart on her kitchen wall, commenting on how she must have been able to see Cap Gris Nez twice as the tide took her up and down the coastline.

'Yes, I knew exactly where I was heading,' said Julie. 'But you don't swim towards land - you follow the boat.'

Kevin instructed me similarly. 'I know where the tide is going, where the currents are, and the best way to get you to land. I point the boat, and you use it as a guide.'

For over nine hours, this had worked perfectly. I had indeed been able to see land for some time, and that was encouraging, and when I turned my head to breathe, there was Connemara, faithfully showing me which way to head.

And then the storm struck.

With no forward momentum in the boat, Connemara became

a cork on the sea. Kevin could no more control her than he would have been able to guide a coconut. The only means of him maintaining any steerage was by putting her in gear and swinging the boat back round to face the correct way. But I had no idea he was doing this. I would glance to my right for half a second whilst breathing and see that the prow was facing one direction, and I would correct my own trajectory to match it. I could not see land at all, and for most breaths I could not see the boat either, as it was in a trough the other side of mine. Consequently, the boat could actually be facing 180 degrees in the opposite direction by the time I saw it again. Each time, I'd assume that the waves were knocking me off course, and I'd 'correct' my angle of swim. From the boat, it must indeed have looked as though I had completely lost the plot. I was indeed disoriented, and this was compounded by the necessity for Kevin to have to swing the boat around.

The second question is more complex, and it involves my conscious decision not to go down to Dover and train with other swimmers. Due to Julie being cut out of the final production, many people logically assumed I was training completely solo. In fact, I received an email from one gentleman telling me that if I ever wanted to do it again, he would happily put me in touch with a good Channel swim mentor.

And as a consequence of Julie being absent from the film, a further misconception also resulted: that there is only one Channel swimming organisation, not two.

Julie Bradshaw is the secretary for the Channel Swimming Association, the original governing body. Historically, Kevin Murphy, the 'King of the Channel' also belonged to the CSA. But differences of opinion were raised, and for various reasons Mr. Murphy and others broke away to form the Channel Swimming and Pilot's Federation.

During my initial research into Channel Swimming, I'd only come across the CSA, and hence logged my attempt through them and got to know Julie. I knew nothing of the CSPF for some time.

Conversely, the film crew had only initially encountered the CSPF, and so the main 'focus' of the production was around the CSPF community. In the film, only my pilot Kevin Sherman and I were not part of this organisation. With no contrast being shown or explained between the two organisations within the film (and admittedly very little need for it), the review in the Daily Express focussed entirely on the CSPF community, presumably because they were completely unaware that the CSA even existed.

Julie and I had certainly discussed the possibility of me going down to Dover. She had encouraged it from a point of view of safety, and for the opportunity to swim with others. But her contrasting concerns were around the 'advice' she was sure I'd be given.

'You are paying me for my experience, expertise and advice. If you go down there, you will undoubtedly hear lots of contradictory suggestions - people telling you that you "must" eat this, and drink this, and how you must train. It can be quite intimidating, and could raise lots of questions in your mind. That's something we do not want during your actual swim. During the attempt, you have to be 100% convinced that you have done everything correctly.'

At first, my real reluctance to go to Dover was more born simply out of logistics. Dover is hugely awkward to get to from Worcester, so I'd somehow have to get there during the week whilst I was in London - during which time the 'community' would not be there anyway. As time wore on, however, I decided I just did not need to swim with other people. Ali was there to look out for me from shore, and I saw little point in swimming alongside a stranger when I was perfectly capable of motivating myself. Julie told me much later, 'People like you and I only need the carrot.' I loved that saying.

So for those watching the film for whom the whole thing was a mystery, it would be easy to incorrectly assume that I was another CSPF swimmer, but that I was reluctant to be associated with my fellow swimmers.

I want to state that I have very little knowledge about the CSPF. I cannot offer any unbiased advice on which of the two organisations a swimmer should register with, as I only know Julie (whom I would certainly recommend). Guidelines and rules for both organisations differ, so anyone unsure of which to register through should conduct their own research before making a decision.

The release of the film, and the subsequent frenzy of Channel swimming talk all made me question the issue of a second attempt. Esta and I spoke about it late one hot July evening, shortly after the film had aired. We were paddling in the inflatable pool outside our new house, trying to cool down. Talk turned to the Channel.

'The big question would be the funding. If someone were to stump up for me to do it, then I would,' I said.

'Do we get no say in it?' Esta asked.

I grinned sheepishly. I'm often guilty of putting myself first.

'We would support you,' Esta continued. 'But you'd have to train differently this time. It was too much of an impact on our family time for you to do things that way again.'

And I agree. I do think I would do things differently, somehow. I'm perfectly capable of getting myself to a high level of fitness, and I can get my mind into the correct positive state required of such an endurance event. What I would have to avoid would be repeating the punishing schedule I'd undergone last time.

Of course, this is all very easy to say on a hot night in July, when the water in the pool is cooling you down, as opposed to making you shiver. It's so easy to forget the pain and the boredom, and to begin to dream about successfully arriving on that beach in France, exhausted but elated. But my attempt was only ever intended to be a one-time venture, and with no sign or real prospect of any funding, a repeat effort is no more than a vague dream.

So for now, all I can say is, never say never.

Acknowledgments

Without help and support from the following, my Channel attempt would never have been possible:

Permission and acceptance of my mad endeavour by my family; Dovetail, Hallmark Hulme, Kendall Wadley, Rybrook of Worcester and Spire South Bank Hospital for their vital financial support; David Lloyd's for the generous access to amazing training facilities; Vita Coco and Glaxo Smith Kline for drinks and gels; Zoggs for the brilliant anti-fog goggles; and Dr. Julie Bradshaw MBE for exceptionally experienced advice and guidance.

Thanks too, to friends, neighbours and work colleagues for your support. 14 months is a long time to stick at something like this, so your little snippets of encouragement really were helpful.

Printed in Great
Britain
by Amazon